This book is dedicated to
Austin T. Turk, my mentor and colleague,
who introduced me to the academic fields of
criminology and criminal justice, and who
taught me that in professional life, theoretical
and methodological differences among scholars
should be friendly and facilitative.

Contents

List of boxes, figures and tables

Boxes

Figures

Tables

About the author

Jeffrey Ian Ross, PhD, is a Professor in the School of Criminal Justice, College of Public Affairs, and a Research Fellow of the Center for International and Comparative Law at the University of Baltimore, Maryland, USA.

He has researched, written and lectured primarily on corrections, policing, political crime, violence, and crime and justice in American Indian communities for over two decades. Ross's work has appeared in many academic journals and books, as well as popular media. He is the author, co-author, editor, and co-editor of a number of books including most recently *Policing issues: Challenges and controversies* (Jones and Bartlett Learning, 2012).

Ross is a frequent and respected subject matter expert for local, regional, national, and international news media. He has made live appearances on CNN, CNBC, and Fox News Network. Additionally Ross has written op-eds for *The* (Baltimore) *Sun*, *The* (Maryland) *Daily Record*, *The Gazette* (weekly community newspapers serving Maryland's Montgomery, Frederick, Prince Georges and Carroll counties), the *Baltimore Examiner*, and the *Tampa Tribune*.

From 1995-98, Ross was a social science analyst with the National Institute of Justice, a Division of the US Department of Justice. In 2003, he was awarded the University of Baltimore's Distinguished Chair in Research Award. During the early 1980s, Jeff worked for almost four years in a correctional institution. His website is www.jeffreyianross.com

Acknowledgements

The process of developing, researching, and writing this book has been a journey of sorts. Maintaining my focus has been a constant challenge, given the competing pressures on my time.

In any given project, however, there are many people to thank, and this one is no different. I would like to extend my appreciation to the staff at The Policy Press, including Karen Bowler, Senior Commissioning Editor, for signing this book, demonstrating impeccable patience and maintaining confidence that this typescript would eventually make its way into print. Thanks to Laura Vickers, Editorial Assistant, for keeping me on track. Kudos also to Kathryn King, Marketing Manager, for helping to shape the appropriate language, look and feel for the book. Thanks to the production people at The Policy Press such as Laura Greaves and Dave Worth, and their production subcontractors.

I would like to thank Rachel Hildebrandt, who tidied up my prose when it was clear that my thoughts were a bit scattered. I also extend my gratitude to my students – some of whom are former or current convicts, while others are criminal justice and national security practitioners – for enduring portions of this work through lectures and/or required readings.

Thanks to my many invaluable sources, who over the years gave freely of their time to respond to my numerous questions and to help me contextualize this material.

I am also indebted to Fran Buntman, Morad Eghbal, Allen Hornblum, Lee Michael Johnson, Brian Martin, Stephen Muzzatti, Marvin Ross, Phil Stinson, and Aaron Winter, who volunteered (or, pressed into service) to look at selected chapters. I also extend my gratitude to several anonymous reviewers throughout the years for their helpful comments; these individuals encouraged me to rethink many of the ideas I initially presented at both the proposal and the typescript review stages.

Thanks to David O. Friedrichs for writing the foreword. I would also like to extend my appreciation to various colleagues, such as Gregg Barak, David Charters, Raymond Corrado, Frank Cullen, Morad Eghbal, Jeff Ferrell, Peter Grabosky, Ted Robert Gurr, Frank Hagan, Mark S. Hamm, Keith Hayward, Richard Jones, Victor Kappeler, David Kauzlarich, Ron Kramer, Peter Manning, Gary Marx, Ray Michalowski, Greg Newbold, Stephen Muzzatti, Stephen C. Richards, Dawn Rothe, Alex Schmid, Frank Shanty, Michael Stohl, Ken Tunnell, Austin T. Turk, Trey Williams, and Ron Weitzer, who over the years have provided a supportive intellectual community in this field of study.

I extend my never-ending gratitude to my wonderful family. I thank Natasha J. Cabrera, my wife and fellow scholar, for providing encouragement and feedback at several critical times, and for serving as a sounding board for my ideas. I also recognize Keanu and Dakota Ross-Cabrera, our children, who are a constant source of inspiration and joy.

Foreword

David O. Friedrichs

In the spring of 2011 news stories once again reported that "crime is in decline," and in some cases, that within the context of difficult economic circumstances some experts were surprised by this. But what did this mean? These stories were reporting on declines in conventional crimes such as assault, burglary, and theft, as measured by the Federal Bureau of Investigation's (FBI) Uniform crime report. It is far from clear that the most consequential forms of crime, including white-collar crime and political crime, are in decline. On the latter form of crime a much bigger story being reported throughout 2011 – popular uprisings and rebellions against autocrats and their regimes across North Africa and the Middle East – brought into especially sharp relief some of the complex and sometimes contradictory dimensions of political crime. The uprisings were inspired by the widely diffused perception that the citizens of these countries had been victimized, over a long period of time, by large-scale political crimes, especially the severely autocratic and repressive policies and practices of the leadership – including the torture and execution of political dissidents – and by systematic theft of the national wealth, to the tune of billions of dollars. The autocrats in these countries – notably in Egypt, Yemen, Libya, and Syria – characterized protesters and rebels as "terrorists" and traitors, in effect as political criminals using illegal means to try to bring down the legitimate regime of the country. Many thousands of people were killed in this context, principally by security forces acting on behalf of the regimes being challenged. In some of the countries autocrats were forced to flee, were taken into custody to be tried or were captured and executed, with steps taken to establish a new (and ideally democratic) form of government; in other countries – at least at the time of writing – the autocrats were holding onto power. But one of the big questions in all of this was whether the uprisings would ultimately lead to more or less political crimes, more or fewer victims of political crime in these countries. The cautionary lessons of history in the Middle East (and other parts of the world) have hardly provided a basis for uniform optimism on this score.

In the US at present there has been much commentary on the increasing and dramatic disparities in the distribution of wealth, and the ongoing desperation of millions of unemployed people, homeowners losing their homes, and savers contending with drastically reduced investment accounts. The job prospects for a large cohort of college graduates are especially worrisome. Public disenchantment with the political system is, by some measures, at a record high. In the fall of 2011 an Occupy Wall Street movement spread across the country, as well as in other countries. The protesters are largely united in their view that the Wall Street financial sector is promoting obscene wealth for the "1%," while too many in the remaining "99%" are struggling. Further, the Wall Street investment bankers, whose fraudulent, reckless, and wholly self-interested actions led to the financial meltdown of 2008 and subsequent taxpayer bailout, have not been called to account for these actions. The inherently corrupt symbiotic relationship between Wall Street and Washington is one subtheme of these protests, and implicit if not explicit recognition of a "political crime" dimension to present circumstances. Will the US witness outbreaks of rioting and possibly serious challenges to the existing order, as has happened not only in the Middle East but also in at least some measure in major European cities such as London, Madrid and Athens? Is a fundamental transformation of the whole architecture of the political economy on the horizon? This remains to be seen.

Also in the fall of 2011, the 10th anniversary of 9/11 was commemorated. In the Western world, at least, there is a high level of consensus that the 9/11 attacks, leading to the loss of some 3,000 lives, was a monstrous political crime. But it remains to be determined whether the responses to 9/11 – including the pre-emptive invasion of Iraq ("Operation Iraqi Freedom") – will ultimately be viewed by history as political crime on a large scale. Certainly many parties presently hold that view, especially in the Arab world, but also among many Westerners as well. And many of the other responses of the Bush administration to 9/11 – including the use of torture against suspected terrorists and their allies and a range of infringements on due process – have been quite widely viewed as the manifestation of state-organized political crime.

An introduction to political crime offers a highly instructive mapping of the broad terrain of activities that have been encompassed under the term "political crime," including acts of political insurrection on the one hand, and crimes of states on the other. The author, Jeffrey Ian Ross, has been an early and active promoter of more criminological attention to crimes of states – and political crime more broadly – in the recent era. His former professor Austin Turk (originally of the University of Toronto) and William J. Chambliss (of George Washington University) were relatively lone voices in the criminological vineyards during the 1970s and 1980s in calling attention to political crime, and state-organized crime. But over the past two decades or so this situation has changed, and there is now a significant group of criminologists – young, middle-aged, and older – who are focused on such crime. Jeff Ross deserves significant credit here, with books such as *Controlling state crime* and *Varieties of state crime,* for making the case for political crime as an appropriate and indeed imperative project for the criminological enterprise. The present book has the potential to recruit a whole new generation of students to become engaged with political crime. Hopefully at least some of the student readers of this book will be inspired to undertake serious scholarly explorations of one or more of the countless questions suggested by the discussion here.

This new edition addresses political crime in a post-9/11 world, and a world where the internet plays an increasingly important role. It incorporates the significant criminological scholarship on political crime that has been published in recent years, makes some new conceptual distinctions and addresses dimensions of political crime not discussed in the original edition, as well as many recent cases of political crime.

–

If most criminologists focus on conventional crime and its control, how is it that some criminologists become interested in political crime, and crimes of the powerful in particular? In my own case I believe this interest is not unrelated to the fact that my parents were refugees from a criminal state, Nazi Germany, and that I came of age during the era of the 1960s. The Civil Rights Movement and the Anti-War Movement targeting the US military campaign in Vietnam were key events of this era, and my participation in both movements impressed on me the significance of crimes emanating from the powerful and not the powerless segments of society. There are other paths to an interest in political crime, but for the student of criminology some initiative and possibly a measure of professional career risk may be involved. Above all, in my experience, criminological students of political crime tend to believe passionately in the immense importance in being part of a larger, interdisciplinary project of trying to make sense of such crime and generating effective responses toward its containment.

A concern with political crime, and especially those forms of such crime perpetrated by the powerful, has, within criminology, been principally embraced by critical criminologists. But recently some prominent criminologists essentially associated with the mainstream – but in any case not with critical criminology – have turned their attention to political crime. John Hagan, John Braithwaite and Joachim Savelsberg are three prolific and highly regarded criminologists who have called for more criminological attention to crimes of states, and have produced books addressing some forms of such crime. John Hagan fled the US during the Vietnam War error to avoid the draft, John Braithwaite's father was among the very few survivors of a notorious "death march" in the Pacific region during the Second World War, and Joachim Savelsberg grew up in a country contending with the monstrous crimes of the Nazis. Students of political crime and crimes of states may be especially drawn to these topics by personal and family-related experiences.

If conventional crime will surely continue to be a source of considerable harm and suffering, the conviction here is that during the course of the 21st century the overwhelming challenge will be to effectively address political crime, broadly defined. The potential scope of harm emanating from such crime is monumental, with the possibility of nuclear terrorism or nuclear war as just one especially frightening instance of a form of political crime with a level of harm almost beyond imagining. A criminology that aspires to remain relevant in the 21st century must fully engage with the whole range of political crimes, and the challenges of controlling such crime. This book provides students (as well as scholars) with a broad overview of and a basic point of departure for the in-depth study of political crime and its control.

David O. Friedrichs
Professor and Distinguished University Fellow
University of Scranton (Pennsylvania), USA

Preface

My book *The dynamics of political crime* (hereafter *Dynamics*), published in October 2002, consists of 12 chapters, each covering a different basic element within the field of political crime (that is, both oppositional and state crimes). It provides definitions, typologies, and a brief history of each subtype of political crime that has occurred in the US, Canada, and the United Kingdom (focusing on the 1960-2001 period), and discusses the causes and effects of each subtype. Kenneth D. Tunnell, a well-known critical criminologist and the editor of *Political crime in contemporary America* (1993), wrote the foreword. At the time, the only other publication comparable to *Dynamics* was Frank Hagan's *Political crime*, published in 1997 by Prentice Hall; this book has since gone out of print. As yet no other introductory books taking a comprehensive approach to political crime have been published in the intervening years, and there remain no other equivalent studies.

History of *Dynamics of political crime*

Dynamics was the subject of three detailed reviews in scholarly venues. First, Tim Prenzler, in *Australian Journal of Politics and History* (vol 50, no 3, 2004), wrote that the book "represents a voice of moderation and reason in an area where the voices – and actions – of extremists seem to predominate" (p. 465). It is "written in a very basic textbook format for undergraduates, with plenty of sub-headings, textboxes, and sample test questions. The readability, succinctness, explanations of terminology, and structuring of concepts all make it attractive for students. It is nonetheless an extremely useful resource for other audiences ... as well as the interested lay person..." (p. 465). He added, "Overall ... this book provides a valuable contribution to understanding political crimes. And the whole style of the book is itself a partial antidote to extremism. There should be more academic books like this – well researched, smart, but graphic, clear and friendly" (p. 465).

Second, Christopher A. Simon, writing in *Terrorism and Political Violence* (vol 17, no 4, 2005), stated, "Ross does a very good job of demonstrating to students and to instructors that he is cognizant of extant theory.... His writing is very solid and the reader can sense Ross's thought processes here" (p. 663).

And Livy Visano, in *Criminal Justice Review* (vol 31, no 2, 2006), argued that "his treatment of political crime [is] provoking and insightful" (p. 175).

> This book is not only an excellent and up-to-date review of the literature on political crime, but it also builds on the strengths of previous research in developing an interdisciplinary explanation that implicates individuals, situations, organizations and resource adequacies.[...] The book is a well-informed, balanced, and compelling presentation of traditional and contemporary theoretical concerns

that confront directly the interaction between antisystemic crime and state crime. (p. 175)

The rationale behind the new edition

Since the publication of *Dynamics*, a number of significant political events have occurred and a respectable amount of academic literature has been published, thus making *Dynamics* obsolete. For example, the book does not include a discussion of the impact of The USA PATRIOT Act, the prisoner abuses at Abu Ghraib and Guantanamo, or the numerous high-level politicians in the US (and elsewhere) who have been accused and convicted of corruption.

It is time, therefore, for an updated, more current and user-friendly version of *Dynamics*. In order to signal these significant changes in terms of content, length and updating, the publisher and I believed that the "second edition" should be titled *An introduction to political crime*. This second edition retains many of the elements reviewers originally found helpful, but goes beyond these.

What the new edition is about

An introduction to political crime is an updated text written in a way that makes it appropriate for classroom adoption and the general public. In general, the revision involved updating the existing text, reviewing additional scholarly literature that has been published since the original version, and adding a discussion of other noteworthy incidents and episodes from current affairs. This new edition also includes more case studies, either in the form of boxes or within the actual text, and updated statistics, particularly for the chapter on oppositional political terrorism (see Chapter Two).

Chapter One examines the obstacles to understanding and interpreting political crime. It also clarifies the definition of political crime, explains why political crime has changed over the past decade since *Dynamics* was published, details the typologies and categories of political crime, and outlines what the book aims to accomplish. Political crime, and its subcomponent parts, is a controversial and highly contested topic. The introduction therefore attempts to explicate some of the general misperceptions of political crime, and the subsequent chapters, each of which each focus on one specific political crime, also shed light on these controversies.

Chapter Two examines the need for a theory of political crime, reviews the varying explanations of political crime, discusses psychological theory and structural theory as the basis for a new theory, and outlines my individual, situation, organization, and resources (ISOR) explanation.

Chapter Three defines political crime and the difficulty with this process.

Chapter Four provides a more detailed, nuanced, and historical rendering of nonviolent oppositional political crimes than what was presented in *Dynamics*, including a longer review of the numerous cases of dissent, sedition, treason, and espionage in different countries that have occurred since the 1960s. The concepts of resistance and civil disobedience are reviewed in this chapter.

Chapter Five incorporates new material, drawing from relatively recent research produced since the original book's publication. The section on assassination has been significantly expanded, and there is new material on political riots and sabotage.

Chapter Six is an introductory chapter on the subject of state crime, and deals with definitional issues and typologies. It reviews the considerable amount of material written on this subject between 1989 and 2012.

Along with definitional issues, types and causes, Chapter Seven has been revised to address a number of well-known cases of political corruption, including US politicians such as Congressmen Dan Rostenkowski and Randy "Duke" Cunningham. Also reviewed is the case of US lobbyist Jack Abramoff. This chapter also includes a more detailed explanation of police corruption, its causes and controls.

Chapter Eight provides an extended discussion of the controversial USA PATRIOT Act and noteworthy incidents of illegal domestic surveillance conducted by various spy/intelligence agency activities since the 1960s. There is also a greater focus on more contemporary intelligence scandals in Canada and the UK.

Chapter Nine presents a comprehensive analysis of human rights violations and a review of the most important debates that have occurred over the last decade. Because of its topicality, the chapter reviews the abuses (and public reactions to them) at Guantanamo, Cuba.

Chapter Ten deals with numerous types of state violence committed in the US, UK and Canada by state criminogenic agencies, including, but not limited to: torture, deaths in custody, police riots, police use of deadly force, and correctional officer violence.

Definitional issues, typologies and a comprehensive review of the history of state-corporate crime are provided in Chapter Eleven. Throughout the past six years, significant scholarship in this area has been conducted by individuals such as David O. Friedrichs, David Kauzlarich, Ronald C. Kramer, Raymond Michalowski, Dawn L. Rothe, Steve Tombs, and David Whyte, and their work has been integrated into this chapter. They have reviewed the Challenger and Columbia space shuttle incidents, Imperial Foods, Firestone tires, Goodyear tires, Halliburton, Blackwater, ValuJet, Carlisle, and various arms smuggling cases.

The book concludes with an expanded Chapter Twelve, which has been revised to draw together additional insights from the preceding 11 chapters.

An introduction to political crime will be useful for upper-level criminology/criminal justice classes, including "special topics in criminology." It can also be used in political science departments, particularly ones that have classes on "public administration," and in sociology departments for class topics such as "political sociology."

An ancillary website is available to be used with this book, where students can find end-of-chapter question (www.policypress.co.uk/resources/ross).

ONE

Introduction

Political crime is rarely examined when studying the dynamics of crime, justice, and law. Yet understanding political offenses or illegalities[1] is fundamental to comprehending the workings of a criminal justice system that selectively defines what is criminal, enforces criminal laws, and adjudicates who are defined as criminals (Kirchheimer, 1961). As a variety of scholars, jurists, policymakers, legislators, and activists have argued, the law and (by extension) crime, qualify as political acts. Hence, interpreting law, crime, and criminals requires a political focus (see, for example, Quinney, 1970, 1977; Miller, 1973; Allen, 1974; Chambliss, 1976; Chambliss and Seidman, 1982).[2]

Indeed, various criminal acts are explicitly political. For example, sedition and treason have traditionally been viewed by states as political offenses because of their real or alleged threats to order (public, social, or otherwise) or national security.[3] As a result, these behaviors have been codified in law.[4] However, some state reactions to dissent are, in various cases, almost or actually criminal. This is the case when governments occasionally engage in repressive actions, during which law-abiding individuals are placed under surveillance and/or harassed, or groups are infiltrated and/or destabilized.

These escalating state responses are rarely recognized in domestic criminal law. Both types of actions, oppositional and state-initiated, are increasingly understood by many scholars and activists as political crime. Likewise, and according to recent theoretical advances in criminology, sociology, political science, and law, many controversial behaviors are considered politically and socially harmful, yet are not presently classified in legal codes as criminal.

In order to accommodate changes in current thinking, this analysis recognizes that legal definitions of crime are often too narrow and that the law is, by nature, dynamic. In other words, we cannot impose the kind of neutrality on the law that might be implicit in the statement, "Equal justice under the law."

Thus, an alternative, more contemporary, and inclusive definition and conceptualization of crime is needed. One definition that is gaining increasing legitimacy recognizes that crime is not only a type of deviance that has been codified or has been conceptualized as a violation of a criminal law, but it can be interpreted by the wider body politic as any social harm, moral transgression, and/or civil or human rights violation (see, for example, Sutherland, 1949a, 1949b; Schwendinger and Schwendinger, 1975; Bohm, 1993).[5]

This "social justice" perspective acknowledges that some behaviors are not traditionally labeled criminal, but should be, and that certain activities that do not violate the existing law, yet possess the previously mentioned characteristics, should be considered crimes. This notion would accommodate not only the actions of individuals and organizations, but also those of states, their employees, and their contractors.[6] Thus, political crime is a more far-ranging label than those previously considered.

Obstacles to understanding and interpreting political crime

As the previous discussion suggests, it is difficult to understand political crime, and several reasons contribute to this state of affairs. In general, there is often a lack of consensus with respect to a definition, availability of reliable information, rigorous analysis, and/or interest in political crimes.

Undoubtedly, considerable confusion exists about what constitutes a political offense. Experts are often divided over how to define political illegalities, and many seem to either avoid defining it, or purposefully define political crime without considering other existing definitions. Moreover, information presented by the mass media (for example, movies, books) and the news media (for example, newspaper, radio, television) minimizes the ability of citizens to understand political crimes without a great deal of confusion (see, for example, Barak, 1994; Warr, 1995).

Although this is less true for oppositional political crimes (for example, terrorism), the mainstream media construction of state crimes (for example, genocide) often presents them as unavoidable illegalities, the "just deserts" inflicted on "irrational" dissidents, or the collateral damages of war. Perhaps more importantly, the identification of crimes by one's own state is not a popular activity. Many people do not criticize their own political systems' legitimacy because of high levels of trust, patriotism, deference to authority, apathy, or repeated experiences of powerlessness (see, for example, Dionne, 1991; Ross, 2000a, Chapter 5).

Similarly, citizens may not participate in their polity's political process because they are cynical, skeptical, and/or complacent with respect to these matters. For most people, the principles of universally applied justice and equality before the law remain central to their idea of the criminal and civil justice process. The notion that their own democratically elected government may commit crimes is unthinkable/deplorable, thus the result is a citizenry that fails to believe that these political offenses are present and/or widespread. Consequently, the citizenry fails to act in the righting of wrongs. On the other hand, one of the interesting and sometimes disconcerting by-products of many high profile dramatic political crimes (especially assassinations and terrorist events) are the numerous conspiracy theories that develop. Well-intentioned individuals and groups often look for or are willing to believe alternative explanations alleging far-ranging conspiracies for these tragic events, dismissing government inquiries by labeling them as whitewashes and/or cover-ups. On the surface, these explanations seem plausible, but they are often seriously flawed.

In many respects, the scholarly study of political crime and the pedagogy surrounding this subject has been marginalized and/or ignored. Criminologists and other social scientists have been slow or reluctant to incorporate the study of political crime into their research agendas. Thus, rarely do scholarly journals in the field of criminology/criminal justice have articles dealing explicitly with political crime, and few academic books are published on this subject.

Four decades ago, scholars and students would have been hard-pressed to find an introductory criminology textbook that provided a substantial discussion about the role of politics in the creation of crime, much less an entire chapter devoted to the concept of political crime (Moran, 1974, Chapter 2). Today, however, most reputable entry-level criminology texts include this material (Tunnell, 1993a). This is not necessarily because there has been an increase in the amount of political crime or scholarship, but because the subject matter is now considered by instructors, textbook editors/publishers, and perhaps students to be worthy of coverage.

Needless to say, the higher education curriculum is generally reluctant to include classes focusing specifically on political offenses. Few criminology and criminal justice departments at colleges or universities offer courses on political crime. This may be the result of a disproportionate focus on street crime and a lack of training

Box 1.1: Getting a paper published in a peer-reviewed journal

After academic investigators have conducted research, they typically compile their findings in a paper and may present their results at a public forum such as a conference and/or submit it to a respectable and/or recognized peer-reviewed scholarly journal. The journal editor (or board) makes an initial determination about the suitability of the paper (if he or she thinks that the subject matter and approach of the paper will be of interest to its readership and of appropriate academic credibility).

If the paper holds merit, the editor then sends it out to three or more subject matter expert reviewers. The writer's identity is concealed, as is the identity of the reviewers (also known as referees). This process of quality control, called 'blind review', is meant to guard against bias. Reviewers try to determine if the paper is thorough, if it offers an empirical analysis, and whether the methods, data tested, and results seem appropriate. Referees generally make one of three recommendations: accept, reject, or revise and resubmit. Authors may resubmit, but if their work does not show improvement, the editor may refuse the writer/s the opportunity to submit again.

Hopefully the findings from the research process will have an impact on policy and practice, but due to a multitude of factors, unfortunately this is rarely the case. Peer-reviewed research is more credible than non-peer-reviewed research. Peer review strengthens the validity and reliability of the paper. It is the highest standard of research in academia. It is important for the career of a scholar to be published in a peer-reviewed journal. Not all academic or scholarly journals are peer reviewed, however. In order to determine whether a journal is peer reviewed, you have to check the submission criteria, typically listed at the back of the journal or on the journal's website. Also, a paper is not an article until it has been published.

and expertise among professors in the fields of criminology/criminal justice. The subject of street crime dominates the material that the typical undergraduate learns in the average US university department of criminology/criminal justice (Rothe and Ross, 2008). Moreover, with the increase in the number of PhD programs in criminology/criminal justice, and a desire by many departments to hire graduates only from this specific discipline, the field typically reproduces itself.

Furthermore, with the exception of terrorism, the wider problem of political crime, as defined as such, does not appear to be a major governmental policy concern. And if the lack of research funding is an indicator of government and private foundation interest, enthusiasm is clearly lacking in both sectors.

Clarifying the nature of political crime

As previously indicated, not only should definitions of political crime start with a contemporary understanding of what a crime consists of, but it must acknowledge research that has been conducted on "political deviance" (for example, Corrado, Olivero, and Lauderdale, 1992). The term "political deviance" has been periodically and selectively used (1967-1992) by some scholars, but perhaps because of its dependence on normative behavior as a defining term, has been used as frequently as the term political crime. Although numerous definitions of political crime exist, one of the most useful is the one developed by Beirne and Messerschmidt (1991, p. 240). They define political crimes as:

> ... crimes against the state (violations of law for the purpose of modifying or changing social conditions) ... [and] crimes by the state, both domestic (violations of law and unethical acts by state officials and agencies whose victimization occurs inside [a particular country]) and international (violations of domestic and international law by state officials and agencies whose victimization occurs outside the US).

Given this categorization, a domestic political crime in the US could involve a correctional officer, for example violating a prisoner's civil, human or constitutional rights (Ross, 2008). On the other hand, an international political crime could include the destabilization of a foreign government, as the US was accused of attempting in Allende's Chile in 1970 (Agee, 1975). Alternatively, the 1998 bombing of the US embassies in Kenya and Tanzania, allegedly committed by the al-Qaeda terrorist organization, would also qualify as an international political criminal action.

Jurists usually distinguish a crime by referring to the existing criminal code, and if this is insufficient, they examine the context. The context includes the perpetrators' motives, affiliations, targets/victims, and the effects of the action (see, for example, Koistra, 1985; Ross, 2003). Context allows us to examine the victims and the perpetrators, and the kind of harm that has been inflicted.

Motives

In general, an actor has committed a political crime if he or she has a political or ideological intention or motivation to cause harm. The most clear-cut example of an oppositional political offense is to illegally force a change or overthrow the existing government of a country. A state-motivated political crime would consist of an action perpetrated by a government in an illegal manner to minimize or eliminate threats to its rule.

Caution, however, is paramount when analyzing political crime, because some kinds of actions are conducted in a political context but are appropriately not labeled as political crimes. For instance, unless one delves deeply into the psyche of the perpetrator, an assault against a police officer by a protester at a political demonstration, such as the anti-globalization protests in Seattle (1999), Washington, DC (2000), and Genoa (2001), is not commonly thought of as a political assault. Alternatively, the US-based Black Liberation Army (BLA) and its direct targeting and killing of police officers in New York City during the 1970s was suitably labeled as a political crime (Bell and Gurr, 1979).

If the intent of an action is in opposition to the state, then the act is generally considered a political crime. This argument, however, gets slippery in situations where intent is dubious and the possibility of multiple interpretations exists.

Take, for example, an engineer who works for an airplane manufacturer that builds a new version of a fighter jet. In an effort to raise his standard of living or to pay off creditors, he sells the plans of the aircraft and other useful information to a foreign spy. Although the engineer is cognizant of the implications of his actions, he is not motivated by opposition to his country's defense policies or practices, nor is he necessarily in favor of or in ideological alignment with the foreign government to which he sells the plans. Instead, the engineer sells the information for the financial gain he wants or needs.

Nevertheless, because potential harm to the national security of the state is present, the engineer's actions should be classified as a political, rather than nonpolitical, crime. As this example should demonstrate, intent is neither necessary nor sufficient for an action to be labeled a political crime.

Membership/affiliations of the perpetrator

To further clarify, some crimes can be identified as political based on the affiliation of the individual. Occasionally, we can distinguish a political crime based on the membership of the perpetrator. If the person is part of a recognized terrorist organization, then it is highly likely, but not certain, that his or her action had a political intent. Others, such as Theodore (Ted) Kaczynski, the "Unibomber," did not have an affiliation, but it is clear, through his manifestos, that his letter bombs and parcels had a political/ideological intent.

The kind of victim/target

In addition to the unique nature of political crime, the majority of these kinds of offenses are perpetrated by or against a recognized governmental entity (at the federal, state, provincial, county or municipal level). At other times, individuals, organizations, and corporations are used as the conduit by which perpetrators communicate discontent to the government.

The crime's effect

Finally, political crimes can also be identified by the effect of the criminal action on the government and the public. If the harmful event is committed against the state or by the government against a citizen, then we can say a political crime has occurred. In this context, the state is the apparatus of the government, interests identified with the government and people who work for the government (bureaucrats, administrators, politicians) (Carnoy, 1984; Evans et al., 1985).

In sum, a political crime can be identified by triangulating among the existing laws that are broken, the perpetrator's motivations (aka intent), the affiliations of the perpetrator, the kind of victim/target attacked, the result/effect of the actions, and/or more simply, the context of the action.

Why political crime has changed over the past three decades

Over the past three decades, since the publication of Turk's seminal book (1982a), historical events leading to new policy concerns have affected the nature of and response to political crime. Many longstanding threats to homeland and national security have disappeared, and new ones have developed.[7]

1990s

With respect to the US, in 1990, shortly after the election of Boris Yeltsin, the formerly Communist Soviet Union and many of its satellite countries dissolved into a loose confederation of states. Two years later (February 1, 1992), it was officially acknowledged that the Cold War between the US and the Soviets had ended. Most of the former Soviet states countries were now making their first steps towards Western-style democracy.

In March 1990, the South African Apartheid system ended. In 1994, the country elected Nelson Mandela, its first black president, who had been incarcerated for almost 27 years as the leader of the outlawed African National Congress (ANC). In April 1994, Rwanda witnessed fighting between the Hutu and Tutsi tribes, resulting in one the worst genocides of that period.

On August 2, 1990, Iraqi tanks crossed the border into Kuwait. An international armed force sponsored by the United Nations and led by the US was assembled, and it successfully pushed the Iraqi military. Although the Persian Gulf War was successful in its intent (with a surrender signed on February 24, 1991), Saddam Hussein remained in power as the President of Iraq because the UN mandate was observed and followed.

In the early 1990s, it appeared that peace was finally coming to the Middle East. After a decade-long Intifada (a low-intensity resistance by Palestinian youths to the continued Israeli occupation of the West Bank and Gaza), the Palestinian–Israeli (Oslo) Peace Accords (1993) were signed. For once, there was hope and evidence that a democratic Palestinian state was being established that could coexist beside Israel. This historic agreement culminated with Yasser Arafat, leader of the Palestinian Liberation Organization (PLO), shaking hands with Israeli Prime Minister Yitzhak Rabin, with President Bill Clinton in attendance, all on the White House lawn.

Elsewhere, in February 1994, Bosnian Serbs attacked an open-air market in Sarajevo, unleashing the beginning of a major civil war in the former Yugoslavia, which included war crimes, ethnic cleansing, and genocide. This precipitated a refugee crisis and the involvement of the United Nations (UN) forces for almost a decade.

On November 4, 1995, an Israeli citizen opposed to the Peace Accord assassinated Rabin, and subsequent political change was slow. Within a few years' time, increased violence on both sides, including the death of Arafat (2004), the election of Hamas (2006), and the Gaza War (December 2008-January 2009), called into question the possibility of long-term peace between the Palestinians and the Israelis.

During the 1990s, charges of state crimes were not limited solely to countries outside of the US. On March 3, 1991, four white Los Angeles policemen were caught on videotape severely beating African-American motorist Rodney King. This led to their suspension and the filing of criminal charges. On April 29, 1992, when the all-white jury in neighboring Simi Valley, California, acquitted the officers, Los Angeles became the scene of a major riot that lasted close to a week.

In August 1992, in Ruby Ridge, Idaho, federal agents tried to arrest avowed white supremacist Randy Weaver on weapons charges. The armed standoff resulted in government snipers killing Weaver's wife and child. In February 1993 in Waco, Texas, the Bureau of Alcohol, Tobacco, and Firearms (formerly a division of the US Department of Treasury) tried to arrest David Koresh, the charismatic leader of a Christian millenarian sect called the Branch Davidians. The situation led to another standoff, this time at the Davidians' compound. After 51 days, the final assault, led by the Federal Bureau of Investigation (FBI), resulted in the compound becoming a veritable inferno. Eighty-six cult members, including children, died. Unintentionally, these two incidents bolstered a fledgling militia movement in numerous states.

Meanwhile, highly visible Truth and Reconciliation Commissions, with the purpose of bringing perpetrators of genocide, human rights violations, and war crimes to justice, have begun in numerous countries (for example, South Africa,

1995-98, Rwanda, 2006-09, Bosnia-Herzegovina, 2001-present), and through the world court in The Hague (The Netherlands).

In addition, arguably the best-known type of political crime – terrorism – has increased in many countries. During the past two decades, US soil has experienced some of the most dramatic acts in the nation's history.

On February 26, 1993, members of al-Qaeda placed a truck bomb in the underground parking garage of the World Trade Center in New York City. Although the bombers' original intent was to fell one of the buildings, the resultant blast failed to demolish the structure, although it killed six people and injured 1,042 others (Reeve, 1999).

The US has not been the only target of political terrorist acts that have injured and killed numerous people. On March 20, 1995, members of Aum Shinrikyo, an anti-government religious cult operating in Japan, released sarin, a deadly nerve gas, in Tokyo's subway system. This resulted in the death of 10 people and more than 5,000 injured.

On April 19, 1995, decorated Persian Gulf War veteran Timothy McVeigh, with the assistance of Terry L. Nichols and Michael Fortier, detonated a Ryder truck bomb that destroyed the Alfred P. Murrah Federal Building in Oklahoma City. One hundred and sixty-eight people were killed, including several children in the building's second-floor daycare center. Another 680 individuals were injured. McVeigh, who was later apprehended and given the death penalty, said that he committed the action because of his disappointment with the federal government's handling of the Ruby Ridge and Branch Davidian incidents (Hamm, 1997).

On April 3, 1996, Theodore (Ted) Kaczynski (known as the "Unibomber") was finally arrested and charged with a series of mail bombings he had perpetrated. These were ostensibly directed against supporters of technology and those who were hurting the environment. In January 2001, President Clinton left office under a shroud of controversy because of a number of scandals in which he (and sometimes, his wife) was alleged to have been involved in (Whitewater, abuse of power, and romantic or sexual involvement with assorted women). Additional tension was produced by President Clinton's unsuccessful impeachment.

2000s

On September 11, 2001, 19 al-Qaeda members hijacked four airplanes and flew two of them into the two towers of the World Trade Center, one into the Pentagon and one into a rural field in Pennsylvania. This act alone probably stands as one of the most important US political crimes, leading to 3,000 deaths and 6,800 injured.

Although not nearly as dramatic or deadly, autumn 2001 witnessed the sending of a number of deadly anthrax-filled letters through US post offices, some addressed to well-known television broadcasters and others to politicians. The attacks led to the deaths of three people, the hospitalization of others, and the slowdown and virtual shutdown of the US postal system. In 2008, following a series of US law enforcement failures, and multiple interpretations, the FBI conceded that Bruce Ivans was the likely culprit. Ivans committed suicide before formal criminal charges could be laid against him, was a disgruntled federal government biodefense researcher who had experienced psychological problems.

Since 9/11, members of al-Qaeda have been implicated in various terrorist actions around the world: the bombing in Bali, Indonesia (October 2002); the commuter train bombing in Madrid (March 2004); the London Underground bombing (July 2005); and the armed attack in Mumbai, India (November 2008).

In 2003 the US, in conjunction with the United Kingdom, attacked Iraq under the pretext that Iraq possessed Weapons of Mass Destruction. The military incursion (known as Operation Iraqi Freedom) led to the toppling of Hussein, regime change, and the presence American troops in Iraq for close to nine years.

In sum, over the past 50 years the political actors, technology, laws and ideas/values have changed significantly. These developments have implications for the study of and response to political crime.

Typologies and categories of political crime

Besides a brief review of the motives, membership/affiliations, targets, and effects of political crimes, it is helpful to discuss in detail two major distinctions that are important in the context of such crimes: targets and perpetrators.

Targets

Although a variety of specific types of political crimes are covered in different sections of this book, they can be classified into two types: oppositional (or anti-systemic) and state (or pro-systemic). The former refers to those actions committed by individuals, groups, and countries that want to change or dismantle a particular political or economic system, its institutions, the state, and/or interests aligned with the state (for example, major corporations).[8] The latter types of political crime encompass those actions committed by the state's criminogenic agencies (for example, the police, military, and national security agencies), including their managers and agents. These actions are orchestrated against a country's own citizens, foreigners, or other foreign governments (Roebuck and Weeber, 1978; Ross, 1995/2000, Chapter 1, 2000b).

Generally, research on political crime does not accommodate both types of crime, or even link them together. However, in order to understand thoroughly the full scope of political crime, it is necessary to appreciate the interdependency (both definitional and substantive) of oppositional and state political crime.

Perpetrators

Various categories of political criminals (or perpetrators) (for example, organizational, occupational, and individual) also exist (Roebuck and Weeber,

1978, pp. 7–8). The first type, organizational, refers to situations in which crimes are committed on behalf of or for the benefit of a collection of people who are part of a particular unit, whether that is a terrorist group or a national security agency.

The second category, occupational, encompasses crimes committed by individuals in the course of their jobs or professions for their own personal gain, both pecuniary and nonpecuniary (for example, corruption).[9] Some occupations are structured such that individuals performing them are frequently put in situations where they occasionally break the law in order to achieve the goals of the organization for whom they work.

Lastly, some political crimes are committed solely by individuals acting independently. These occur without any organizational involvement or support, and benefit only the perpetrators participating in the misdeeds.

Furthermore, the reader should keep in mind that political criminals usually do not define their actions as illegal. They minimize conceptualizations of themselves as criminals through complicated mechanisms of denial, rationalization, and neutralization (Sykes and Matza, 1957). These mental processes allow individuals to justify their violations of the law or of other norms, and this interpretation helps to minimize and/or negate any self-identification as criminals. In this context, individuals can rationalize their behavior before or after the deviant act (Coleman, 1994, p. 202).

Why is this distinction important?

Political crime is dependent on the tensions among people, occupations, and organizations. For instance, the problem of mobilizing appropriate resources to organizational breaches is an important problem in many administrative settings. Individual terrorists, for example, may not want to wait for the group to which they belong to take action, or they may share sympathies to reach a consensus, before political action takes place.

The difference between organizational, occupational, and individually based political criminals is fundamental to any discussion of political crime that attempts to understand the various causes and effects of political crime. Organizationally based crimes are potentially much more egregious than occupational or individual crimes. Put simply, groups can typically marshal more resources and can, thus, have a greater detrimental or adverse impact on civil rights, personal liberties, freedoms, property, and lives than individuals acting alone.

Where does state crime fit?

Although democratic governments and their employees are bound by specific laws and statutes forbidding them to engage in particular illegalities (typically embedded in criminal and administrative law), they periodically violate these rules for special purposes. Crimes committed by the state are somewhat unique because they include illegalities committed by the government as a whole, by organizational units of the state and by individual officials who break the law for their own personal or their agency's gain (Ross, 1995/2000, 2000b). These types of crime differ because the former is organizationally based whereas the latter is regarded as individual crimes of occupational corruption. Just as some types of white-collar crime are organizationally based (for example, the Ford Pinto case of violence against consumers; see, for example, Cullen et al., 1987), some specific political state crimes are also considered organizational (see, for example, Kauzlarich and Kramer, 1993, 1998). For instance, the FBI's ongoing illegal surveillance of US citizens (1925-72; see Chapter Seven, this volume) was an agency-wide operation, conducted with the guidance of top FBI officials, and involved almost every field office in the US (Churchill and Vander Wall, 1990, 1998; Davis, 1992). Finally, these actions should not necessarily be viewed as conspiracies where government actors (managers and bureaucrats) secretly and systematically plan and commit crimes, but as unsavory outcomes of organizational goals and constraints (Parenti, 1995, Chapter 8).

What this book seeks to accomplish

Although a considerable number of academic articles and book chapters have been written on the subcomponents of political crime, only a handful of English-language books (sole-authored or edited) have been published on the general subject, including Proal's *Political crime* (1898/1973), Schafer's *The political criminal* (1974), Roebuck and Weeber's *Political crime in the United States* (1978), Ingraham's *Political crime in Europe* (1979), Turk's *Political criminality* (1982a), Kittrie and Wedlock's *The tree of liberty* (1986), Tunnell's *Political crime in contemporary America* (1993b), Hagan's *Political crime* (1997), Kittrie's *Rebels with a cause* (2000), Ross's *Dynamics of political crime* (2003), and Head's *Crimes against the state* (2011). This literature has contributed to our understanding of the role of politics in the creation of and response to criminal acts.

Some of the early scholarship, however, suffered from problems that were inevitable, since they were produced at a time when few studies on the subject had been published. These difficulties, listed in increasing importance, include:

- the analysis is ahistorical, there is little appreciation of the longstanding difficulties connected with political crime;
- the publications ask more questions than they answer;
- the writing is overly pretentious, polemical, or philosophical;
- the writing style is conservative in tone;
- the examples marshaled are confined mainly to discussions of political crime in Western democracies;
- the literature is dated;
- the research is highly anecdotal or focuses primarily on the description of specific cases;

- the publications are based primarily on collections of government or nongovernmental organization (NGO) reports;
- theoretical explanations of causes are overly simplistic or questionable;
- the types of political crime are not integrated;
- few implications for policy are drawn from these studies;
- the explanation of the effects of political crime is limited;
- the studies focus mainly on anti-systemic political crimes; and,
- there is little appreciation of the interconnectedness of causes and effects.

In other words, analysts in the past primarily embraced a static perspective.

This early work on political crime reflected the embryonic state of the field, although some of the problems listed above are still present in the current literature. It is not my goal to correct all of these issues, only the most important. However, I do intend to contribute in some way to the knowledge base.

Although political crime is as old as the creation of the first state, this book focuses solely on advanced industrialized democracies during the contemporary period (1960-present)[10] – in particular the three dominant Anglo-American democracies (the US, Canada, and the United Kingdom) – and strives to explain the nature and dynamics of political crime in these geographic contexts. These countries stand in stark contrast to lesser-developed states, which are commonly ruled by authoritarian and/or totalitarian governments and economies are primarily based on agricultural production and/or raw material extraction. Most state agencies in advanced industrialized countries are subject to a variety of controls. When intolerable levels of state crime come to public attention, the results often involve public and governmental indignation, scandal (Markovitz and Silverstein, 1988), and/or a crisis of legitimacy (Habermas, 1975). Unlike the totalitarian and authoritarian states, Anglo–American countries facilitate the expression of public discontent and publicize inquiries into political crimes.

The past six decades have been selected for study because during that time, perhaps more than ever, elaborate controls have been established and the legitimacy of state actions called into question. During the 1970s and 1980s, the three countries in this study were affected by "belt-tightening" policies and practices situationally referred to as Reaganism, Thatcherism, or Mulronyism (Ratner and McMullen, 1983). This led to a decline in the provision of social services and, in many cases, an increase in public security functions. This situation created the conditions for a variety of injustices, including state crimes. In addition, Canada and the US are the world's largest trading partners, and their economies are intimately linked through such arrangements as the North American Free Trade Agreement (NAFTA). Finally, this period also corresponds to what some analysts (see, for example, Ingelhart, 1977) call the post-industrial era, one of the most significant historical changes in recent time.[11] Some scholars have argued that the past two decades qualify as an era of liquid modernity (see, for example, Bauman, 2000), in which globalization and communication technology have altered both human relations and the forces of capitalism. In this context, political crime stands at the nexus of these trends.

This book builds on the strengths of previous research and analysis, and is interdisciplinary in scope. In general, all evidence has been garnered from open source literature, including scholarly and "popular" books and articles, and news media stories. Additionally, a number of interviews were conducted with individuals called "sources," as part of their job involved prosecuting or defending so-called political criminals.

Equally important are the types or subtypes of political crime. Each chapter in the book focuses on a dominant variant of political crime. The most important subtypes of political crime are reviewed, including, but not limited to, corruption, illegal domestic surveillance, human rights violations, and state-corporate crime. Almost every conceivable political crime is covered, but an attempt was made to focus on some issues rather than others.

In addition, a discussion of genocide best rests with totalitarian and authoritarian states, which this book does not explore. "State crimes of commission and omission" are addressed in the general chapter on "state crime" (Chapter Six); "torture" is covered in a chapter on "state violence" (Chapter Ten); "war crimes" is not covered because few individuals were charged and/or convicted of this offence during the contemporary period in the US, Canada, or the United Kingdom.[12] The conclusion attempts to deal with the dialectical strategies that pertain to controlling political crime.

Summary

The previous discussion introduced a definition of political crime and its various types, while also sensitizing readers to the dynamics of political illegalities. The following chapter reviews the varying theoretical explanations of political crime and clarifies how this phenomenon is the product of individuals, situations, organizations, and resource adequacy (referred to by the acronym, ISOR). The remainder of this book covers each type of political crime, with special attention to its definition, types, history, conceptual issues, typologies, frequency and impact, and causes and effects. A variety of examples are provided to explicate the processes.

The first half of the book focuses on oppositional political crimes. Eight major crimes against the state are recognized: assassination, espionage/spying, political rioting, sabotage, sedition, subversion, treason, and terrorism. In the second half of this study, five state political crimes – political corruption, illegal domestic surveillance, human rights violations, state violence, and state-corporate crime – are examined. After demonstrating the weaknesses of our current system for dealing with political crime, the conclusion outlines the difficulties in articulating appropriate measures for controlling it.

An introduction to political crime is an encompassing treatment of the general subject of political crime. This conceptualization goes beyond traditional ones by including activities resulting in social harm, moral transgressions, and civil and human rights violations. This broader definition includes activities that until recently were excluded from most studies of political crime.

Notes

[1] The terms political crimes, offenses and illegalities are used interchangeably throughout this book.

[2] Scheingold (1998) continues this tradition. He labels this kind of activity as "political criminology"; this approach, however, confuses traditional political crime with the political ramifications of crime policy.

[3] Some, but not all, political crimes can be identified as crimes against the social or public order. Violations of this nature "disturb or invade society's peace and tranquility" (Schmalleger, 2002, p. 431).

[4] While state means a governmental entity, a nation is typically composed of a group that shares the same language, history and customs. Thus, it is technically a mistake to confuse a nation with a state or even a country.

[5] These alternative definitions began mostly with the scholarship of Sutherland (1949a, 1949b), who encouraged a definition resting on socially injurious behavior. Two decades later, Schwendinger and Schwendinger (1975) expanded the scope of crime by calling for a definition resting squarely on human rights violations. For them, a criminal was an individual, organization, state, or social relationship that denied individuals the right to realize their human potential (see also Bohm, 1993). Racism, sexism, and economic exploitation resulting from profit-maximizing social relations have also been treated as crimes as they violate individuals' basic human rights (see, for example, Quinney, 1977). Bohm (1993) has argued for a more inclusive definition of crime, focusing on human rights violations conducted by the state, which are considered political crimes.

[6] This concept is sometimes referred to as crimes by the powerful (Pearce, 1976; Tombs and Whyte, 2003). Crimes by the powerful include not only actions by the state, but elites and corporations too. Although useful, it takes the conversation into a direction that is somewhat tangential to my current concerns.

[7] Although there are a number of books reviewing the history of the past two decades, both Joseph (1994) and Flexner and Flexner (2000) are helpful.

[8] And for whatever reasons, they are willing to participate in the "political process" of the very states that these forces seek to alter.

[9] One of the problems with political corruption is the uncertainty of whether or not it qualifies as a political crime, and second, whether it is a crime against the state or a crime by the state against its citizens. See Chapter Seven, this volume, for a detailed discussion of this issue.

[10] In general, data is easiest to access in advanced industrialized democracies; thus, the findings should be more accurate.

---

[11] The post-industrial era involved a shift in the dominant bases of the economy from manufacturing to the provision of services. There has also been an attendant change in the issues that concern the public, particularly a movement from material concerns to those of quality of life.

[12] Since the 1960s, the charge of war crimes has often been used as a rhetorical device by political activists in order to draw attention to their displeasure with their countries and foreign policies and participation in war efforts in other countries (for example, Vietnam, Iraq, Afghanistan).

TWO

Theoretical explanations
of political crime

Introduction

Theories are developed and designed to explain the causes and effects of processes and phenomena, and to predict likely outcomes. Social science theories, including those that cover the subjects of criminology and criminal justice, are no different in this regard. Needless to say, not all theories are viable. Often there is a quest to create the "best" theory and this may require the expenditure of considerable resources. Students, scholars, and practitioners should bear in mind that theories should not be judged on whether they are "good" or "bad," but rather on their utility.

In order to determine the usefulness of particular theories, academics have advanced criteria. One such effort identifies five basic qualities of a useful theory: testable, logically sound, communicable, general, and parsimonious (Manheim and Rich, 1986, pp. 19-20). To assess utility, theories (more appropriately, their hypotheses) can be tested, and those that demonstrate merit can be translated into policies or practices, reified and/or abandoned (and not necessarily in that order). This process may provide some scholars with a certain degree of contentment or complacency by reassuring them that theories are important. It may also be a welcome distraction from other more pressing social and political problems. In order to understand better the dynamics of political crime, I briefly review not only the general theories of crime that are relevant to political crime, but also the small number of explanations that have been designed with political illegalities in mind. I then sketch the outlines of a preliminary framework for a revised theory, building on differential association and routine activities theories.

Is a theory of political crime necessary?

There are two dominant explanations concerning the necessity of a theory of political crime. Those in favor of a theory of political crime might argue that if political crime is ever to be understood, controlled, or eliminated, then we need to have a sophisticated explanation. Thus, we must understand why political crime happens and who participates in this type of offense. Once these components are determined, we can propose some general causal principles, rigorously test them, and then develop and implement better policies and practices designed to control political crime. If responding to political crime is successful (however defined), then in the case of anti-systemic political crime, we can better protect our democratic system of government against unsavory sentiments and elements in the population, and in the case of state crime, we can restore trust in the government and minimize its negative effects. Such action will also allow us to better allocate the scarce resources that are invested in controlling political crime. By extension, some people argue that if no theory exists, then people may become cynical, lose faith in their leaders, representatives and experts, and become apathetic about the possibility of social change. Subsequently the democratic political process could collapse, and the state would deteriorate.

On the other hand, some may suggest that although a theory of political crime would be helpful in understanding this kind of behavior, it is not necessary. Developing a theory is no guarantee of a peaceful existence or coexistence, or the resolution of conflict. Those who doubt the importance of a theory of political crime may also argue, for example, that the premise that the general public, scholars, and practitioners need a theory in order to properly identify the actions of someone like Osama bin Laden, the former head of al-Qaeda, or Colonel Oliver North, who was closely connected with the Iran-Contra scandal, is questionable.

Is it possible to have a theory of political crime?

A major difficulty in developing a theory of political crime is that political crime can be comitted by a diverse range of actors. In order to control or reduce political crime, a society may benefit from a theory that explains why or how these kinds of crimes are committed. Once the point of origin is found, reformers may take steps to resolve the problem, restore accountability, and enable good government. Since the types of political crimes are very broad, however, perhaps several theories need to be developed/integrated for dealing with the different manifestations of political offenses. In other words, and in all likelihood, there cannot be a general "catch-all" theory to explain political crime, but there may be an approximation.

Theories of political crime

No widely accepted causal theories of crime, including political crime, exist. Although this hinders our ability to specify an appropriate explanation for political offences, we can talk about relevant theories. Few scholars have developed a theory of political crime.

Merton (1938, 1964, 1966) provided one of the earliest explanations that, in part, touches on political crime. According to his anomic theory of deviance (that is, strain theory), individuals live in societies that have a considerable amount of "structural dysfunctionalism." This, in turn, leads people to experience an ends/ means discrepancy. These processes combined together create stress. In order to minimize discomfort, individuals have five options, one of which is rebellion (nominally, a type of political crime). Merton's anomic theory of deviance, which partially explains political illegalities, is used by Kelly (1972) and Alexander (1992a,

1992b). Unfortunately, Merton's theory, regardless of who uses it, is too limited for a more encompassing understanding of political crime (see Box 2.1).

Box 2.1: Robert King Merton (1910–2003)

Robert King Merton was born on July 5, 1910, in Philadelphia, Pennsylvania. He earned his PhD in Sociology from Harvard University in 1932. His last teaching position was as Professor of Sociology at Columbia University. Merton was also designated as a distinguished lecturer to many universities, institutes, and organizations in the US and overseas. During his career, he was a member of several important delegations and committees, including the American Sociological Association, of which he was once president. In 1994, Merton won the National Medal of Science, and in 1996, he was awarded the Edwin Sutherland Award from the American Society of Criminology. He is known for originating such terms as "self-fulfilling prophecy" and "role models," and his specializations included anomie, deviance, sociology of science, mass media, history, and literature. Merton is the author of numerous publications, including *Social theory and social structure: Toward the codification of theory and research* (1949), *On theoretical sociology: Five essays, old and new* (1967), *The sociology of science: Theoretical and empirical investigations* (1973), and *Contemporary social problems: An introduction to the sociology of deviant behavior and social disorganization* (1961), with Robert A. Nisbet. Merton's works have been translated into numerous languages.

Source: Literature Resource Center; Kaufman (2003)

Similarly, Moran (1974) describes "sequential stages which in successive combination might account for the development of a political criminal" (p. 73). The first step involves what Moran calls "predisposing conditions or background factors, the conjunction of which forms a pool of potential political criminals. These conditions exist prior to an individual's decision to commit a political crime and by themselves do not account for his behavior" (pp. 73-4). The aforementioned conditions include the concept of strain and "a political problem solving perspective." The latter consists of "situational contingencies which lead to the commission of political crimes by predisposed individuals" (p. 74). Moran advocates a five-stage "developmental model" consisting of the following steps: (a) strain; (b) "political problem solving perspective"; (c) a turning point event; (d) commitment to act; and (e) engaging in the political crime. Although he recognizes many of the limitations of his idea, the cases on which Moran builds his model may be too ideographic to legitimately support the kinds of generalizations he makes.

Turk (1982a) has offered an alternative perspective. His structural conflict theory posits that although power and inequality are important factors in explaining political crime, the cultural gap between offenders and authorities is the primary factor that leads to the commission of political crime. Turk's theory is interesting, but it is limited in its explanatory power (see Box 2.3).

Box 2.2: Richard Moran (1944–)

Richard Moran is Professor of Sociology at Mount Holyoke College and the author of *Knowing right from wrong: The insanity defense of Daniel McNaughtan* and *Executioner's current: Thomas Edison, George Westinghouse, and the invention of the electric chair.* He has written numerous scholarly articles and reviews. He also served as a commentator for five years on National Public Radio, Morning Edition, and has written OP-EDs for *The New York Times, Wall Street Journal, Washington Post, Boston Globe, Los Angeles Times, Newsweek* and *Time Magazines*, etc. He is the winner of the 2004 Hugo Adam Bedau for his scholarly contributions to the research literature on capital punishment. His current research is on creating a nonprofit prison system as an alternative to public/private prisons, and unlawful convictions in capital cases.

Box 2.3: Austin T. Turk (1934–)

Born in 1934 in Gainesville, Georgia, Austin T. Turk is Professor of Sociology at the University of California, Riverside. His research and writing focus primarily on relationships among law, power inequality, and social conflict. Major publications include: *Criminality and legal order* (1969), *Legal sanctioning and social control* (1972), and *Political criminality: The defiance and defense of authority.* Turk is a Fellow and former president of the American Society of Criminology. He has been a Trustee of the Law and Society Association, as well as Chair of the American Sociological Association's Section on Crime, Law and Deviance. Turk's most recent publications include "Political violence: patterns and trends," in R.A. Silverman, T.P. Thornberry, B. Cohen and B. Krisberg (eds) *Crime and justice at the millennium: Essays by and in honor of Marvin E. Wolfgang* (2002); "Policing international terrorism: options," *Police Practice and Research: An International Journal* (2002); "Sociology of terrorism," *Annual Review of Sociology* (2004); "Policing revolutionary and secessionist violence: an overview" (guest editor's introduction, special issue), *Police Practice and Research: An International Journal* (2005); and "Criminology and conflict theory," in S. Henry and M.M. Lanier (eds) *The essential criminology reader* (2006).

Merton, Moran and Turk's theories are useful in describing, and in some cases explaining, various types of political crime, but they are not very helpful in accounting for all types of this phenomenon. The dynamic nature of such activities needs to be more thoroughly explored, and furthermore, the macro- and micro-level processes in political crime should be linked (see, for example, Frenkel-Brunswik, 1952).

The broader context

Often, research about political crime uses a static perspective or maintains that political crime primarily results from either state or oppositional activities. Like many other phenomena in the social and natural sciences, the process of political crime follows an interactive, iterative or what I call, "dynamic" pattern. In short, building on Newtonian physics and political conflict research (for example, Holsti, Brody, and North, 1981; Lichbach, 1987), nothing in nature is static, and neither is political crime. One of the central hypotheses underlying political crime is grounded in the interaction between anti-systemic political crime and state crime (Ross, 2003, Chapter 2).

In an effort to illustrate how dynamic political crime can be, we should look at an example of a pattern whereby state crimes can cause oppositional crimes and vice versa (similar to the concept of Morphing; see Ross, 2006, pp. 13-14). The history of the country of Israel is replete with periods of Israeli state terrorism (as well as anti-Arab settler violence) that motivated Palestinian anti-systemic terrorism, which in turn caused Israeli security responses against the Palestinian people and "terrorist organizations" (Chomsky, 1983; Miller, 2000). When this complex dynamic, as exemplified by the Israeli–Palestinian issue, is recognized, blame can be directed against all participants in a conflict (that is, individuals, organizations, and countries) and not simply towards one party. This is not to say that the claim that oppositional political crime leads to state crime and vice versa is a sufficient explanation to understand this phenomenon, but it is a reasonable hypothesis.

Political crime does not exist in a vacuum. Rather, as previously mentioned, it is affected by a series of factors that are endemic to the people who commit the crimes, the occupations they hold, the organizations that employ them (or of which they are members), and more generally, the context in which a particular crime exists. Since political crime is affected by an individual's state of mind, we need to initially turn to psychological theories. Political crime is also contingent on cultural, economic, organizational, political, and social influences, usually collectively referred to as "social structure." Thus, political crime is a response to a variety of subtle, ongoing, interacting, and changing psychological and structural factors manifested by perpetrators, victims, state agencies, and audiences.[1]

A vast array of theories shed light on various aspects of political crime. Moreover, one must accept the possibility that each type of political crime may have a different cause. The relative explanation of a particular political crime, therefore, depends on the situational dynamics. One category of theories are "micro" in focus because they explain phenomena pertinent to people, their differences, their mental states, and their interactions. The micro theories typically explain individual-level behavior and encompass explanations subsumed by psychology. On the other hand, "macro" theories are relevant because they clarify how environmental factors (including institutions, economics, political systems, and cultures) affect individuals and groups. Among the macro theories are sociological explanations, sometimes called structural explanations.

Linking macro and micro theoretical explanations helps to make sense of political crimes. Relying on these theories forces us to appreciate the actions of specific individuals in tandem with the environment in which they live and work.

Although each of these broad paradigms subsumes several theories, subtypes of each category are proving to be even more useful, and they are now enjoying wide currency among scholars as explanations of political crime. In the area of structural theory, the social conflict approach has utility. On the other hand, differential association is a pertinent category of psychological theory (Sutherland, 1947).

Regardless, the most dominant cause behind acts of political crime (oppositional or state) is the desire to maintain or expand power for an individual and/or his or her organization. In general, political crime is motivated by a quest for power in all of its ramifications. People or groups may lack power or fear that their power is being threatened. Individuals may want power because of greed, feeling oppressed, opportunity, and/or recognition (that is, hubris). They may distrust those who are in positions of power, they may have lost power because of general chaos and destruction that has ravaged their community, city, state, or country, or they may have experienced the death or injury of friends and loved ones in their lives. If successful, political crime can lead to a change in political leadership and the way a government (especially a bureaucracy) conducts its business. In short, success (and failure) can lead to material and psychic losses and gains.

Psychological theory

Psychological theories are rooted in individual-level processes. Differential association theory (see, for example, Sutherland, 1947) fits conveniently into this paradigm.[2] Sutherland's theory was first used to explain the process by which adolescent males become deviant and engage in delinquent behavior, including joining gangs. Later he reformulated and expanded his theory to include the illegal actions of the wealthy, whom he labeled white-collar criminals (Sutherland, 1949a, 1949b). Sutherland's theory, by logical extension, is applicable to political crime and criminals.

Differential association theory purports that crime is learned behavior that one adopts through affiliating and interacting with others. Favorable attitudes, as well as logistical information about how to commit crimes, are learned from close friends or acquaintances. In addition, one is socialized into having favorable definitions or attitudes about crime. This later process is pertinent to understanding how individuals come to regard crime as a viable course of action.[3]

In particular, Sutherland argued that criminal behavior is learned in a process of symbolic interaction with others, primarily in groups.[4] Although Sutherland organized his theory into nine statements, it is the sixth that he claimed as the principle of differential association. It argues that a person commits crimes because he or she learned "definitions" (rationalizations and attitudes) favorable to violation of the law in "excess" of the definitions unfavorable to breaking the law (Akers, 1994, p. 93).

Sutherland did not simply purport that association with "bad company" leads to criminality. Rather, he implied that one learns criminal behavior in intimate communication with criminal and noncriminal "patterns" and "definitions." Criminal behavior is explained by one's exposure to others' favorable definitions of crime that are weighed against one's contact with conforming, noncriminal definitions. The process varies according to the "modalities" of association. "That is, if persons are exposed first, more frequently, for a longer time, and with greater intensity to law-violating definitions than to law-abiding definitions, then they are more likely to deviate from the law" (Akers, 1994, p. 93).

Sutherland's theory is as pertinent to political crime and criminals as it is to juvenile delinquency and the vagaries of white-collar crime. It follows that political criminals acquire their behaviors through interactive learning with others. Although there will always be "lone wolves," it stands to reason that political offenders develop a belief that their actions offer positive outcomes when the definitions favorable to violation of the law exceed those definitions unfavorable to committing crimes. Whether considering oppositional terrorism by nationalist-separatists or human rights abuses by military officers, it is logical to assume that these behaviors are learned and conducted by individuals within various networks where a system of shared norms and values exists.

Sutherland's theory explains people's actions as learned within an environment that formally and informally instructs them that criminal behavior (or at least, certain types of political actions) are favorable, indeed more desirable than behaviors that do not violate the law. Thus, systematic violations of citizens' rights sanctioned by an organizational program within MI5 (a British national security agency) or the FBI (the US agency that is primarily tasked with investigating domestic terrorism and other criminal offenses of a national nature), for example, can in part be explained by this micro-theoretical perspective.

It also follows that Sutherland's theory is able to explain the process by which otherwise law-abiding police officers, acting within their bureaucracy, can violate both the law and individuals' human rights, knowing all the while that their actions are illegal and should be kept secret (see Chapters Six and Seven, this volume).

Structural theory

In general, structural theories posit that the causes of political crime can be found in the environment and/or the political, cultural, social, and economic structure of societies. Social-psychological theories specify and explain group dynamics, why individuals join organizations, and how participants (perpetrators, victims, and audiences) affect the commission of acts. Structural theories explain human behavior by focusing on the social structures within which individuals function and on the organizational dictates that affect varieties of behavior. Despite their diversity, these theories share a main concern in explaining societal organization and the ways that people are affected by institutions, culture, economies, and conflict.

Although several structural theories may be relevant to a discussion of political crime, many scholars regard conflict theory as the most valuable or useful explanation. To make matters more complicated, a variety of different conflict theories have been formulated. They range from conservative to radical perspectives, but they all agree that conflict is a naturally occurring social phenomenon. Special attention should be given to the variety of radical and critical theories, including but not limited to Marxist, neo-Marxist, and conflict approaches (Ross, 1998/2009). Radical conflict theory, some theorists suggest, explains the roots of much political crime that is situated in and emanates from social, political, and economic processes (Roebuck and Weeber, 1978, p. 7). Conflict theories differ specifically in their origins, their persistence, their ability to create change, and their contribution to understanding criminal behavior.

Even though many theories that have emanated from the radical/conflict tradition are parsimonious in nature, they have considerable explanatory power over various actions and are widely accepted by many criminologists, as evidenced by their inclusion in a large body of literature pertaining to political, white-collar, and state crime research (Ross, 1998/2009). Nonetheless, these theories are difficult to apply to practical policy concerns.

Radical conflict theory traces its origins to the work of Karl Marx (1818-83). He (along with Friedrich Engels) suggested that conflict in society is the result of a scarcity of resources (that is, property, wealth, power, and jobs). This creates inequalities among individuals and constituencies, which in turn lead to a struggle between those who possess these resources and those who do not (Marx and Engels, 1848/1948, p. 9). During the 1960s, a number of theorists applied these theories to crime. These neo-Marxist or "radical" conflict theorists (see, for example, Quinney, 1974, 1977) suggested that class struggle affects crime in at least three ways.

Quinney, a leading radical conflict theorist, argued that all crime in capitalist societies (which stresses individualism and competitiveness) should be considered a manifestation of the class struggle, whereby people strive for wealth, power, money, status, and property. In countries dominated by a capitalist mode of production, a culture of competition arises. This is seen as normal and desirable, and takes many forms, including criminality (Quinney, 1977, pp. 53-4; see also Bohm, 1982, p. 570).

Traditional neo-Marxists can be criticized for the disproportionate emphasis they place on the working class and poor (what Marx calls the "dynamite") as a catalyst of change. The working class and poor levels of society rarely participate in the political process (Lukes, 1974; Gaventa, 1980). Furthermore, the types of activities that are legislated as criminal, and that are responded to by the crime control industry, are often those behaviors most often engaged in by the poor and the powerless (Reiman, 1998).

New improved explanation

Clearly, a number of theories are more relevant (and useful) than others in explaining political crime in general and the different types in particular. In sum, political crime is the result of a complex interplay among individuals (I), situations/opportunities (S), organizations (O), and resource adequacy (R) (see Figure 2.1). I call this the ISOR relationship and explain it in detail below.

Figure 2.1: The individual-situation-organizational facilitation-resource adequacy (ISOR) explanation of political crime

Individuals who commit political crimes

Some people are more predisposed to break the rules than others. Often called nonconformists or malcontents, they have difficulty with sustained relationships (especially ones that involve issues of power and authority) and with organizations/institutions, whether a marriage, school, or corporation. In short, they do not like being told what to do, when to do it and how to do it. Nonetheless, individuals do not automatically take up arms or break the laws that exist in the society in which they live. In this respect, situational theories may shed light on our endeavor. Typically, however, situational theories have focused on crime prevention and opportunity structures (Clarke, 1992). Clearly, other kinds of opportunities also present themselves to individuals and organizations.

Situation presents itself

On a daily basis, many people and organizations are presented with situations and opportunities that can be perceived as providing some kind of benefit. At the same time, these individuals/entities are frustrated in their attempts to achieve certain goals. They may play by the rules (conform to generally accepted norms, including abiding by the law), or they may selectively or randomly break them.

Organization facilitates illegal/deviant behavior

Collectivities, also known as organizations, groups, and so on, whether we are talking about terrorist groups or national security agencies, may have as their primary mission the desire to overthrow a government, or quash dissent, respectively. An organization may be structured so it provides incentives, or it may have poor controls over its members' behavior. Although some scholars argue that all humans have a sense of bounded rationality (Simon, 1982), individuals, consciously or unconsciously, make cost-benefit calculations about whether they will uphold the law or break it.

Individuals/organizations have necessary resources

Organizations need the ability and capacity to mobilize resources (that is, money, personnel, training, technology, etc.) in order to accomplish their goals. For example, an untrained army may be equipped with the most modern equipment (for example, weapons), but unless it has proper training, it may not be able to mobilize properly (see, for example, Tilly, 1978). Shifting to a governmental context, states have a variety of resources that can be leveraged including information control, threat, coercion, infrastructure, organization, and experience. Moreover, technology (especially information and electronics) has improved and is now widely used, increasing the ability of both oppositional and state actors to engage in political crimes (see, for example, Ackroyd et al., 1980).

Whether the political crime is committed by government officials in the name of the state, individual bureaucrats acting for their own personal gain (self-interest), or people and groups desiring to change political and economic systems, each example is the result of the mobilization of available organizational or situational resources (for example, power).

In many respects, this theory of political crime is similar to Tilly's (1978) resource mobilization argument, but it differs in the following areas. Tilly suggested that the reason why groups rebel is not because of a relative deprivation, manifested through a process of frustration aggression (see, for example, Gurr, 1970). Rather, he argued that it was a combination of circumstances that included timing.

Anti-government groups may demand better housing, education, jobs, wealth redistribution, social support programs, and universal medical care. They may attempt to organize, protest, march, and strike. In advanced industrialized democracies, most of these actions are considered examples of democratic political participation and are protected by the country's constitution. This, however, does not mean that such activities are welcomed by the state; instead, they may be met with resistance from the state and its coercive agencies.

Just as important are the illegalities that the state and its agents commit when segments of the population appear threatening to the political status quo (Turk, 1982a, Chapter 4). Wiretapping, illegal surveillance, opening of mail, harassment, intimidation, and even overt force, for example, have all been used by states to contain the rising tide of democratic participation.

Summary

Although many political crimes are committed by groups that are formally or loosely structured, whether oppositional or state organizations, these activities are, in the final analysis, committed by individuals. These people are working within the structural confines of informal or complex organizations, political systems, political economies, and different cultures. They make decisions and act, while often denying that they are not engaged in any kind of wrongdoing.

In general, government response to political crime ranges from apathy to policy advocacy or organizational or political change.[5] In general, anti-systemic political illegalities are commonly met with either state-level resistance or change, whereas state crimes are met with apathy, resistance, or demands for change from the public or its elected representatives. Apathy and resistance are the most disconcerting responses to state crime because they prevent its control and encourage future commission. For example, a state that is the victim of espionage can simply ignore that a threat to national security has taken place. Alternatively, it can analyze the event or can engage in counterespionage. The ISOR relationship is not simply a resource mobilization theory or crime prevention through environmental design theory. Although it has the advantage of breaking up behavior into an easily understandable process, not all outcomes can be explained.

Even though conflict and differential association theories were originally developed for understanding nonpolitical crime, they can easily explain political law breaking and, as a result help us to understand the dynamics of political crime. Conflict in general, rather than that motivated by economic factors alone, is the most important reason why people engage in political crime. Groups and in-group socialization are equally important and powerful motivators.

This chapter has provided a backdrop to an applicable theory of political crime. One must recognize that although creating a theory of political crime may be difficult, it is a necessary although not wholly sufficient step in the process of understanding this phenomenon and establishing better controls or methods of prevention. The following sections are not tests, but contain descriptions and analyses of the most dominant political crimes in contemporary advanced capitalist societies (in particular the US, UK and Canada). The next chapter starts with an analysis of oppositional political crimes, which have attracted the lion's share of public, governmental and academic attention.

Notes

[1] Depending on the circumstances, any of these actors can be audiences.

[2] In particular, Burgess and Akers (1968) explained the rich meanings and relevance of differential association by extending it through a synthesis with learning and behavior modification theories.

[3] After some revision, differential association theory was detailed by Sutherland in nine points or statements, all of which are important for understanding the process by which one learns favorable attitudes for doing crime (Sutherland, 1947, pp. 6-7).

[4] Many political crimes (for example, espionage, treason, sedition, terrorism) are committed by individuals without any group support.

[5] See Ross, 2000a (Chapter 2), for a similar explanation of police responses to incidents of police violence/excessive force that have come to public attention.

THREE

Oppositional political crimes

Introduction

Oppositional political crimes is not simply a term that is found in a dusty old book you may stumble upon in a library, nor did it somehow just magically appear in the public mind. It is part of a larger understanding of crime and serves to organize a variety of diverse actions. Oppositional political crimes are a subset of "crimes against the administration of government" (Schmalleger, 2002, pp. 454-63). This broader rubric includes treason, misprision of treason,[1] rebellion, espionage, sedition, suborning of perjury, false swearing, bribery, contempt, obstruction of justice, resisting arrest, escape, and misconduct in office. Some, but not all, of these crimes have a political motivation. Treason, misprision of treason, rebellion, espionage, sedition, bribery, and misconduct in office are traditionally considered political crimes, while resisting arrest, bribery, and misconduct in office are not necessarily political offenses. The following reviews political crimes that are directed against government.

Delimiting and defining oppositional political crime

Although the labels and actions that individuals, organizations, and states have ascribed to anti-systemic political crime differ, this type of action has existed since the birth of the first state. Over time, the term has been clarified and the actions to which it refers delimited. This has been accomplished through scholarly debate and the practical difficulties experienced in applying the term and its component parts (and actions) to various anti-government behaviors. Definitions of political crime have also been shaped through the tendency of governments, when developing their criminal codes or legislation, to look at other countries for examples. According to Ingraham and Tokoro (1969), since the late 19th century "the doctrine of political crime has become increasingly limited in its scope and application and hedged with exceptions in those European democracies and constitutional monarchies which had adopted it into their codes" (p. 147).

Historically, oppositional political offenses have often exacted the most repressive responses from government. Indeed, before the French Revolution (1789-99), "these crimes were ... normally requited with the most severe and barbaric punishments, since an attack against the holders of power was ... an attack on the society itself, comparable to the attack of a foreign country" (Ingraham and Tokoro, 1969, p. 145).

A commonly accepted view is that the largest proportion of political crimes are anti-government in nature. However, the definitions and the characteristics attributed to political crime have varied considerably over time.[2] Proal (1898/1973), who wrote one of the classic books on political crime, introduced a broad interpretation that included anarchy, assassination, political hatreds, political hypocrisy, political spoliation, the corruption of politicians, electoral corruption, the corruption of law and justice by politics, and the corruption of manners. Many of his terms, however, particularly when interpreted through a 21st-century lens, appear ambiguous, archaic, or irrelevant to present-day behavior and laws. Today, we might question why Proal chose to identify many of these actions as political crimes.

It was not until the 1960s that considerable research and writing on the subject of political crime appeared. Schafer (1971, 1974), contrary to the scholars who preceded him, believed that political crime was a type of altruistic behavior motivated by ideological considerations. The actions of political offenders are not entirely selfless, however, as many engage in this activity to satisfy their own needs, too.

Box 3.1: Stephen Schafer (1911–76)

Stephen Schafer was born on February 15, 1911 in Budapest, Hungary. In 1933, he graduated from Eötvös Loránd University (Budapest) with a doctorate in jurisprudence. In the earlier part of his career (1933-43), he was a practicing attorney in Budapest; later (1947-51) he was Professor of Criminal Law at the University of Budapest. He moved to the US in 1961. During the last part of his career, he was Professor in the Department of Criminal Justice at Northeastern University (Boston, Massachusetts). His accomplishments include serving on the President's National Crime Commission, and in 1969, he worked on the President's Violence Commission. Schafer's numerous publications include: *Restitution to victims of crime* (1960), *The victim and his criminal: A study in functional responsibility* (1968), and *The political criminal: The problem of morality and crime* (1974).

Source: Literature Resource Center

Sagarin (1973), in an effort to clarify the meaning and usage of the term, argued that a political crime is "any violation of law which is motivated by political aims – by the intent, that is, of bringing about (or preventing) a change in the political system, in the distribution of political power or in the structure of the political-governmental bodies" (p viii). So, for example, violations of campaign funding laws and civil disobedience might fall under his definition. Although both oppositional and state crimes may be covered by this effort, Sagarin neglects to address the possibility that violations of civil law may also be considered political crimes.

Ingraham (1979), in his most classic piece of scholarship, suggests that political crimes are "acts which officials treat as if they were political and criminal regardless of their real nature and the motivation of their perpetrators."

Turk (1984) defines political crime as "whatever is recognized or anticipated by authorities to be resistance threatening the established structure of differential resources and opportunities" (p. 120). Turk (1982a), like Sagarin, does not consider state illegalities legitimate political crimes. He argues that "[n]o matter how heinous such acts may be, calling them political crimes confuses political criminality with political policing or with conventional politics, and therefore obscures the structured relationship between authorities and subjects" (p. 35).

Consequently, Turk suggests that oppositional political crime should be limited to four types: dissent (for example, sedition and treason), evasion (for example, income taxes, draft dodging), disobedience (for example, civil disobedience), and violence (for example, terrorism, kidnapping, and assassination). Turk's definition, however, is both under- and over-inclusive. He rejects state crimes and mentions a number of actions that, while they may have political overtones, are not political crimes in the strict sense of the term (for example, income tax evasion and kidnapping).

Finally, Hagan (1994, 1997) describes political crime, regardless of the source, as "criminal activity committed for ideological purposes" (p. 2). According to this perspective, shoplifting by members of a terrorist group might be equated with sedition by a person opposed to his or her government's policies and practices (see Table 3.1).

Table 3.1: Definition comparison chart

	Proal (1898)	Sagarin (1973)	Ingraham and Tokoro (1969)	Turk's (1982)
Sedition		x	x	x
Treason	x	x	x	x
Kidnapping		x	x	x
Assassination	x	x		x
Terrorism	x		x	x
Political corruption	x			
Anarchy	x			
Civil disobedience		x		x
Income tax evasion				x
Electoral corruption	x	x		
Political spoliation	x			
Political hatreds	x			
Draft dodging				x
Political hypocrisy	x			
Corruption of manners	x			
Corruption of law and justice by politics	x			

Typologies

In an effort to improve definitions of political crime and move towards a more analytic perspective, some experts have outlined acts that can and should be subsumed under the concept of political crimes. Others have marshaled typologies of political offenses. There is, however, considerable debate over which political offenses in general, and which anti-systemic political crimes in particular, are to be grouped into these categories.

Packer (1962) subdivided oppositional political crimes into "conduct inimical to the very existence of government, and offenses which affect the orderly and just administration of public business. Treason ... sedition or advocacy of overthrow, and espionage are examples of the former," whereas "perjury, bribery and corruption, and criminal libel and contempt by publication" (p. 77) are examples of the latter.

Ingraham and Tokoro (1969) divided political crimes into two types based on intent: pure and mixed/relative ones. Pure political offenses were those behaviors "which, by their very nature, tend to injure the state or its machinery of government either internally, or externally with regard to foreign powers" (p. 196). This delineation includes such crimes as treason and sedition. "Mixed" or "relative" political crimes, on the other hand, included "all criminal acts, regardless of kind, which have as their motive or object some rearrangement of political power within the state and which entail at the same time both an attack on the state and the private interests of citizens" (Ingraham and Tokoro, 1969, p. 146). In other words, acts such as an "assassination of a political figure, robbery, theft or vandalism during an insurrection" would be included in this category.

In another context, Ingraham (1979) further refined this distinction by creating a three-part typology of political crime to include: "acts of betrayal," "challenges to political authority and legitimacy," and "hindrance of official function." The first refers to behaviors "which deal with the safety and security of the nation and or society with respect to a foreign enemy." The second involves "those which concern the safety and security of rulers and the legitimizing principles on which their right to rule and their authority depends." And the last includes "those which involve impediments or embarrassments to rulers in carrying out functions of government such as foreign relations, taxation, coinage of money, raising armies, or the administration of law" (pp. 21–3).

Unlike Ingraham, Kittrie (1972) employed a target-based approach and divided political offenses into five categories, including those intended to: "weaken or destroy central political systems" (for example, treason and sedition); "weaken independent segments or subsystems of the political structure" (for example, "disruption of vital industries," etc.); "personal violence and harassment of individual representatives of the political system" (for example, "capitalists," politicians, etc.); "fund raising, designed to underwrite underground political crime phenomena" (for example, robberies, etc.); and "activities designed to produce visibility and public support for ... the protesting political group" (for example, "disruption of traffic," "unauthorized assembly" etc.). With the exception of "activities designed to weaken or destroy central political systems" (for example, treason and sedition), other activities identified fall under Ingraham and Tokoro's mixed or relative categories, which are excluded from this treatment of political crime.

Box 3.2: Barton L. Ingraham (1930–)

Barton L. Ingraham was born on June 10, 1930 in Paterson, New Jersey. He earned his BA from Harvard University in 1952, his JD (Juris Doctor) from Harvard University in 1957, and his DCrim (Doctor of Criminology) in 1972 from the University of California, Berkeley. During an earlier part of his career, he was a practicing attorney, but later became a professor. Ingraham's last academic job (1970-92) was as Associate Professor at the Institute of Criminal Justice and Criminology, University of Maryland, from which he retired. His publications include *Political crime in Europe: A comparative study of France, Germany, and England* (1979), *The structure of criminal procedure: China, the Soviet Union, France and the United States* (1987), and (with Thomas P. Maurillo) *Police investigation handbook* (1990).

One of the most useful typologies, perhaps because of its simplicity, is one that divides political crimes into those actions committed by opponents to a regime and ones perpetrated by a state (that is, the political leadership and those who work for the government bureaucracy) (Sagarin, 1973, p. viii; see also, Roebuck and Weeber, 1978). Finally, an equally important typology cutting across these two broad divisions includes two other types of oppositional political crimes: nonviolent and violent (Beirne and Messerschmitt, 1991, p. 241).

In sum, scholars interested in the typologies of political crime, albeit primarily anti-systemic political offenses, have categorized these actions based on a variety of factors: intent, target, degree of harm done to the target, situational location/profession of the violators, and degree of violence associated with the crime.

Table 3.2: Typology of political crimes

Level of violence	Government/state	Anti-government
Violent	Genocide Police violence	Assassination Terrorism
Nonviolent	Corruption Illegal domestic surveillance	Sedition Treason Espionage/spying

Box 3.3: Nicholas N. Kittrie (1928–)

Born on March 26, 1928 (aboard a Polish ship), Nicholas N. Kittrie arrived in the US in 1944 and became a naturalized citizen in 1950. That same year, he received his LLB (Bachelor of Laws) from the University of Kansas and his MA (Master's) a year later. He received his LLM (Master of Laws) in 1963 from Georgetown University and his SJD (Doctor of Juridical Science) from the same institution in 1968. In addition to being Professor Emeritus of Law at the American University (Washington, DC), Kittrie is also a practicing attorney and has been a visiting professor at various universities. He is a member of numerous international committees dealing with international and criminal law. His books include *The right to be different: Deviance and enforced therapy* (1971), *The tree of liberty: A documentary history of rebellion and political crime in America* (1986/98, edited with Eldon D. Wedlock Jr), *The war against authority: From the crisis of legitimacy to a new social contract* (1995), and *Rebels with a cause: The minds and morality of political offenders* (2000).

Source: Literature Resource Center

Summary

The previous section outlined seven distinctions discussed in the scholarly literature concerning classifications of anti-systemic political crimes. Nominally, nonviolent political offenses include sedition, treason, and espionage, and the next chapter focuses on these actions and related political crimes. Although these activities may be mentioned in constitutional or criminal law and a variety of legislative acts, because of the problematic nature and lack of frequency of these actions and their prosecution, the state generally uses other mechanisms to exert some form of social control against so-called political criminals or resisters (Torrance, 1977, 1995).

Notes

[1] Misprision of treason is a criminal charge applied to a person who knows that treason is going to occur but does nothing to stop it, in particular reporting it to the authorities.

[2] It is interesting to note that almost all of the individuals who have offered definitions of political crime have been male. This may signal an opportunity for the development of a feminist theory of political crime.

FOUR

Nonviolent oppositional political crimes

Introduction

In contemporary times, there is a subtle difference between nonviolent actions which are directed against the state (that is, dissent and civil disobedience) and those behaviors that the legal system (including some, but not all, scholars, policymakers, politicians, activists, and jurists) defines as anti-systemic political offenses (that is, treason, sedition, and espionage/spying).[1] Thus misprision of treason[2] and criminal syndicalism,[3] mentioned in the last chapter, have been recognized as oppositional political crimes, but in the last three decades these charges have been rarely applied by courts against political criminal defendants. Despite the existence of well-articulated laws concerning treason, sedition, and espionage/spying, criminal justice and national security agencies disproportionately arrest, charge and sanction "political" offenders using traditional criminal laws (Kittrie and Wedlock, 1986, p. xi).

In general, sedition, treason, and espionage are typically included in many of the criminal codes and in legislation governing the security and intelligence agencies of advanced industrialized countries.[4] All of these actions have existed since the creation of the first state; however, their codification in legal statutes has varied among countries due to the sophistication of legal codes and the availability of alternative mechanisms for quelling dissent. This chapter defines these actions and offenses and places them in a historical context.[5]

This categorization of what constitutes oppositional political crime varies across Anglo-American democracies. But to put matters in context, most of the laws have their origins in England, and over time, these concepts were integrated into the legal systems in the US and Canada when these countries were forming their respective criminal codes. Although England and Wales do not have a formal criminal code (Spencer, 2000), Canada has a federal criminal code. In Canada, the principal groups of oppositional political crimes are "(1) treason, intimidating Parliament, sedition, sabotage, presently found in Part II of the Criminal Code (hereafter Code); and (2) espionage and leakage, currently dealt with in the Official Secrets Act" (Canada, 1986a, p. 1). In the US, on the other hand, while many of the state criminal codes include political offenses, at the federal level, the most recent US Sentencing Commission guidelines manual lists "offenses involving national defense and weapons of mass destruction," "offenses involving the administration of justice," and "offenses involving public safety" as typical political crimes (www.ussc.gov/Guidelines/2011_Guidelines/Manual_PDF/Chapter_2_L-X. pdf). In the UK, many of the oppositional political crimes can be found in the Official Secrets Act, which "covers areas where the state wishes there to be no further threat or debate around certain sensitive security matters."[6] In addition, many of the political crimes are spelled out in anti-terrorism and emergency powers legislation used in connection with the "Troubles" in Northern Ireland.

Historical perspective

One of the oldest political crimes is treason. In short, treason is "an attempt to overthrow the government of the society of which one is a member" (Schmalleger, 2002, p. 454). In "early common law it was considered 'high treason' to kill the king or to promote a revolt in the kingdom" (Schmalleger, 2002, p. 454). Charging an individual with treason, however, was a convenient way to eliminate those that a king or queen deemed traitors, although this tactic was primarily used as a means to silence real or supposed threats to his or her power. The history of England's the Tower of London, for example, is shaped by stories of such acts. Those who were found guilty of the charge of treason were usually taken to nearby Tower Hill for public execution and were commonly beheaded by an executioner. Once the deed was done, the axe man would hold up the head for the assembled crowd to see, it would then be placed on a pole and paraded around the streets of London. And in a final act of barbarity, the head and pole would be placed on London Bridge (one of a handful of bridges that cross the River Thames), while crows, ravens, and other birds would strip the head of its flesh. Eventually the skull would fall into the river. It is alleged that almost 1,500 people were executed in this way (Ackroyd, 2001).

The British law of treason dates back to the Treason Act of 1351. Although revised several times, it outlines four basic conditions under which an individual can be charged: killing or advocating the death of the sovereign (that is, king, queen); having sexual relations with the King's mistress, unmarried oldest daughter, or wife of the King's oldest son; engaging in war against the king or providing support to the King's enemies; and killing a member of the executive in including justices at different levels (Head, p. 96). The Treason Act of 1702 added the offence of frustrating those next in line to the thrown (Head, pp. 96-97). Since that time numerous prominent trials of individuals charged with treason occurred (including those who participated in the Irish rebellions of 1916), and many persons so convicted were put to death (Head, pp. 98-99). William Joyce, "a pro-fascist politician and Nazi propaganda to the United Kingdom during World War II," was the last person to be executed for treason in 1946 (Head, p. 99).

In contemporary times, although treason is mentioned in the US Constitution (Article III) and several federal statutes, the legislation concerning sedition, sabotage, and espionage is embedded in a variety of Congressional acts and other important documents (Archer, 1971). Some of these include the Espionage Act (1917), Sedition Act (1798/1918), Smith Act (1940), McCarran Act (1950),[7]

Internal Security Act (1952),[8] and Communist Control Act (1954).[9] Needless to say, "similar, and often even more sweeping, laws (such as those against 'criminal syndicalism') have been enacted by state legislatures and by local governments" (Turk, 1982a, p. 59).

In England, in 1889, the Official Secrets Act was passed. "This law made it a misdemeanor punishable by imprisonment for up to one year or fine for a person wrongfully to communicate information which he had obtained owing to his position as a civil servant" (Ingraham, 1979, p. 297). In 1911, the Act was revised, making it a felony with a possible sentence of three to seven years if an individual "'for any purpose prejudicial to the safety or interests of the State' to approach any military or naval installation or other prohibited place or to make, obtain, or publish or communicate with others information, sketches, or notes which might help an enemy" (p. 298). Also in England, during the past century, two Acts set controls over anti-government demonstrations by various dissenters: the Incitement to Disaffection Act (1934) and the Public Order Act (1936).

The special case of emergency legislation

During times of emergency (for example, war, widespread natural disasters), most advanced industrialized countries have emergency legislation that gives the state additional powers. Typically, this allows the government to suspend certain constitutional protections. Indeed, these laws have strong political overtones, including provisions that would be considered violations of generally accepted civil liberties during normal times (Scheppel, 2006).

The United Kingdom has also relied on a number of pieces of legislation including the Terrorism Act of 2000, Anti-terrorism, Crime and Security Act (2001), Terrorism Act (2006) and the Counter-Terrorism Act (2008). This legislation has been used frequently in connection with policing in Northern Ireland (Ross, 2000c) and in the post 911 era.

Similarly, Canada utilized the War Measures Act (which was replaced in 1985 with the Emergencies Act); this was implemented during the two world wars and the 1970 "October Crisis" (Ross, 1995c; Corrado and Davies, 2000). The United Kingdom has also relied on a series of special legislation to address these kinds of situations. During the First and Second World Wars, British Parliament passed the Defence of the Realm Act (DORA) laws. These allowed the leadership "unlimited power" in its efforts to maintain public safety and national security (Ingraham, 1979, p. 292). "The regulations were not limited to combating external political crime.[...] They regulated virtually any aspect of civilian life which the Government felt was expedient or necessary for public safety or the defence of the nation" including banning "dog shows, the supplying of cocaine to actresses, as well as limiting freedom of the press" (pp. 292-3). Initially the 250 DORA laws were enforced by the military, but when these became too great a drain on resources, "civil magistrate courts could conduct trials for minor offences and exercise summary jurisdiction" (pp. 292-3). In 1939, on the eve of the Second

World War, the British government passed new special legislation called the Emergency Powers (Defence) Act. Although the Act was slightly revised in 1940, it was similar in content to the previously instituted DORA laws, but now encompassed 500 laws (Ingraham, 1979, pp. 294-5). This Act was eventually terminated after the war.

In the current century new emergency powers legislation has been passed (i.e., Civil Contingencies Act of 2004) which needs little more than "Her Majesty in Council" to believe that an emergency is about to happen, is currently occurring or will happen in the future. The Act trumps all existing legislation short of the Human Rights Act (Head, p. 251). Many constituencies believe that the Civil Contingencies Act is the most draconian of laws passed over the past century in the United Kingdom.

In the US, in the wake of the attacks on the World Trade Center and the Pentagon on September 11, 2001, Congress passed The USA PATRIOT Act, which has given both state and federal law enforcement more power in investigating and charging individuals suspected of or engaging in terrorism. This type of legislation and its attendant procedures is considered by many to be quite controversial. In short, during times of national emergency, by attempting to combat real or imagined threats, the government and its criminogenic agencies may violate basic values of due process and fairness (Mannle and Hirshel, 1988, p. 178). The war on terror and the emergency legislation that was passed in its wake has created a permanent state of affairs where the public considers this normal.

Moreover,

> Diverse mechanisms and criminal or quasi-criminal sanctions for the control of political offenses and the punishment of political offenders likewise have been established. Federal and state laws have relied not only on penal sanctions but also on loyalty oaths, security investigations, the exclusion and expulsion of politically suspect aliens, the calling up of the military, the imposition of martial law, and the confinement of suspect populations in special camps as tools to maintain political order. (Kittrie and Wedlock, 1986, p. xii)

Nevertheless, these crimes represent "the most serious offenses ... [mainly] because such conduct jeopardizes the security and well-being of the whole nation and its inhabitants ... these acts are rarely committed and even more rarely charged" (Canada, 1986b, p. 1).

Regardless of where the codification of these offenses is located (penal codes, special legislation, etc.), most informed analysts believe that these crimes threaten the security of the state and its society. Because security is an amorphous term and practice (Saltstone, 1991), it makes identification, arrest, and prosecution of individuals committing so-called political crimes variable. This has inspired Turk (1982a) to comment that "among the distinguishing features of such laws are their explicit politically, their exceptional vagueness, and their greater permissiveness with respect to enforcement decisions and activities" (p. 54). Later he adds: "Not only is it inherently difficult to specify the meanings of … many political crimes it is generally in the interest of authorities to leave themselves as much discretion as possible in dealing with intolerable political opposition" (p. 62).

This situation has stimulated a number of reforms within various countries' criminal codes, especially those sections that deal with political offenses.[10] Before reviewing the different anti-systemic political crimes, a discussion of dissent (which is easily, typically, and mistakenly confused as oppositional political crimes) is provided as a necessary backdrop.

Dissent

The simplest definition of dissent is a "difference of opinion." In the context of political crime, dissent is an "ideological label" given:

> … by national security agencies or those assuming this mandate to social conducts and/or opinion held by citizens of diverging political learning [...] dissent cannot be recognized by a determined behavior of social actors, but rather by the limits (of either an ethical or a formal nature) set to what is considered acceptable social and political behavior. (Faucher and Fitzgibbons, 1989, p. 139)

Further complicating matters is the fact that dissent, and the behaviors it refers to, are intricately linked with other political crime concepts and practices. According to Turk (1982a), "[d]issent includes any mode of speaking out against the personages, actions, or structures of authority. [...] Each form of resistance may vary in regard to whether it is calculated or spontaneous (or instrumental versus expressive) and organized" (p. 100). Regardless, dissent is:

> … characteristically a higher-class form of resistance, particularly insofar as it is an articulate elaboration of a reasoned political philosophy. Grumbling, diffuse complaints, or emotional rhetoric with little if any empirical grounding or logical coherence are more likely to characterize the 'dissent' of those lower-class persons who do speak out against the given order. (Turk, 1982a, p. 100)

Almost anyone can express dissent; thus, the characteristics of those who engage in this behavior are numerous. Dissenters include anyone or any group that holds and expresses an opinion that differs from the status quo (for example, media personnel, politicians, clergy, conscientious objectors, and social movements; see, for example, Hagan, 1997, Chapter 4).

Moreover, "[i]n the absence of a developed political consciousness, or sensitivity, dissent is likely to be an expression of a more or less vague resentment of one's political fate rather than an instrumental action intended to achieve any specific changes in the political environment" (Turk, 1982a, p. 101).

Undoubtedly, both governments and states have flexible criteria for identifying and responding to "acceptable and unacceptable dissent." Franks (1989) suggests that dissent can be classified into four categories based on the dimensions of legal–illegal and legitimate–illegitimate (that is, legal–legitimate, legal–illegitimate, illegal–legitimate, and illegal–illegitimate). Typically, authorities (law enforcement and national security) accept legal–legitimate dissent but reject illegal–illegitimate dissent. "The other two categories are contentious. From a liberal-democratic viewpoint, a goal of government and society should be to include as much as possible in the legal–legitimate category" (Franks, 1989, pp. 6-7).

The legal mechanisms for controlling dissent have been criticized because they typically "directly sanction or prohibit unwanted behavior by labelling it illegal. Instead, the law permits authorities to investigate, study, and report. This results in indirect penalizing" (Franks, 1989, p. 1), or what Whyte and MacDonald (1989) term "partial sanctioning."

This includes "hidden penalties such as negative personnel reports, or refusal to hire. [...] These sorts of activities do not fit within the liberal-democratic legal tradition. They are outside standard legal and judicial concepts and practices" (Franks, 1989, p. 1). Whyte and MacDonald (1989) conclude that Western democracies have lost the ability to use legal concepts in the field of national security regarding dissent. Consequently, "this leads to extreme problems in making a distinction between legal and illegal dissent" (Franks, 1989, p. 11).

Dissent is expressed through a variety of different means (including letter writing, guerilla theatre, vandalism, demonstrations, etc). Dissent can involve masses of people participating in a World Day in support of nuclear disarmament, G20 protests, or the numerous Occupy movements, or coordinated protests against US involvement in Iraq or Afghanistan, or it can involve the singular action of an individual who creates a blog and posts regularly on it. In our hyper-fast late modern world, where individuals living across the street or across the globe can communicate with others electronically through smart phones, Facebook, and Skype, the possibilities and prospects for dissent are almost endless. This was evident during the Arab Spring in 2011, during which citizens in Algeria, Egypt, and Libya rose up against longstanding dictatorships and overthrew them.

Resistance

A complementary term is resistance. Indeed both powerful and powerless/marginalized individuals and groups have contested what they perceive or know to be the unjust policies and practices of the state and its criminogenic agencies. Over the past two decades, numerous studies have been done that outline the "weapons of the weak" from both violent to nonviolent activities (Scott, 1985). Some actions are criminal, while others (pirate radio, graffiti, etc.) are not (for example, Ferrell, 2001). The public fails to recognize that marginalized and powerless groups have a number of resources at their disposal to respond to government. Nonetheless, considerable sectors of the society remain apathetic in the wake of government abuses. Perhaps at an earlier time, these groups were quite active, but they now realize that they have more to lose than to gain from contesting the state and thus often decide to withdraw from the political process (see, for example, Lukes, 1974; Gaventa, 1980). Although some individuals and groups articulate their displeasure through various forms of political activism, protest, and violence, others resist the power of the state through so-called weapons of the weak, which are low-level acts of resistance.

The powerless have a number of evolving methods with which they can combat large powerful interests, but not all of these are successful. Shortly after the invention of the printing press, those opposed to perceived and actual injustices and political opponents made pamphlets and distributed them. The origin of the fourth estate (for example, beginning with pamphleteers, samizdats, newspapers and evolving into the media of today) was, in large part, a response to elite power by various individuals and groups. Modern-day resisters utilize such nonviolent actions as culture jamming, adbusting, and graffiti/street art.[11]

Civil disobedience

Many times the public believes that existing laws and practices are unjust or unfair. Whether these are voting rights, seatbelt laws, curfews, or racial quotas, in order to challenge these laws people may purposely break the law. The hope is that they will clog the criminal justice system and that it will shock the conscience of the wider public, judiciary, or politicians, and that laws and practices will be changed. Although the arrests of those breaking the law may involve excessive force, the violation of the law is meant to be nonviolent. There has been a long tradition of civil disobedience. It was popularized by Mohandas Gandhi (1930-42) against the British occupation of India and then again during the 1960s in the US by the Civil Rights Movement when African-Americans participated in strikes and sit-ins. Although civil disobedience is an action that is in opposition to the state, it is not in and of itself an oppositional political crime because there is no attempt to change the entire regime, just selected aspects of it (Bay, 1968).

Sedition

In its basic sense, sedition involves advocating (typically through speech and other kinds of communications) the overthrow of a government. In other contexts, it is "communication or agreement intended to defame the government or to incite treason" (Schmalleger, 2002, p. 456). In Canada, the Criminal Code identifies as guilty of sedition any individual who "teaches or advocates ... the use, without authority of law, of force as a means to accomplish a governmental change within Canada" (Borovoy, 1985, p. 156). In the US, the Sedition Act of 1798, chapter 74, 1 Statute 596, criminalized any scandalous article written about the President or

Congress. Later, in response to the Red Scare, and as a way to deal with acquittals produced by the Espionage Act, Congress passed the Sedition Act of 1918. It provided sanctions against individuals and organizations that published statements that were Anti-American and/or argued against American participation in wartime efforts (Stone, 2004, p. 186). In 1920, the government overturned the Sedition Act of 1918, only to reenact it in 1940 before the US entered World War II. In order to strengthen the Act, Congress also passed the Alien Registration Act (aka Smith Act) "which required all resident non-citizens to register with the government, streamlined deportation procedures" (Head, p. 48) for individuals

> with intent to cause the overthrow or destruction of any such government, prints, publishes, edits, issues, circulates, sells, distributes, or publicly displays any written or printed matter advocating, advising, or teaching the duty, necessity, desirability, or propriety of overthrowing or destroying any government in the United States by force or violence, or attempts to do so; or...organizes or helps or attempts to organize any society, group, or assembly of persons who teach, advocate, or encourage the overthrow or destruction of any such government by force or violence; or becomes or is a member of, or affiliates with, any such society, group, or assembly of persons, knowing the purposes thereof. (54 Stat. 670)

Shortly after the passage of the Smith Act, close to 5 million people registered. The Act was used to prosecute a number of prominent left-wing political parties operating in the United States. According to Head, "prosecutions continued until Supreme Court decisions in 1957 made them more difficult, but the court upheld a major conviction in 1961, and the statute remains on the books" (p. 77). Later federal law defined seditious conspiracy as follows:

> If two or more persons in any State or Territory, or in any place subject to the jurisdiction of the United States, conspire to overthrow, put down, or destroy by force the Government of the United States, or to levy war against them, or to oppose by force the authority thereof, or by force to prevent, hinder, or delay the execution of any law of the United States, or by force to seize, take, or possess any property of the United States contrary to the authority thereof. (18 US Code, Section 2384)

More commonly, those determined by authorities to have engaged in sedition are charged with seditious libel (Thomas, 1972; Stone, 2004). Thus, the problem is embedded in the larger issue of freedom of speech, especially that which criticizes a government (Borovoy, 1985; Foerstel, 1998, Chapter 1). Furthermore, the criteria for defining acts as seditious libel are dynamic and subject to changes in political, economic, and social conditions. In its most expansive form, however, seditious libel may be said to embrace any criticism – true or false – of the form, constitution, policies, laws, officers, symbols, or conduct of a government (Stone, 1983, p. 1425).

Understandably, the biggest difficulty with the crime of sedition is the ability to specify "at what point in the continuum between the thought and the deed is it appropriate for the law to intervene" (Borovoy, 1985, p. 156). In general, "speech which is likely to result in imminent violence is arguably dangerous enough to warrant legal intervention. On the other hand, speech which is not likely to culminate in this way does not warrant such intervention" (Borovoy, 1985, p. 156).

Sedition laws date back to early English history (Head, pp. 150-157); originally, the criminalized act was called "seditious libel." In short, this involved saying something negative about someone in power (that is, kings, queens, and/or their ministers). The truth of a statement was not relevant to the charge. A rule of thumb at that time was that jurists believed that the greater the truth, the greater the libel. Historically, a frequent penalty given those convicted of sedition was to cut off their hands.

The first significant challenge to the sedition laws in the US happened in 1735, when John Peter Zenger, a printer, accused the governor of Massachusetts of being a liar and a thief. In contrast to previous rulings, it was determined that the truth was a valid defense; thus Zenger was acquitted (Foerstel, 1998, pp. 2-3). In 1918, in an effort to shore up support for the entrance of the US into the First World War and to prevent criticism of the war, which would damage recruiting efforts, the Sedition Act of 1798 was amended, and made more specific. During this time, close to a thousand individuals were incarcerated under state or federal sedition laws because they opposed US involvement in the First World War, or because of their "controversial" union activities, or religious and political beliefs (Kohn, 1994). However, it was not until 1971 that the Espionage Act was once again considered newsworthy. In that year, Daniel Ellsberg, a scientist working for the RAND Corporation, a consultant to the Department of Defense, released information to the *New York Times* about Pentagon bombing missions in North Vietnam (Herring, 1993). The government unsuccessfully tried to block the publication through the rarely utilized legal mechanism called "prior restraint" (Foerstel, 1997).

In the US, judges and jurists generally use the so-called "clear and present danger test" to determine whether communications are dangerous and/or seditious. In other words, an individual who says something that could potentially lead to immediate harm, such as shouting the word "fire" in a crowded theater (an example attributable to Justice Oliver Wendell Holmes, Jr, 1919), can be charged and, thus, does not have protection under the free speech guarantees of the Constitution. The issue begs the question of whether or not it is appropriate to label various statements as seditious or merely as expressions of political positions. Individuals are occasionally charged with seditious conspiracy, but it is difficult for the government to secure a conviction for this type of crime.

The charge of conspiracy is established by inference from the conduct of the parties involved. It is very rare that an agreement between parties can be established by direct evidence; the information offered is usually purely circumstantial. To prove the collaboration, evidence such as hearsay, which would normally be inadmissible to establish any other criminal offense, may be admitted to show links in a chain of circumstances from which the common agreement may be inferred (Grosman, 1972, p. 142).[12]

Frequently governments have tried to prevent people and opposition groups from expressing dissent by charging them with sedition. Rather than protecting the common good, however, this kind of charge backfires, because it reinforces the perception, and perhaps the reality, of arbitrary state power. Alternatively, because of the cumbersome nature of the Sedition Act, the government has found it more convenient to frustrate, charge, and in some cases, convict individuals and organizations under a variety of existing laws and Acts. This process virtually places plaintiffs under a gag order. For example, in 1978, *The Progressive*, a left-leaning magazine, was about to publish an article that explained, using readily accessible library resources, how to build a hydrogen bomb. The federal government quickly found out about this, and believing this communication to be harmful to the well-being of the US (and a violation of the Atomic Energy Act), it issued a prior restraint order against the magazine.[13] This legal maneuver prevented the article from being published for six months, but it was eventually printed in November 1979. Similarly, former Central Intelligence Agency (CIA) employees who have published "tell all" books (see, for example, Agee, 1975; Marchetti and Marks, 1975; Snepp, 1977) about their work for the agency have been sued because they violated a secrecy agreement that they signed when they entered government service, which in most cases required them to vet their material through the agency's pre-publication review process.[14]

Treason

Treason refers to overt (that is, nonsymbolic) acts aimed at overthrowing one's own government or state, or murdering or personally injuring the sovereign (king or queen) or the sovereign's family (Chapin, 1964). In Canada, Section 46 (Subsection 1) of the Criminal Code differentiates between high treason and treason. The former crime includes: restraining, injuring, killing, or attempting to kill the king or queen; engaging in war against Canada; and assisting an enemy of Canada in time of war or helping a state engaged in "hostilities" against Canada (Canada, 1986b, p. 12). Treason is defined by the Code, Section 46 (Subsection 2), as the use of force or violence against Canada with the purpose of overthrowing the government. Treason can also involve giving foreign agent information that would affect the safety or proper defense of Canada, or helping an individual commit treason or high treason (Canada, 1986b, p. 13).

In the US, the Constitution (Article III, Section 3) states that, "treason against the United States, shall consist only in levying War against them, or in adhering to their Enemies, giving them Aid and Comfort." Federal statutes use similar language, such as,

> Whoever, owing allegiance to the United States, levy war against them or adheres to their enemies, giving them aid and comfort within the United States or elsewhere is guilty of treason and shall suffer death, or shall be imprisoned not less than five years and fined under this title but not less than ten thousand dollars ($10,000); and shall be incapable of holding any office under the United States. (18 US Code, Section 2381)

Many states, either in their legislation or constitutions, also have specific sections that refer to treason (Schmalleger, 2002, p. 455).

Thus, it is:

> … a criminal offense to publish false, scandalous, and malicious writings against the government, if done with intent to defame, or to excite the hatred of the people, or to stir up sedition or to excite resistance to law, or to aid the hostile designs of any foreign nation against the United States. (Packer, 1962, p. 82)

Given the burden of proof, the appropriateness of the charge of treason is often debatable. Historically, treason has been a slippery concept. Although it is generally recognized as a legitimate criminal offense, the charge is frequently used by authorities, opinion-makers, moral entrepreneurs, and pundits as a label to describe the actions of nonviolent dissenters. Furthermore, few individuals and organizations have been prosecuted for treason.

For example, in the history of the US fewer than 50 cases involving treason have been prosecuted (Hurst, 1983, p. 1562). "[S]ince the adoption of the Constitution there have been few treason prosecutions in United States history (less than forty pressed to trial, even less convictions, and no federal executions" (Ingraham and Tokoro, 1969, p. 148). "The legal history of treason and related offenses in England is similar" (Turk, 1984, p. 121). A review of the historical record reinforces the perception that some events clearly represent textbook cases of treason and others do not. Moreover, two factors are crucial if the charge of treason is to be applied appropriately: the citizenship of the individuals and the place where the action has taken place.

Because treason is a violation of allegiance, for a charge within the US to have merit, one must be a citizen of the US or engaged in the process of naturalization. Thus, resident aliens are assumed to be on their way to becoming citizens. If, on the other hand, one has lost, renounced, or was never a citizen of the US (for example, tourists, temporary visitors, such as students or workers), the charge of treason does not apply (Hagan, 1990, p. 444; Schmalleger, 2002, p. 455).

Normally, the offense of treason needs to be committed inside the US, but jurisdiction has expanded to states outside of the US. For example, during the Second World War several Americans were prosecuted for their broadcasts in foreign countries (Packer, 1962, p. 80). One of the most famous cases was against the rather eccentric, pro-Fascist, US poet-writer Ezra Pound (Cornell, 1969). During the Second World War, the Italian Fascist government allowed him to broadcast in English from Rome. When the war ended, the Allies arrested and charged Pound with treason. During the trial, he claimed that his actions were patriotic since they were aimed at trying to keep the US out of the war and US soldiers safe. Pound was "institutionalized after a questionable trial resulting in a verdict of 'unsound mind' [and] kept in St Elizabeth's Hospital, Washington DC from 1945 to 1958 when upon petition he was released as incurably insane, but not dangerous" (Turk, 1982a, p. 53).

Another interesting case occurred in 1948, when Tomoya Kawakita, who had dual US and Japanese citizenship, was convicted of treason and sentenced to death in connection with his work related activities in Japan during World War II. In 1953, President Dwight D. Eisenhower commuted the sentence to life imprisonment. In 1963, President John F. Kennedy pardoned Kawakita and he was deported back to Japan. Despite political posturing and rhetoric invoking the charge of treason, during both the 1950s (e.g., the Cold War) and 1960s (e.g., Vietnam War), the most recent charge of treason was levied against Adam Yahiye Gadahn, in 2006. Gadahn had posted videos in support of al-Qaeda, the Islamic Fundamentalist terrorist group associated with the 9/11 attacks (Head, p. 103).

Espionage/spying

Spying, also called espionage (the act or practice of spying) or sub-rosa crime, is one of the most well-known acts of treason (Bryan, 1943). This type of political crime refers primarily to secretly obtaining information or intelligence about another, and typically hostile, country, its military, or weaponry (Bryan, 1943; Laqueur, 1985). In short, espionage entails "gathering, transmitting or losing information or secrets related to national defense with the intent or the reasonable belief that such information will be used against the United States" (Schmalleger, 2002, p. 455).

Various types of espionage and spies exist, including "black espionage," a term for such things as "covert agents" involved in classical forms of spying, and "white espionage," which refers to "spying via space satellites, through code-breaking, or technical collection" (Hagan, 1990, p. 444). Considerable effort has been devoted to distinguishing and describing different kinds of spies (Tzu, 1963; Copeland, 1974; Anderson, 1977; Hagan, 1997, pp. 124-31). Although this kind of work is important, it has yet to be utilized for theory building or testing.

Espionage has been practiced since early recorded history, and is mentioned in ancient texts, such as the Bible (for example, when the Israelites surveyed the land of the Canaanites) and Chinese military philosopher and practitioner Sun-Tzu's *Art of war*. In 1917, the US Congress passed the Espionage Act (18 US Code,

Section 2384). Consequently, a handful of prominent individuals were charged, convicted and imprisoned because of this legislation including: Jane Addams, Eugene Debs, Emma Goldman, and Mollie Steimer (Head, p. 41). Despite minimal attention in the criminological literature, the political crime of espionage "is more costly than traditional crime and has altered post-World War II economic and political history. It was estimated that during the cold war, theft of Western technology by the Soviet Union cost billions in future defense expenditures to counter Soviet improvements" (Hagan, 1990, p. 444). The information that has been revealed has not only had an effect on national security, but it led to the deaths of double agents (that is, individuals working for two different countries at the same time).

Numerous reasons exist to explain why individuals, organizations, and states spy. At the level of the individual, some factors include the person's ideology, potential embarrassment over being compromised, ego, and sexual favors. At the organizational or state level, espionage can be part of the broader mission and goals of intelligence gathering, which primarily seeks to gain some sort of competitive advantage (Hagan, 1990, p. 444). And recently,

> … [a] major shift [has been detected] in the motivations of spies East and West from the ideological, Cold War fifties to the materialistic/hedonistic eighties and nineties. The ideological motivation has been replaced for the most part by mercenary considerations. (Hagan, 1990, p. 444)

At the turn of the twentieth century, the British government passed the UK Official Secrets Act of 1911. This was done in order protect the country against the threat of German espionage. Due to various criticisms, the Act was revised and in 1989, the Official Secrets Act was passed. The legislation "largely, but not exclusively, applies only to members of the security and intelligence services, and to other public servants or contractors who work with security and intelligence information" (Head, p. 130). In 1997, David Shayler, a former member of British intelligence was charged with sending official documents to the *Mail on Sunday* newspaper that indicated that MI5 was overly preoccupied with monitoring socialists and made public that MI6 had secretly planned the assassination of former Libyan leader Muammar Gaddafi, and was monitoring several Labour party officials. In 2002, Shayler was convicted of three of the charges and spent six months in prison.

Espionage/spying is conducted by citizens and foreigners alike. The public is usually first informed about these activities when Americans are arrested for spying on behalf of a foreign country in the US. Alternatively, foreigners are arrested for espionage inside the US, and finally there are occasions when Americans are detained and charged with spying in foreign countries. In short, when foreigners are caught engaged in spying, they are usually briefly detained and then deported. When citizens are accused of these types of acts, they are incarcerated and may even be executed.

One of the most well-known cases of espionage in the US concerned the activities of Julius and Ethel Rosenberg. In 1950–51, during the height of the Cold War, they were arrested, tried, and convicted. On June 19, 1953, despite considerable public protest, the Rosenbergs were executed for obtaining classified information on the highly secret atomic bomb for the Soviet Union (Garber and Walkowitz, 1995; Neville, 1995; Hornblum, 2010).

During the past three decades, several FBI and CIA officials and members of the Armed Services have been arrested, charged, and/or convicted of espionage. Usually, these individuals were suspected of selling classified documents outlining details of military weapons, equipment, and capabilities to Soviet or Russian Intelligence sources (for example, the KGB, the national security agency for the former Soviet Union). Many of those arrested had worked in senior positions in government agencies and had engaged in espionage undetected for decades. In 1985, for example, naval Officer John Walker Jr, was convicted of spying on behalf of the KGB for 18 years (Kneece, 1986; Earley, 1988). In 1994, Aldrich H. Ames, a veteran CIA official (and his wife Rosario) were convicted of espionage. Ames was given life in prison, and his wife served five years. In 1996, Earl Edwin Pitts, an FBI agent for 13 years, was arrested, and a year later, he pleaded guilty to espionage. In 1996, Harold J. Nicholson, a CIA station chief, was arrested; two years later he was convicted of espionage (Earley, 1998). In October 1998, retired Army Intelligence analyst David Shelton Boone was convicted of selling secrets to the KGB. For close to a decade before his arrest, Boone had passed on information concerning America's nuclear arsenal.

Box 4.1: Julius and Ethel Rosenberg

In the 1950s, at the height of Cold War hysteria, Julius and Ethel Rosenberg and a small group of their friends, family members (such as David Greenglass, Ethel's brother), and other co-conspirators (such as Harry Gold) were arrested, charged and convicted of conspiracy to commit espionage: specifically, passing secrets of America's atomic bomb to Soviet agents. Although denying these charges right to their deaths, it did not help that both Julius and Ethel had been, at one time, members of the American Communist Party. They were both sentenced to death, and on June 19, 1953, despite their claims to innocence, considerable debate about the quality of the evidence presented at their trial and about the impartiality of the judges, a large public protest, a stay of execution, appeals to the Supreme Court and the president of the US, and the fact that the couple had two small sons, they were electrocuted at Sing Sing Penitentiary in Ossining, New York.

Despite deals struck with the prosecution, the co-conspirators received sentences ranging from 15 to 30 years. The Rosenberg case has been the subject of numerous articles and books, both popular and scholarly. Two documentaries have also been produced: *The Unquiet Death of Julius and Ethel Rosenberg* (1974), and *Landmark American Trials: Julius and Ethel Rosenberg* (1999).

In the spring of 2001, Robert P. Hanssen, a senior FBI agent, was accused and convicted of having illegally transferred sensitive documents to Soviet, and later Russian, intelligence agents and their organizations since 1985. Hansen was in a unique position because of his contacts with the CIA and the State Department. By what means he managed to evade detection for a decade-and-a-half were matters of grave concern to US intelligence officials (Havill, 2001).

Most of the individuals described above as convicted "spies" were sentenced to long stints in maximum security or at the federal Supermax penitentiary (ADX Colorado), some of them only marginally avoiding death penalty sentences. The information these individuals provided to the Soviets/Russians had the unfortunate consequence of leading to the deaths or executions of counter- and double agents (that is, Soviet/Russian citizens who were spies on behalf of the US).

On the other side of the coin, in February 2001, US student John Edward Tobin, who was also a member of the Army Reserve, was arrested by Russian officials on charges that he was spying on behalf of the US. Also in 2001, a handful of Chinese-American scholars (Li Shaomin, Gao Zhan, and Qin Guangguang) working in the People's Republic of China were arrested and accused of spying by the PRC. After several months in detention, they were ultimately released back to the US ("China Expels Convicted US 'Spy'").

After the Second World War, in the United Kingdom, a number of British citizens who were working in senior intelligence capacities and acting as spies for the Soviet government were detected. These people included Michael Bettaney, George Blake, Anthony Blunt, Guy Burgess, Donald Maclean, Kim Philby, Anthony Price, and John Vassall (Boyle, 1979; Sutherland, 1980). Their presence "proved that internal security was still deficient, causing new problems between Britain and her allies" (Laqueur, 1985, p. 208). Like the US spies, their activity had been going on for decades.

In Canada, in September 1945, Igor Gouzenko, a rather low-ranking Soviet cipher clerk, walked into the *Ottawa Journal* and then the Department of Justice, and confessed that the Soviet Union had been spying on Canada. Shortly thereafter, 39 individuals were arrested in two sweeps, including Fred Rosenberg, a Member of Parliament. This led to the establishment of the Kellock-Taschereau Royal Commission of Inquiry (1946), which determined that a large spy ring existed in Canada for obtaining atomic secrets (Canada, 1946). Approximately half of those arrested were convicted of their charges (Sawatsky, 1984).

Between 1956 and 1979, at least 32 government workers from various countries, such as Cuba, Czechoslovakia, Hungary, Iraq, the People's Republic of China, Poland, and the Soviet Union, were expelled from Canada or their governments were informed that these individuals could not return to Canada because they were attempting to illegally obtain military secrets or industrial information, to recruit spies, or to engage in "unacceptable behavior" (Sawatsky, 1980, Appendix A).

Most notably during this period, in 1967, Bower Featherstone, a mapmaker working for the Canadian government, sold classified naval maps to a Soviet spy. He was charged and convicted under the Official Secrets Act, sentenced to 30 months in prison, and ended up serving 10. During the 1980s, it seemed like a varied stream of foreigners were allegedly spying in Canada, including Americans, Cubans, Koreans, and Israelis. In almost all of the cases, the individuals were expelled from Canada.

In 1978, the US government passed the Foreign Intelligence Surveillance Act (FISA). This was a response to the perceived excesses of the Nixon administration in connection with spying against political groups that engaged in legitimate political dissent. The passage was also interpreted as a reaction to the revelations of the Church Committee. FISA was designed to monitor communications between foreigners outside of the US; it was not intended to monitor domestic communications. FISA was amended in 2001 because of The USA PATRIOT Act. The legislation was once again changed in 2007 with the Protect America Act, but because it expired a year later and was considered seriously flawed, a new FISA was passed in 2008.

Finally, in 2011, Julian Assange, the director of the controversial organization WikiLeaks, facilitated the dissemination of US Department of States diplomatic cables. Not only was the information contained in the cables controversial, but the US Department of Justice (under the direction of Eric Holder at the time) also considered charging Assange with espionage under Section 3 of the Espionage Act, which specifies that if a person "receives or obtains or agrees or attempts to receive or obtain from any person, or from any source whatever, any document ... respecting the national defense with intent or reason to believe that the information is to be used to the injury of the United States, or to the advantage of a foreign nation."

Summary

Objective study of nonviolent anti-systemic political crimes is complicated by the subtle nuances in the different definitions, the tendency of the state to downplay the political context of charges, the use of obscure political crime laws, and the application of traditional criminal laws against so-called political offenders (Torrance, 1977, 1995). Other relevant factors include the proliferation of mass media misinformation and political propaganda that contributes to public ignorance. Some of the commonly applied, but generally obscure statutes that the state uses relate to inciting a rebellion, obstructing military operations, and sabotage (Mannle and Hirschel, 1988, p. 170). Conventional criminal laws that governments may use to quell political dissenters include violations of city ordinances, disturbing the peace, resisting arrest, and conspiracy to cross state lines to commit a crime (Mannle and Hirschel, 1988, p. 170). When the political situation appears to be in crisis, not only will governments rely on these kinds of statues, but they will also hastily develop and pass seemingly comprehensive emergency legislation. Alternatively, "most insurrections have been local affairs and have usually been handled under state treason, sedition or subversive conspiracy statutes or under statutes designed to control riots and public disturbances" (Ingraham and Tokoro,

1969, p. 148). Moreover, in the US, despite the perception that "illegal forms of political dissent [are viewed] as immoral and dishonorable, as well as impermissible," juries typically hesitate to convict political criminals; the state frequently grants "pardons, amnesties, or suspended sentences" after the conditions that motivated the individual have subsided, and if convicted and sentenced to federal prison, the prisoners are often treated more leniently (Ingraham and Tokoro, 1969, p. 149). Although the widespread harm that can be caused by treason, sedition, and espionage are noted, violent events are more dramatic, gain more media attention, and are often more disturbing to the general public and government. During recent times, however, the majority of oppositional political crimes and those that have garnered the greatest amount of scholarly, government, and media attention have been violent in nature (for example, sabotage, subversion, assassination, and terrorism). An analysis of these actions is treated in the following chapter.

Notes
[1] For a history describing this legislation concerning offenses against the state of Canada, see Canada (1986a, 1986b), and for a history of legislation about political crimes against the US, see, for example, Kittrie and Wedlock (1986).

[2] In short, "the concealment or nondisclosure of the known treason of another" (Schmalleger, 2002, p. 455).

[3] In sum, "advocating the use of unlawful acts as a means of accomplishing a change in industrial ownership, or to control political change" (Schmalleger, 2002, p. 455).

[4] In general, political crimes can be divided into violent and nonviolent types. Admittedly, we could probably devote a chapter to each of these types of nonviolent oppositional political crimes; however, since treason, sedition, and espionage charges are rarely applied in the contemporary period, we do not.

[5] Noticeably absent is a discussion of civil disobedience. Despite the political nature of civil disobedience, it is largely ignored by most reviews of political crime.

[6] Personal correspondence, Steve Wright, February 2002.

[7] It required the registration of all Communists and their organizations that existed in the US.

[8] Also known as the McCarran Walter Act, it outlined the conditions under which aliens who were suspected of disloyalty to the US could be expelled.

[9] For a review of these Acts, see, for example, Packer (1962). Some of these laws have been struck down as unconstitutional (Turk, 1984).

[10] For example, in 1986 the Law Reform Commission of Canada noted a series of problems with offenses against the state and suggested that, "Part II of the Code and the Official Secrets Act are riddled with defects of both form and content" (Canada, 1986b, p. 25).

[11] See Klein (2000) and the adbuster organization and magazine they produce to get an idea of this trend.

[12] Cultural criminology has elucidated two terms: subversive symbol inversion and creative recoding. Seditious conspiracy is found in Section 60(3) (4) of the Canadian Criminal Code.

[13] Prior restraint enables the government to prevent the printing or broadcasting of material that it believes could be harmful in advance of a determination being made by a court. The constitutionality of this power is hotly debated.

[14] Some of the authors have detailed this experience in either the prefaces to their books or in follow-up memoirs (see, for example, Snepp, 1999).

FIVE

Violent oppositional political crimes: assassination, riot, sabotage, subversion, and terrorism

Introduction

Numerous actions fall under the heading of violent oppositional political crimes. These include political assassination, riot, sabotage, subversion, and terrorism.[1] This chapter defines these various practices and places them into a historical context. To the greatest possible extent, this chapter also seeks to explain the causal dynamics and effects of this phenomenon.

Political assassination

Although assassination is part of the arsenal of tactics used by terrorists, "pure assassination" is an attempt to eliminate a person and not necessarily to strike fear into the citizens of a country. As a subset, political assassination is the deliberative murder of a specific individual (typically, a political figure) for strategic purposes, without the intent of creating fear among the wider population.

The history of assassination is long and rich. There have been numerous assassination attempts of political figures (that is, from aldermen to mayors to governors to presidents). Not only have the assassinations of John F. Kennedy (US, 1963), Martin Luther King Jr (1968), Robert Kennedy (1968), Indira Gandhi (India, 1984), Anwar Sadat (Egypt, 1981), Yitzhak Rabin (Israel, 1995), and Benazir Bhutto (Pakistan, 2007) been the subject of copious news media attention, but they have garnered high-level political examinations and commissions of inquiry into the circumstances surrounding the security lapses.

In the US, where the majority of scholarly research and actions have been documented, one can find numerous instances of individuals who have attempted to assassinate mayors, governors, and presidents. A handful of studies have looked at this phenomenon over time. Clarke (1982), for example, identified five types of assassins: political, egocentric, psychopathic, insane, and atypical. Although all of these types of individuals have committed a political crime, the political assassin has explicit political motives. For example, during the 1960s, the assassinations of prominent politicians and figures, including President John F. Kennedy (1963), his brother Senator Robert Kennedy (1968), civil rights leader Martin Luther

King Jr (1968), and Black Muslim leader Malcolm X (1965), would fall into this category. One of the most dominant aspects of the discussion about political assassination is the degree to which the perpetrator may suffer from a mental illness and to what extent some mental illnesses may mitigate the political motivations of the perpetrator. Within this paradigm, Clarke is the most critical of earlier scholars, suggesting that the information on which interpretations have been built have disproportionately relied on secondary sources that attribute the causes to single sources and neglect the complexity of human behavior and contextual circumstances.

In advanced industrialized democracies, reliance on assassination, "a politically motivated killing in which the victims are selected because of the expected political impact of their dying" (Turk, 1982b, p. 82), has been limited. Usually, such a killing is the work of a person of sound mind and not by a mentally deranged person. Political assassinations have prompted not only a news media frenzy, but in the case of John F. Kennedy, the murder resulted in the creation of the Warren Commission that investigated the incident, while in the case of King, widespread riots took place in many inner cities. The Select Committee on Assassinations also came into being as the result of political assassinations.

Political riot

History is littered with examples of riots by nongovernmental actors such as students, workers, peasants, and activists supporting varied causes. In many respects, all riots are political if they involve powerless people and organizations protesting against those more powerful than they are. Riots have been prompted over numerous matters including religious differences, housing/living and food shortages and conditions, work opportunities, government oppression, and other collectively perceived injustices. During the course of the riot, both property (public and private) is often damaged and those participating in the riot may be injured and or killed, as can the police, military or militia who are called out to maintain order (Marx, 1970a; 1970b). Over time, the legal penalties for instigating, planning and participating in riots have changed from death to imprisonment (Head, p. 221).

Because of overreaction by the military and/or police (see, discussion of police riots in chapter 10), over time most advanced industrialized democracies have abandoned specific anti-riot legislation and embedded it under public order laws. In 1973, for example, the United Kingdom abandoned the Riot Act of 1714 and relied upon the common law offense of riot. This law was superseded by The Public Order Act of 1986 which embedded riot as one of several violations (Head, p. 226). The United States incorporated elements of the British Riot Act into its Militia Act of 1792 (Head, p. 228). This law was later revised into chapter 15 of title 10, of the United States Code, and present in section 2012 of title 18 of the Code. That being said, it must be understood that, in the US, each state has their own criminal code and some of them have defined riots in that legislation too. Canada has embedded its Riot Act into two sections of the Criminal Code revised in 1985.

Sabotage

Sabotage is the deliberate destruction or damage of property and is typically carried out for military or political objectives. Sabotage may be committed during times of war, revolutions, protests, etc., but it can also surface during labor disputes, such as when workers destroy machinery in a factory. Not every work related sabotage, however, is intended as a protest against the government. One legal definition for sabotage is: "the willful destruction or injury of, or defective production of, war-material or national-defense material, or harm to war premises or war utilities" (Black's Law Dictionary, p. 1335). In this context, there are some debates over what, exactly, constitutes war and national defense material. According to the US Code, Title 18 (Crimes and Criminal Procedure), Chapter 105 (Sabotage), Section 2151 (Definitions), "war and national defense material includes arms, armament, ammunition, livestock, forage, forest products and standing timber, stores of clothing, air, water, food, foodstuffs, fuel, supplies, munitions, and all articles, parts or ingredients, intended for, adapted to, or suitable for the use of the United States or any associate nation, in connection with the conduct of war or defense activities." In more recent times the targets of sabotage have been expanded to computer systems and networks.

Sabotage is often accomplished by using equipment and machines in a manner in which they were not intended (including "monkey-wrenching" or purposely breaking equipment and machines); this is a frequent occurrence in factories and the industrial sector (Abbey, 1975). Many such instances involve acts of low-scale, unorganized rebellion, a reflection of frustration with poorly functioning or maintained equipment/machines or of difficulties with the management of an institution. Specifically, if equipment/machines do not work properly, there may be a tendency among workers to inflict further damage, either as a demonstration of their frustration or as a means to compel their administrators to finally replace the faulty equipment. Such damage may also be perceived by workers as an acceptable way to "pay back" administrators for capricious and arbitrary supervision, management, and leadership.

In the United States Chapter 105, of the US Code outlines the crime of sabotage during wartime and against military targets. Section 2153 deals with "Destruction of war material, war premises, or war utilities." Section 2155 focuses on sabotage committed during peacetime. And Section 2151 identifies "national defense" related targets that can be considered sabotaged (Head, p. 142). According to Head, "These measures require a specific intent or purpose to damage the national defense of the United States. Nevertheless, pacifists and other anti-war activists have been convicted under these provisions for seeking to expose and oppose military operations, particularly those involving nuclear warfare. Courts have firmly rejected defenses based on good faith, belief in the lawfulness of the protest and the illegality of the war preparations" (p. 143).

Subversion

Subversion refers to the act of "overthrow[ing] that which is established or existing" and is "used to delegitimize ideas and activities opposed to the established order, and hence to legitimize the states' acting against them, even through those ideas and activities are lawful" (Franks, 1989, p. 10).[2] Building on Franks' typology, the state defines subversion as an action that is "legal but illegitimate. Subversion is defined through a supposed link between internal dissent and so-called deviant foreign influences" (pp. 10-11) In the United Kingdom, the 1989 Security Service Act defines subversion as "actions intended to overthrow or undermine parliamentary democracy by political, industrial or violent means" (Section 1[2]). According to Gill, "This definition clearly includes political and industrial activity that is both peaceful and lawful" (1995, p. 91).

During the early part of the 20th century, in many Western democracies, individuals and organizations espousing, advocating, and/or practicing a variety of different political ideologies (for example, anarchism, bolshevism, communism, fascism, nationalism, Nazism, pacifism, socialism, separatism, etc.) were labeled as "subversives." These groups were blamed for widespread industrial unrest, including bombings. They were feared by governments, their bureaucracies, and the elite (see, for example, Goldstein, 1978).

In both Canada and the US, for example, the Royal Canadian Mounted Police and the Department of Justice, respectively, formed "Radical" or "Red-hunting" squads. These groups frequently infiltrated, arrested, and, in some cases, deported alleged, suspected, or self-confessed subversives (Brown and Brown, 1978; Sawatsky, 1980; Ellis, 1994, pp. 39-59).

During the 1960s in the US, the term subversive was used by authorities and moral entrepreneurs to describe many student protesters, the New Left, and Black, Chicano, and Native American nationalists. These political and social movements led, in some cases, to spin-off political parties, militias, and terrorist organizations such as the Weathermen (later called Weather Underground), the Black Liberation Army, and the Symbionese Liberation Army. In Canada, the Rasemblement pour Resistance inspired the formation of a variety of Québécois nationalist separatist terrorist groups (Ross and Gurr, 1989; Ross, 1995c). And in the UK (Northern Ireland in particular), during the 1960s, police crackdowns and confrontations with civil rights protestors resulted in the rekindling of Irish Roman Catholics' hatred of the British and an increase in IRA terrorist activity.

In short, because of the subjective nature of interpreting acts of subversion, many jurists and observers find the term very contentious (see, for example, Spjut, 1974). Due to this debate, prosecutors often try to charge defendants with other kinds of criminal charges with which they might be more likely to secure a conviction.

Terrorism

Although the crime of rebellion, defined as "deliberate, organized resistance by force and arms, to the laws or operations of the government committed by a subject" exists in federal legislation (Schmalleger, 2002, p. 455), over the past four decades it has been rarely applied to individuals and groups. More common have been numerous acts of oppositional political terrorism occurring in countries throughout the world (Ross, 2006).

Since the early 1960s, anti-systemic political terrorism has generated considerable attention.[3] By far the greatest number of incidents of oppositional political crime in advanced industrialized countries during recent times has been classified as terrorism.[4] Understandably, the meaning of the term has been fervently debated and politicized because it is used as a label that powerful individuals and organizations, especially states, apply sometimes indiscriminately to perceived and actual enemies (Herman, 1982; Jenkins, 1988). This simplistic thinking has encouraged so-called conspiracy theories of terrorism. For example, one theory argued that the former Soviet Union and its satellite countries, Cuba, Iran, Libya, and North Korea, launched an offensive against the West through a well-organized and well-financed network of terrorist organizations (see, for example, Sterling, 1981). Although some evidence pointed to communist support for a number of national liberation organizations, the charges against the "evil empire" appear to have been exaggerated.

Definitional and conceptual issues

Although most countries, in particular their legal systems, criminal justice agencies, and national security apparati, have constructed definitions for terrorism in order to guide their work, the academic community has generally adopted Schmid's (1983) conceptualization:

> ... terrorism is a method of combat in which random or symbolic victims ... become target[s] of violence.... Through ... the use or threat of violence, ... other members of that group [eg, class, nation, etc] are [placed] ... in a state of chronic fear.... The victimization of the target is considered extra-normal by most observers, ... [which] creates an ... audience beyond the target of terror ... the purpose of ... [terrorism] ... is either to immobilize the target of terror in order to produce disorientation and/or compliance, or to mobilize secondary targets of demands (eg a government) or targets of attention (eg public opinion). (p. 111)[5]

This definition has many advantages (Ross, 1988a, 1988b), and with four qualifications, it is relatively appropriate. First, not every element of the definition must exist for an action or campaign to be labeled terrorist. Second, while terrorism sometimes appears random in its targeting, it may actually be selective (for example, directed against particular groups).[6] Third, violent attacks on symbolic, nonhuman targets (for example, statues, buildings, etc.) that meet the definitional criteria are also considered acts of terrorism.[7] And, fourth, only acts that have a political motive can justifiably be defined as terrorist incidents (see, for example, Hacker, 1976). Conversely, events that are mainly "criminal" in nature (for example, extortion) or acts committed by psychologically "abnormal" people and that are not politically motivated are excluded from the broad category of terrorism.[8]

Typologies

Several different types of oppositional terrorism (that is, domestic, state-sponsored, and international) exist. Thus, it seems logical that each kind has a slightly different pattern of causation and that the relative importance of each contributing factor varies according to the type of terrorist act, the group that commits it, and its location in space and time.

Figure 5.1: Typology of political terrorism[a]

		Direct involvement of nationals/citizens of more than one state	
		Yes	No
Government-controlled or directed	Yes	Interstate/state-sponsored	State terrorism
	No	International/ transnational terrorism	Domestic terrorism

Note: [a] This figure is based on Mickolus (1981).

Jongman (1983) described an array of typologies linked to terrorist actions: actor-based, political orientation, multidimensional, and purpose-based typologies. The first typology distinguishes between state and nonstate actors. The second differentiates between terrorism motivations from either above or below and distinguishes between right-wing and left-wing terrorism. The third typology subsumes distinctions based on Thornton's (1964) and Bell's work (1978). Jongman concluded that "one of the problems with typology building is the absence of a commonly agreed-upon definition of terrorism" (Jongman, 1983). Jongman constructed his own definition through the means of an actor-based typology, classifying the state and the nonstate participants as the major actors (see Box 5.1).

Historical perspective

Terrorism, both a political and violent crime, is not a new phenomenon. It has a lengthy history that can be classified into three time periods: ancient, modern, and contemporary (Ross, 2006, Chapter 2). Each period had dominant groups and causes during which terrorism was used.

Box 5.1: *In the Name of the Father* (1993)

This film, directed by Jim Sheridan, details the exploits of Gerry Conlon, a petty thief suspected of being a member of the Irish Republican Army (IRA). Based on Conlon's autobiography, *Proved innocent*, the movie depicts Conlon leaving Belfast for London and going to a squatters' house. He and a friend then break into a prostitute's apartment, steal her money, and return to Belfast, after which Conlon and his friends and family are implicated in the IRA's Guildford pub bombing (October 5, 1974) in which five people were killed and 75 injured.

In response to the bombing, British Parliament hastily passed the Prevention of Terrorism Act, which allows the government to detain an individual for seven days without charging him or her. Through their interrogation techniques (particularly sleep deprivation), the London Metropolitan Police managed to make Conlon confess to the bombing. His father, Giuseppe Conlon, and other relatives and friends were also arrested and incarcerated for lengthy prison terms.

The film depicts Ms. Gareth Pierce, a prominent human rights lawyer, coming to visit the prison. Conlon explains his innocence and that of his father (Giuseppe's health deteriorates, and he eventually dies). Pierce is allowed to inspect the Giuseppe Conlon files in a government archive, where she discovers a file that says, "not to be shown to defense". The evidence implicates the government detectives in a cover-up to secure Conlon's conviction, and the case against Conlon is dismissed. Conlon was incarcerated for 15 years before he and the others who were convicted in the same case were released.

Since December 29, 1992, in particular, we have seen a number of terrorist incidents committed by members of al-Qaeda against US targets or citizens. These have gained worldwide attention, including the 1993 bombing of the World Trade Center (New York), the 1998 bombing of US embassies in Kenya and Tanzania, the 2000 incident against the USS Cole in Yemen, and the attacks of 9/11. To add insult to injury, al-Qaeda or terrorist groups with allegiances to this organization, exploded powerful bombs killing and injuring numerous individuals in Bali, Indonesia (2002), Madrid, Spain (2004), and London, England (2005). An armed assault committed by Muslim extremists in the Indian capital of Mumbai (2008) also led to the deaths of 164 people.

The public, journalists, and politicians tend to get caught up in the spectacular terrorist events and ignore the long-term patterns. In order to have a better understanding of the contemporary patterns of terrorism, the following section provides a description of a number of trends, including the frequency of terrorism, geographic spread, targets, tactics, and terrorist groups. However, before analyzing this, we need to understand how these data are derived.[9] Specifically, it is important to examine the sources for the information we have on terrorism.

Data sources

Prior to the mid-1970s, the majority of information on terrorism was presented in case studies of particular movements, groups, and individuals that used terrorism, and in case studies of countries that experienced terrorism. This material – developed by scholars, journalists, and government agencies – was generally descriptive, atheoretical, and primarily normative.

In the mid-1970s, however, some scholars, private research companies, and governmental departments attempted to systematically collect data on the actions and characteristics of terrorism. The majority of these efforts were rudimentary quantitative studies, which unlike the descriptive studies, allow us to speak with greater precision about terrorist phenomena. The most basic statistics for the study of terrorism are events data, important information gathered on each incident over a specified period of time.

This approach to the study of terrorism helps us in a variety of ways: to spot trends; to understand how the tactics and targets of terrorism have changed over time; to develop and test hypotheses; and to approach terrorism in a scientific fashion to help predict future events. This methodology has allowed researchers and policymakers to understand the frequency of terrorism and, occasionally, to test hypotheses.

There are several advantages to events databases. They give us a better idea of the scope, nature, and intensity of terrorism over time, and they provide us with a historical context. An events data focuses on the discrete incident as its unit of analysis. This method has been used in the creation of numerous large-scale studies of political conflict (see, for example, Gurr, 1966). Most of these projects did not, however, incorporate a separate variable for terrorism, but instead included terrorist acts among other types of violence. During the early 1970s, however, events data methodology was eventually applied to international terrorism.

Since the mid-1970s, there has been an increase in attempts to collect quantitative data on terrorism. Nevertheless, these datasets suffer from a number of problems, including: overly broad definitions of terrorism; limited public availability; a focus on regional tallies rather than on country totals; a lack of distinction between domestic and international events; inclusion of acts of violence that are not terrorism; and a readiness to include events that are not confirmed as being motivated by terrorist goals.

Similar to what happens in the business world, many of the incident-level datasets on terrorism have been combined with others, are unavailable to the public, or no longer exist. Meanwhile, new datasets have entered the academic, corporate, and state marketplace (Ross, 1991). Nevertheless, three datasets have managed to withstand the resource-intensive demands of maintaining a data collection enterprise. When a data source is cited in a terrorism study, it is commonly based on data from the Control Risks Group Database, RAND Corporation Database, or the State Department/CIA/International Terrorism: Attributes of Terrorism Events (ITERATE) I, II, and III datasets.

The economic obstacles to creating and maintaining a dataset are most evident when one observes that the first two of the previously mentioned databases were created by private research organizations, and the latter – at least ITERATE I and II – by Mickolus, a private enterprise, with funding from the CIA. Although all of these datasets have been criticized on several accounts, they also have practical advantages.

Between 1996 and 2003, the US State department, Office of the Coordinator for Counter-Terrorism, issued an annual Patterns of global terrorism report. The publicly available dataset is limited to international terrorism and is presented in an aggregate format. The database includes hoaxes and threats, which tend to over-count the number of actual incidents. In April 2005, the US State Department formally announced that it would no longer disseminate global reports on terrorism.[10] Instead, this function would be handed over the National Counterterrorism Centre (NCTC), which is part of the Office of the Director of National Intelligence.

The data were managed by the National Memorial Institute for the Prevention of Terrorism (MIPT), located in Oklahoma City. According to the database's website, the new database Terrorism Knowledge Base (TKB) was collected from the RAND Terrorism Chronology (1968-97), Rand-MIPT Terrorism Incident database (1998-present), Terrorism Indictment database (University of Arkansas), and DFI International's research on terrorist organizations.

Since the spring of 2008, however, the federal government decided to discontinue MIPT's TKB, the general public, students of terrorism, and experts no longer have easily digestible relatively comprehensive data on oppositional political terrorism. One must go either to the National Counterterrorism Center (NCTC) database, copy down each and every act of terrorism in the database, and then perform basic descriptive statistics, or download the University of Maryland's START database and do the same. This process is rather onerous for the average person, student, and expert.

Despite the previously mentioned drawbacks, the majority of the datasets show the same general patterns. However, not all databases answer the basic questions of who, what, when, where, and why in a comprehensive manner. Thus, for the purposes of this chapter, statistics are based on a variety of sources. Where appropriate State Department information was not available, the RAND reports or MIPT (TKB) data were utilized. Readers must be made aware that data for 1968-97 covers only international incidents, whereas the statistics for 1998-June 30, 2004, covers both domestic and international incidents.

Another caveat is also in order. Although many acts of terrorism are successfully thwarted by the combined efforts of law enforcement and national security agencies, because of fears that sensitive information will be leaked, thus jeopardizing ongoing investigations or the likelihood of conviction, these successes are rarely made publicly available (Jenkins, 2003, pp. 126-7). This information should help us better contextualize the empirical data on real or actual terrorist acts. In other words, the available databases may underestimate the actual terrorism that is perpetrated or in the process of being organized. Unlike previous databases, this one selectively integrates domestic terrorism.

Annual statistics

From 1968 through July 30, 2005, approximately 9,720 international political terrorist events occurred, ranging from a low of 103 incidents in 1969 and 2000 to a high of 440 in 1985. This statistic breaks down to an average of about 259 incidents each year (www.tkb.org).[11] The prevailing impression given by the media, public officials, and some experts concerned with international terrorism is that this type of political crime is on the increase. For the most part, increases are relative to the time period under investigation, and they are not linear, as media accounts might imply. As far back as the 1960s, the frequency of terrorism has been cyclical, with several peaks and valleys occurring over the years. This is not surprising, as terrorism fluctuates due to general factors involved in causation and decline. In 2004, for instance, the total number of international terrorist incidents was 330 – 56 events more than in 2003. However, not all events are of the same magnitude and intensity. For example, the magnitude of the September 11, 2001, attacks on the World Trade Center and the Pentagon might lead to the conclusion that there has been a steep increase in the number of terrorist events overall, which is not actually the case.

Geographic spread

The number of countries experiencing some sort of terrorist activity annually has gradually increased. In the late 1960s, international terrorist incidents occurred in an average of 29 countries each year. This number climbed to 39 countries in the early 1970s and to 43 by the end of the decade. Between 1980 and 1983, the average number of countries experiencing international terrorist incidents was 51, and for the period from 1983 to 1985, the average was 65 incidents.[12]

Although terrorism is experienced throughout the world, some regions currently suffer a disproportionate amount of the world's terrorism. Regions experiencing the largest number of terrorist activities change almost every year. Between 1968 and 2005 (June 30), for example, the Middle East received the brunt of terrorist attacks (6,743 incidents), and East and Central Asia incurred the lowest number of incidents (198) (www.tkb.org).[13] Approximately 20 countries account for between 75 and 90 percent of all reported incidents. The top three countries that experience the largest amount of terrorism (approximately 75 percent) are, in descending order of frequency: Israel (including the Gaza strip and the West Bank), Pakistan, and Colombia.

Targets

Since the 1960s, the range of terrorist targets has expanded. In the early 1960s and 1970s, terrorists concentrated their attacks mainly on property and institutions, whereas in the 1980s, they increasingly targeted people. Almost every conceivable structure and mode of transportation has been hit, including embassies, factories, airliners, airline offices, tourist agencies, hotels, airports, bridges, trains, train stations, reactors, refineries, schools, restaurants, pubs, churches, temples, synagogues, mainframe computers for large businesses and organizations, data-processing centers, and office towers.

A considerable amount of public and media attention has been directed toward the possibility of terrorist attacks on nuclear facilities and the potential of fallout. Indeed, there have been breaches of security at these places; however, most of the incidents were carried out by anti-nuclear protestors trying to halt or delay the construction of new nuclear facilities rather than destroy existing ones.

Americans, the British, the French, Israelis, and Turks account for approximately half of all the nationalities victimized by terrorists.[14] The individuals attacked include diplomats, military personnel, tourists, businesspeople, students, journalists, children, nuns, priests, and the Pope. According to MIPT/TKB statistics, since 1968, the majority of targets have been private citizens and property (3,821). From 1968 to June 30, 2005, out of the 22,457 incidents, there were a total of 75,245 injuries and 29,642 fatalities. Based on 2004 State Department figures, about 16 percent (2,998 individuals) were US citizens.

By the end of 2001, largely because of the events of September 11, the number of deaths rose to over 3,000 individuals. Typically, only 15 to 20 percent of all terrorist incidents involve fatalities; of those, 66 percent involve only one death. Less than one percent of the thousands of terrorist incidents that have occurred in the past two decades have involved 10 or more fatalities. Incidents of mass murder, sometimes achieved through suicide bombings, are truly rare. This has led some experts, like Jenkins, to repeatedly suggest that, "terrorists want a lot of people watching rather than a lot of people dead" (Jenkins, 1979, p. 169). During the 1990s, however, with the increase in suicide attacks, this statement was less applicable as it appeared that if a lot of people are dead, then a lot of people would be watching.

Tactics

Terrorists operate with a fairly limited repertoire of attacks. Seven basic tactics have accounted for 97 percent of all terrorist incidents: bombings (13,217), assassinations (2,182), armed assaults (3,657), kidnappings (1,652), arson (868), hijackings (232), and barricade and hostage incidents (201) (www.tkb.org).[15] In short, terrorists blow things up, kill people, or seize hostages. Every incident is essentially a variation on these activities. Bombings appear to be the most deadly.

Although the use of chemical, biological, radiological, and nuclear (CBRN) weapons, is a topic of constant concern, bombings of all types continue to be the most popular terrorist method of attack. Approximately 50 percent of all international events are bombings. This is followed, in terms of numbers, by armed attacks, arsons, and kidnappings. In addition, the number of arson incidents, bombings, attacks on and assassinations of diplomats has increased in the past few years.

While the majority of bombs are simple incendiary devices, terrorists have made and often use more sophisticated explosive weapons. Rudimentary bombs in particular are easy to construct. Bombings also typically involve the least amount of group coordination and thus are one of the easiest terrorist tactics to employ. Additionally, they are relatively cheap; a group can get a considerable amount of "bang for its buck" through using bombs.

Terrorist groups

Some terrorist organizations show considerable endurance, operating for a lengthy period, replacing their losses, preparing for new attacks, and turning into semi-permanent subcultures. Other groups have fleeting existences.

In 1991, for example, Crenshaw examined the longevity of 76 terrorist organizations. According to her study, many groups exhibited remarkable stability and tenacity, but almost half of the organizations either no longer existed or no longer committed acts of terrorism at the time of her research. However, at least 10 groups – including al-Fatah, the Popular Front for the Liberation of Palestine-General Command (PFLP-GC), and Euzkadi Ta Askatasuna (ETA) – have been in operation for 20 years (Crenshaw, 1991). The MIPT/TKB database (7/30/2005) lists 792 terrorist organizations, although probably no more than 200 are active in any given year.

Over the past 37 years most terrorist incidents have been attributed to "Other Group" or "Unknown Group." This means that the organizational affiliation could not be positively identified. In situations where the organization was positively identified, Hamas (446), Basque Fatherland and Freedom (ETA) (387), and the National Liberation Army (in Columbia) (282) have committed the greatest number of incidents. Those groups that are responsible for the highest number of fatalities are al-Qaeda (3,521), Hezbollah (821), Tanzim Qa'idat al-Jihad fi Bilad al-Rafidayn (a Palestinian group) (615), and Hamas (577).

Research and theoretical implications[15]

One enigma emerging out of terrorism research is the overabundance of descriptions and the relative dearth of empirical causal studies.[16] The most prominent theoretical explanations are: structural, social-psychological, and rational choice.[17] In an effort to explain the dynamics of terrorism, this chapter reviews the structural and social-psychological explanations by consolidating five principal structural factors. Variables that are logically connected and amenable to empirical testing are outlined. These factors include a complex array of processes derived from research descriptive of and associated with the dynamics of terrorism. Although there is considerable diversity among terrorists and their organizations, if analyses are to move beyond case studies, we need to formulate hypotheses, collect better data, and test the propositions that we have developed.

As a general proposition, the greater the number of and intensity of structural and social-psychological causes of terrorism (the independent variables), the higher the number of terrorist acts perpetrated for any particular terrorist or organization (the dependent variable). If these factors are causally related, then the systematic elimination or lessening of them should lead to a decrease in terrorism.

Causes

Few researchers have developed a general model or theory of the causes of terrorism. More common are studies that list several possible factors but fail to specify their interactions. However, there have been five well-known attempts to create or test structural theories and models of terrorism or to explain the processes of the political offense that merits attention (see, for example, Gross, 1972; Hamilton, 1978; Targ, 1979; Crenshaw, 1981; Johnson, 1982, Chapter 8).

Although these authors produced a highly important knowledge base from which to conduct further study, they have a number of difficulties (Ross, 1993a, 1994, 1996, 1999). The benefits of the previous works on the causes of terrorism are maximized by specifying causal relationships between variables.

A phenomenal body of literature on the psychological causes of terrorism reflects several research strategies. First, there is a series of case studies of individual terrorists (see, for example, Bollinger, 1981; Knutson, 1981; Caplan, 1983; Kelman, 1983). Second, there are a number of studies of terrorist groups or subtypes thereof (see, for example, Morf, 1970; Hubbard, 1971; IJOGT, 1982a, 1982b; Clark, 1983; Russell and Miller, 1983; Weinberg and Eubank, 1987). Third, and closely connected to analyses of certain terrorist groups, are psychological interpretations of terrorism that are place/country-specific (see, for example, Ferracuti and Bruno, 1981). Fourth, a considerable amount of research ascribes the psychological causes to one or two theoretical explanations (see, for example, Morf, 1970; Miron, 1976; Gutmann, 1979; Ferracuti, 1982; Caplan, 1983; Crayton, 1983; McCauley and Segal, 1987; Crenshaw, 1990a; Pearlstein, 1991). Fifth, some literature primarily critiques other research (see, for example, Corrado, 1981; Crenshaw, 1990b; Reich, 1990). Finally, by far the majority of work consists of literature reviews (see, for example, Hubbard, 1971, 1983; Hacker, 1976; Cooper, 1977; Margolin, 1977; Crenshaw, 1985; Taylor, 1988).

Various problems also plague psychological explanations of terrorism, including, but not limited to, the relevance of causes, assumptions that terrorism is different from other types of violent political or criminal behavior, use of psychological explanations of terrorism, psychological health of terrorists, methodologies used for psychological studies of terrorism, contribution of nonpsychological causes to the commission of terrorism, and trade-offs between overgeneralization and reductionism (Ross, 1994). None of these criticisms, however, eliminates the utility of continued theorizing about and research on the psychological causes of terrorism.

Although this information has contributed to our knowledge of terrorism, there is no grand theory that can explain why terrorists do what they do and who will become a terrorist. Since each type of terrorism has a different pattern of causation, the relative importance of each independent variable depends on the context, including the type of perpetrator, terrorist act, target, country, and time period.[18] A broad theoretical framework that can accommodate some of these ideas may be achieved through integrating both structural and psychological explanations.

Structural explanations

There are at least 10 structural explanations of terrorism. In general, most of these factors act as independent variables, while occasionally acting as dependent factors in causal ordering. Following Crenshaw's (1985) distinction, these explanations may be divided into permissive and precipitant causes. Regardless of the complexity of the command structure and the size of the organization, acts of terrorism may be carried out by individuals alone or as group members.

At the core of the precipitant causes are the three permissive factors that are endemic to all societies: geographical location, type of political system, and amount of modernization. These three factors are necessary but insufficient interacting predecessors that create conditions for terrorism. Permissive causes also are considered to be systemic conditions that pre-structure and facilitate the presence of the precipitants.

Precipitant causes are the final triggering mechanisms that motivate people and organizations to engage in terrorism. The most common precipitants are: social, cultural, and historical facilitation; organizational split and development; presence of other forms of unrest; support; counter-terrorist organization failure; availability of weapons and explosives; and grievances (Ross, 1993a).

The permissive causes should structure the type and frequency of precursors to a group's choice of terrorism, which is facilitated by interactive precipitant causes. Even though the seven precipitants may motivate individuals or groups to choose terrorism for obtaining their goals, typically the pattern is more complex. For example, grievances can lead to support, which in turn may lead to grievances or the availability of weapons and explosives. Counter-terrorist organization failure can lead to support, and organizational split and development may lead to grievances.[19]

Social-psychological explanations

In general, there are five interconnected processes that social-psychological theories explain: joining, forming, remaining in, and leading a terrorist organization, and engaging in terrorist actions. Although people can engage politically violent acts alone, the process of committing terrorism is aided by belonging to or leading a terrorist group, and the frequency of one's violent acts likely increases if conducted in a group setting and with organizational support. This interpretation complements the framework of differential association theory, which argues that terrorism, like any other crime, is learned behavior reinforced by socialization into the group.

Seven psychological theories can be applied to explain terrorists' behavior: psychoanalytical (see, for example, Morf, 1970); learning (see, for example, Pitcher and Hamblin, 1982); frustration-aggression (see, for example, Gurr, 1970); narcissism-aggression (see, for example, Pearlstein, 1991); trait (Russell and Miller, 1983); developmental (Sayari, 1985); and motivational/rational choice (see, for example, Crenshaw, 1990a). These theories are accepted as partial explanations because none is, in and of itself, a sufficient social-psychological cause of terrorism. An alternative strategy proposed here is to integrate these theories into a single approach.[20]

According to an integrated view, childhood and adolescent experiences condition individuals to develop personality traits that predispose them to engage in terrorism (Ross, 1994, 1996). The development of these facilitating traits can be explained by either psychoanalytic, learning, frustration, or narcissism-aggression theories. The relevant traits motivate people to commit terrorism alone, to form bonds with other people who are predisposed to engage in terrorism, or sometimes to develop, join, remain in, or lead terrorist organizations. Terrorists experience the most important learning opportunities within the group to which they belong. These experiences, in turn, shape the cost-benefit calculus of individual terrorists.

Ultimately, engaging in a terrorist action is a conscious or unconscious rational choice decision, sometimes referred to as an expression of political strategy where expected utility is calculated by individual terrorists and collectively by terrorist groups (see, for example, Crenshaw, 1990a).[21] In other words, terrorists engage in their behaviors because they are relatively rational human beings and not because they suffer from psychological maladjustments (see, for example, Corrado, 1981).

Examinations of terrorists' motivations show a well thought-out logic for their behavior (see, for example, Kaplan, 1978). According to some terrorists, their actions are a cost-effective means to achieve a variety of goals: to obtain individual, collective, tangible, or symbolic recognition, attention, or publicity for their cause; to disrupt and discredit a government or other appropriate target; to create fear and/or hostility in an audience identified as the "enemy"; to provoke a counterrevolution by the government; to create sympathy or acceptance among potential supporters; and to increase control, discipline, and morale building within the terrorist group (see, for example, Hacker, 1976).

Rational choices are linked to the objectives of the terrorist act. In this sense, terrorist practices appear rational (perhaps bounded),[22] because they are committed in order to meet a set of political purposes and goals. These objectives include: "to terrify"; "advertis[e] a cause"; "provo[ke]"; "raise ... morale along with that of whatever group in whose name they claim to be acting by disclosing the vulnerability of their enemies"; "or, if the victims belong to some disliked group (eg, foreign business people) ... [encourage] admiration for their deed among the general population"; and, "sustain ... the group that is responsible for the violence" (Weinberg and Davis, 1989, pp. 9-10). It has been argued that the greater the sophistication, as measured by planning, target selection, and risk, the higher the level of rational choice involved in the process.

> Terrorists may ... perform activities they believe are likely to win widespread approval from their selected audiences ... [and] desist from activities that are too brutal or too difficult to justify on ethical grounds. Terrorists may also fear that inactivity will cause them to lose credibility, support, or the chance to gain new recruits – and that people within the terrorist organization will become restless or depressed. (Jenkins, 1982, pp. 61-2)

Cyberterrorism[23]

Cyberterrorism refers to "the exploitation of electronic vulnerabilities by terrorist groups in pursuit of their political aims" (Yar, 2006, p. 47). There is considerable fear that terrorists will hack into the computer mainframes of critical infrastructures serving transportation, financial, military, and other important areas. Terrorists could then disrupt the computers and cause these industries and organizations to either slow down, make mistakes, or come to a grinding halt.

The threat of cyberterrorism should also be seen in the context of the mythmaking connected to the internet. Numerous stories describe how powerful the internet is and how with a few keystrokes someone or some group with an ideological, political, or religious objective could disable critical computer information systems and cause unprecedented destruction and mayhem. Most of these pronouncements have been exaggerated. On the one hand, programming software architects are the rational people who have predicted these sorts of threats. Thus, they have created backup systems to protect computer systems from the threats. On the other hand, the scares have been advanced by security professionals and wannabes, individuals, and organizations that make their income by protecting computer systems or would like to do so. More skeptical commentators, however, claim there is little empirical evidence to "warrant the level of concern currently being generated over cyberterrorism, nor to justify the sweeping enhancement of state powers that are being instituted in order to respond to the supposed threat" (Yar, 2006, p. 55).

Although attacks committed by terrorist groups have never been confirmed in the US, American computer systems have experienced attacks by foreign governments. It is claimed that two viruses, the Code Red DoS and the Nimda, launched in 2001, were developed by terrorists in order to test the vulnerability of US cyber defenses.

In another case, named Moonlight Maze, investigators established that attacks on the Department of Defense computer systems in 1998 increased as cyber defenses were raised. It was also determined that attackers, traced back to a mainframe in the former Soviet Union, were monitoring US military troop movements. In connection with these attacks, it was further concluded that several suspected al-Qaeda operatives have sophisticated computer science technical backgrounds. Some have experience in infrastructure control systems, and they have used computers outside the US to conduct reconnaissance on national critical infrastructure defense capabilities.

In March and April of 2000, Vitek Boden, an Australian who was denied a job at Maroochy Sire (a sewage control system), launched 46 cyberattacks at the company. While not terrorism per se, these attacks led to the spillage of tons of raw sewage into the surrounding environment. The damage was significant. It caused the death of marine life, darkened waterways, and created an incredible smell.

Terrorist attacks are disruptive to the normal functioning of people's daily routines, business, and government organization. In terms of political crime, terrorism has been a very prominent aspect of modern life. The specter of terrorism has political cache in news headlines and among holiday travelers. And if the events of September 11, 2001, are any indication, terrorism will be with us indefinitely.

Summary

When activists and extremists move from nonviolent to violent actions, this shift increases the amount of attention garnered from both the public and security agencies. Whether it is the destruction of property or injury or death of an individual, the government must respond even if it is through lip service, increased rhetoric, or widespread repression. In many respects, the use of repression is an indication that the government has failed to meet the demands of its opponents and/or mollify them in some respect. When governments respond and end up breaking the law, then they call into question their legitimacy and may even be a cause for increased violent oppositional political crime.

Notes

[1] Since there have been numerous riots with political overtones, including Newark (1967), Chicago-Democratic Convention (1968), Tiananmen Square (1989), the World Trade Organization (WTO) meeting in Seattle (1990), and the European Union (EU) Summit in Gothenburg, Sweden (June 2001), there occurrences will be omitted from review.

[2] Another discussion of subversion can be found in Grace and Leys (1989).

[3] Unless otherwise indicated, all further references to terrorism subsume oppositional and political components.

[4] Oppositional political terrorism is conducted by anti-state and anti-corporate individuals and organizations. There are two types of oppositional terrorism – domestic and international-transnational. Domestic terrorism occurs at a greater frequency than international. Oppositional terrorism contrasts with state terrorism (see Chapters Six, Seven and Eight, this volume), which is carried out by government agencies against real or suspected threats to the regime.

[5] Assassination generally is the work of an individual or organization to kill a person. Unlike terrorism, assassination's goal is primarily focused on simply eliminating the person, rather than to threaten others. Sabotage involves damaging property; if the property is government-owned or contributes to the security of a country, then the action has an explicit political context. The majority of academic literature that examines this practice discusses sabotage in the context of war or war-like conditions, and argues against its political content.

[6] This recognizes that terrorists make cost-benefit calculations regarding targets and methods, which mitigates the perception or charge of randomness.

[7] Terrorist activities are often directed first against non-human targets and then progress to human targets. Most databases on terrorism include this distinction, as well as threats and hoaxes.

[8] In 1988, Schmid revised his consensus definition. Despite his efforts to improve on his previous efforts, many analysts prefer the old definition (1983) over the new one.

[9] This section builds on Ross (1991).

[10] In June 2004, it came to public attention that the data presented in the 2003 annual report had serious problems and had under-reported the amount of terrorism that had occurred that year. The US Department of State took responsibility, but argued that in the interests of getting the report to the printer in time, data collection efforts were suspended before the year's end. On June 22, 2004 the revised database was released, and it is from this report that the figures discussed in this chapter are drawn.

[11] This website is no longer in operation.

[12] www.mipt.org

[13] See note 11.

[14] Why is this the case? Israel, because of its seemingly nonstop conflict with the Palestinians, and the Americans, French, and British largely because of their transnational corporations.

[15] See note 11.

[16] This section builds on Ross (1993a, 1994, 1996, 1999).

[17] For a review of the merits and limitations of the literature on oppositional political terrorism in the US and Canada, respectively, see Ross (1988a, 1988b, 1993b).

---

[18] Reilly (1973) makes the same point with regard to internal war. Romano (1984) divides the causes into the biological, psychiatric, and sociological schools; Mitchell (1985) identifies ideologies, the environment, and individual factors; Turk (1982b) describes criminological approaches to terrorism; and Keenan (1987) outlines sociological and psychological explanations.

[19] Perpetrator characteristics include, for example, age, gender, and ideology (for example, anarchist, communist, nationalist, separatist, and right-wing; see Post, 1986). Regarding terrorist acts, several types of oppositional terrorism are recognized (for example, domestic, international, state-sponsored), and even finer definitions could be made with the addition of different geographic and actor dimensions.

[20] For further details of structural explanations, see Ross (1993a).

[21] Integrating these theories is difficult, especially because they have fundamentally different underlying logics.

[22] This position is not unanimously held. For further coverage of psychological explanations, see Post (1990) and Ross (1994, 1996).

[23] For an explanation of this concept, see Simon (1982).

[24] This chapter builds on Ross (2009, pp. 51-3).

SIX

State crime

Introduction

Until recently, the majority of research on crime has focused on the illegal actions of individuals, gangs, syndicates, and corporations. Less attention has been given to state crimes (Ross, 1995/2000; Ross et al., 1999). When crimes of the state, also known as governmental lawlessness (Sykes and Cullen, 1992, p. 269) and a subset referred to as the "crimes of the powerful" (Pearce, 1976; Tombs and Whyte, 2003) are addressed, they are largely treated as a consequence of or a response to insurgent violence, perceived threats to national security, or the behaviors of authoritarian regimes in second-transitional and third world/less developed countries. They are rarely portrayed as the normal, everyday functioning of governments in their desire to maintain or increase their power.

Since the late 1980s, however, a growing number of criminologists have explored the role of the state in the commission and facilitation of crimes. They recognize that state crime is pervasive and committed with varying frequency by all types of countries, from democracies to totalitarian, from capitalist to communist (Grabosky, 1989; Barak, 1990, 1991; Ross, 1995/2000, 2000b; Friedrichs, 1998a, 1998b; Rothe, 2009). Moreover, the state often is the initiator rather than simply the mediator or target of crime.

So why did it take so long for criminologists to focus on the problem of state crime? As Barak (1993) suggested, it took at least two decades after Sutherland's ground-breaking examination of white-collar crime for social scientists to turn their attention to the crimes of the privately powerful. Now, over three decades after sociologists and criminologists of the early 1970s delineated the category of state crimes, scholarly attention is finally being given to the misdeeds of the governments and their bureaucracies. In general, perhaps because of the controversial nature of state crimes, and the pressures of pedagogy (Ross and Rothe, 2007), it takes time for scholars to accept certain topics for legitimate study. This kind of awareness is not limited to state crime. For example, spousal violence (particularly from a husband to a wife), once something that was rarely condemned, has over the past six decades become criminalized, and there are now laws, policies, and procedures (for example, mandatory arrest in domestic violence calls for service) that many police departments across the country follow.

No state is immune from using repressive tactics, when those in power (that is, leaders, managers, and their agents) define people or groups as threatening to the existing social, political, or economic order. Although private institutions wield coercive power, the state holds an exclusive legal authority to coerce. In fact, theorists from Marx through Weber to Mann have noted the importance of both coercion and criminality to state power. State crime has existed since the formation of the first country, and it has been suggested that it may, in fact, be necessary for the very creation of states (Gurr, 1988).

Box 6.1: Gregg Barak (1948–)

Gregg Barak was born June 29, 1948, in Los Angeles. He earned his PhD in Criminology from the University of California, Berkeley, in 1974. Barak has held professorial positions at seven universities, including as a Distinguished Visiting Professor at Eastern Kentucky University. Barak is currently a Professor of Criminology and Criminal Justice at Eastern Michigan University. He is the author and/or editor of a number of books, including the award winning *Gimme shelter: A social history of homelessness in contemporary America* (1991). Among his most recent books are: *Criminology: An integrated approach* (2009) and *Theft of a nation: Wall Street looting and federal regulatory colluding* (2012).

Barak has served as a board member or officer, including president, for various shelters or programs for the homeless, hungry, and sexually abused and/or assaulted. In 2003, Barak became the 27th Fellow of the Academy of Criminal Justice Sciences, and in 2007 he received the Lifetime Achievement Award from the Critical Division of the American Society of Criminology. In the field of political crime, he is best known for his edited books, *Crimes by the capitalist state: An introduction to state criminality* (1991) and *Violence, conflict, and world order: Critical conversations on state-sanctioned justice* (2007). His website is www.greggbarak.com

---

The notion of the state and/or those employed by it committing crimes is not new. Mills, in his classic book *The power elite* (1956, Chapter 13), explained the notion of "higher immorality." Through this phrase, Mills sought to explain the criminal and unethical actions perpetrated by a country's political, corporate, and military leaders. Mills suggested that when a scandal took place in one sector, it was often linked to ones in another.

Indeed scholars, jurists, and the public have questioned academics about their broad use of the term state crime (see, for example, Sharkansky, 1995). The concept is useful, and with cautious operationalization, it can help us explain the misdeeds of government institutions and agencies, powerful individuals acting in the name of the state, and those acting criminally as enabled by the state power with which they have been vested.

How widespread is the problem?

There are several practical problems connected with monitoring state criminality: it is often difficult to detect; it is hard to prosecute the individuals accused of perpetrating these acts; it is challenging to identify specific perpetrator/s; and, those charged often have considerable resources to mount a sustained defense (Ross and Rothe, 2008).

First, most nonviolent state crimes go undetected because of the ability of the perpetrators to conceal information about this activity (that is, cover-ups, hiding of incriminating or critical evidence or documentation), to destroy documentation, and/or to engineer the disappearance of critical witnesses. Typically, these actions are usually hidden to avoid embarrassment both for the person committing the act and the agency that employs the person. If such crimes are discovered or revealed, this usually occurs years after the fact (Wolfe, 1973; Parenti, 1995, pp. 139-42; Ross and Rothe, 2008). The 1972 Watergate scandal, for example, was discovered only by accident when a security guard stumbled upon "the Plumbers," the people who broke into the Democratic National Committee headquarters (Woodward and Bernstein, 1974). Likewise the US decision to go to war with Iraq in 2003 was in large part predicated on the ability of the Bush Administration to carefully package questionable intelligence regarding Iraq's WMD capability and the power of trusted individuals, such as the then Secretary of State Colin Powell to convince the UN Security Counsel (February 5, 2003) of the US position on Iraq (detailed in the Senate Report on Pre-War Intelligence in Iraq).

Second, those being investigated for state crimes often have considerable resources that allow them to divert, stall, and frustrate (often through legal means, favors, rhetorical powers, or intimidation) investigative inquiries. Many try to claim that their actions were committed in the name of national security, or they rely on "plausible deniability" as their defense. Alternatively, such crimes are hard to prosecute because of solidarity among government workers in tight-knit groups (for example, the "blue wall of silence" engaged in by police officers, the military, etc.). Unless someone has a grudge against a fellow employee or has an overly moral conscience, many bureaucrats look the other way when they see or hear about deviant actions occurring in their place of employment to avoid being perceived as disloyal to co-workers and superiors. Alternatively, they may fear losing their jobs. For a variety of reasons, some individuals may also give false testimony in court. Even when those questionable acts or state crimes come to public attention (although rarely are citizens given the full story), through the media or governmental inquiries, the facts can be skewed or biased. An agency might try its best to cover up a crime, representatives may engage in plausible deniability, considerable red tape might hamper the investigation, or an investigator might be limited to dealing with an offender in a very secretive manner. Alternatively, state crimes that do come to public attention, like the death squad activity in South East Asia (for example, in Cambodia, Vietnam, etc.) during the 1960s and 1970s, and Latin America (for example, in Brazil, Chile, El Salvador, Panama, and Peru), during the 1970s and 1980s, and the use of rendition by the US and its allies in the post-9/11 era (Grey, 2006), are commonly explained by state officials as part of "raison d'état," the right of the state to engage in affairs on its own soil. As for politicians committing a crime, they may be fortunate enough to procure the best kind of legal defense that money can buy, be lightly sanctioned, pay an affordable fine, or have their sentences annulled. In the spring of 2007, for instance, President George W. Bush commuted the prison sentences of I. Lewis (Scooter) Libby, White House insider and adviser to Vice President Dick Cheney, although he had been convicted for obstruction of justice, perjury, and making false statements to federal investigators.

Definitional and conceptual issues

Central questions linked to the issue of state crime include, but are not limited to, the following: "What is the state?" "How did it form?" "What is its nature?" and "How does state crime change over time?" Understanding these concepts is essential to the discussion of who has the power to implement governmental policies and why state employees take particular actions. Of primary importance for our discussion, these questions clarify the notion of state crime. Before continuing, it would be helpful to carefully distinguish and define three terms that many of us take for granted.

A *nation* consists of people who share a common history, language, 'race', and culture, although they may not necessarily live in the same geographic location (for example, Armenians, Palestinians, etc.). A *country* is land that has discernible borders. In general, states have population, territory, government, and sovereignty (Khan and McNiven, 1991, pp. 26-34). According to most state theorists and critical criminologists, the *state* is the political entity that holds a legitimate monopoly on the use of force, law, and administration. The state possesses the balance of power in most political conflicts because it has a disproportionate amount of resources in order to carry out this mandate. Any understanding of contemporary, advanced, industrialized democratic countries is best served by recognizing that the state has not always existed and is typically a product of conflict (Engels, 1942; Tilly, 1985).[1] To maintain power, states (and by extension, regimes) must achieve and sustain legitimacy.[2] This approach is highly relevant to theories of power and interest articulation.[3]

Power and interest articulation

Three interpretations or "faces" of power provide separate but interrelated explanations concerning the role of the government and its purpose in society. These views, it can be argued, are products of their time, and have accordingly been challenged and modified over the past 60 years (Lukes, 1974; Alford and Friedland, 1985).

In the 1960s, the theoretical notion of pluralism was developed (Dahl, 1961; Polsby, 1980). Also known as the "first face of power," or consensus theory, according to this theory, in the political arena everyone has an equal chance of being heard. In conflicts/competitions, majorities prevail and their policy preferences are enacted. Theorists and researchers working in this tradition argued that the state is a neutral entity, a "black box" that simply exists to translate the "will of the people" into policies, legislation, and practices. The state responds to conventional political participation (for example, voting, supporting politicians and political parties, etc.). Pluralists believe that society demonstrates its wishes, and the government responds to and serves its citizens' needs. Pluralists argue that the reason so few people participate in the political process (usually referred to as apathy) is because of their disinterest in politics. In short, pluralism has found a considerable amount of resonance among the US public because this is what Americans are taught to believe from an early age, especially the notion that every vote counts (see Figure 6.1).

Figure 6.1: Outline of the three faces of power

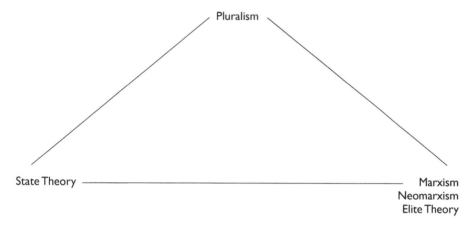

During the late 1960s, both as an intellectual reaction to the shortcomings of pluralist theory and a social response to the events that were taking place in advanced industrialized democracies (anti-war demonstrations, 'race' riots, student movements, demands for the expansion of civil rights), elite (Mills, 1956; Domhoff, 1983), Marxist and neo-Marxist theories evolved (Bachrach and Baratz, 1962; Kasinitz, 1983; Parenti, 1995). Those who advocated this position, also known as the "second face of power," argued that not everyone had the same access to power and not all people could participate in the political process. Moreover, those who had a disproportionate share of resources (for example, the owners and managers of the means of production) were typically the ones who participated politically. Unfortunately, for the powerless in society, the elite's agenda is too often translated into policies and laws. Coterminous with this explanation is Bachrach and Baratz's notion of the "mobilization of bias" (1962). This generally occurs when elite interests can prevent certain groups and issues from reaching the political agenda. Mobilization of bias specifically refers to the practice whereby large powerful entities use their resources to frustrate the wishes of the majority. In these situations, opportunities for confrontation are structured so that political ideas or desires of the less powerful do not come to the table and/or are not aired in public. Within this paradigm, only the strongest and most influential people in our society affect the government. This theory purports that government serves only the affluent and upper-class members.

Finally, in the 1980s, a third variant, called state theory, developed (see, for example, Skocpol, 1979; Carnoy, 1984). State theorists argue that, even though the governments of advanced industrialized democracies are run by elected or appointed officials, the most important political actor is the bureaucracy. Borrowing from the fields of public administration, public policy, and organizational behavior, state theorists suggest that because the state has a disproportional amount of resources, its workers and agents primarily carry out rules and laws in connection with their own views about how things should work. Government workers and administrators are primarily self-interested and, thus, are concerned with career and organizational protection/maintenance and expansion. They will lobby citizens and legislatures on behalf of policies and practices they believe will help their agency. Bureaucracies can also frustrate policies they believe are unfounded, threatening to their agenda, or detrimental to their ability to showcase their skills or talents. Needless to say, the state can facilitate or frustrate political participation (Lukes, 1974; Gaventa, 1980). At the same time, interests can have a history of their own. Repeatedly frustrated by their limited political participation, workers and the general public may become alienated and apathetic, leaving the decision-making process up to others.

Conceptual clarification of state crime

Turk (1982a, Chapter 4) distinguishes between those acts directed against the government as "political crimes" and those acts committed by the government or state as "political policing." Although Turk sensitizes us to the dichotomy between the two actions, it does not appear that he accords state crime the same legitimacy as oppositional political crimes. Perhaps this is why other writers use the term political crime as an umbrella concept for crimes both against and by the state (see, for example, Thomas and Hepburn, 1983; Michalowski, 1985; Gibbons, 1987).

Some of the criminological community and much of society have adopted a double standard regarding definitions of the words crime and criminal. Crimes against the government (or society) have long been regarded as real crimes, that is, serious, harmful acts that are rightly criminalized and receive copious attention from the mass media (Barak, 1994). On the other hand, the abuse of power by the state, particularly in advanced industrialized democracies, is perceived as less egregious and is often designated as a necessary action, which receives erratic public attention. There is rarely a sustained appreciation for the vast harms resulting from the actions of government agencies and agents (Chomsky, 1973; Clinard and Quinney, 1978).

The state and its lawmakers, managers, and bureaucrats are not solely architects and enforcers of the law, but they are also significant players in law violations. Indeed, the state holds a unique position – it is both "a crime-regulating and crime-generating institution" (Barak, 1993, p. 209). With respect to the later behavior, the state has committed such garden-variety crimes as violence and theft, but it has also participated in illegalities available only to those with official state authority and power. Or, as Clinard and Quinney (1978) have outlined: "Those who legislate and enforce the law – and determine what is to be regarded as legitimate – are in the position of violating the laws themselves without being criminally defined" (p. 144).

Given the realities of sovereignty and national security, most states, regardless of their ideological foundations or political-economic systems, seemingly could not survive without some form of secrecy, espionage, and deception (Ross, 1992). The question then becomes, when do such actions violate the law, and whose law is being violated?

Organizational governmental crimes are considered those "committed with the support and encouragement of a formal organization and intended at least in part to advance" its goals (Coleman, 1985, p. 8). The crimes permeate the institution, as illegalities are deemed necessary and functional for the bureaucracy's agenda and mandate, and are considered critical for continuing the dominant political-economic order. Broad organizational support is the defining characteristic of these types of crimes, which are vastly different sociologically from those committed by individuals for their own personal gain.

Naturally, there is some definitional confusion between the concepts of state crime and governmental crime. Although some analysts "treat state crime as a subtype of" governmental crime, quite often these terms are used interchangeably (Friedrichs, 1995, p. 53). To clarify,

> ... the term state refers to a political entity with a recognized sovereignty occupying a definite territory, whereas the term government refers to the political and administrative apparatus of such an entity. [...] Government may also refer to the administrative apparatus of lesser political entities, such as municipalities. The term state crime suggests crime committed on behalf of a state (federal or not), while the term governmental crime [...] can more naturally be applied to crimes committed within a governmental context on any level, and not necessarily on behalf of the state. (Friedrichs, 1995, pp. 53-4)

Friedrichs explains further: "governmental crime [is] used as a broad term for the whole range of crimes committed in a governmental context." State crime "activities," he continues, are those actions "carried out by the state or on behalf of some state agency," while political white-collar crime refers to "illegal activities carried out by officials and politicians for direct personal benefit" (Friedrichs, 1995, p. 54). Because the term state crime is better known, it is used for this discussion.

Although the appropriateness of the term is debatable (see, for example, Sharkansky, 1995), state crimes include "cover-ups, corruption, disinformation, unaccountability, and violations of domestic and/or international laws. It also includes those practices that, although they fall short of being officially declared illegal, are perceived by the majority of the population as illegal or socially harmful" (Ross, 1995/2000, pp. 6-7).[4] This definition squarely puts state crime in the league of actions that are considered social harms (Schwendinger and Schwendinger, 1975).

Typologies

Henry (1991, p. 256), building on the philosophical and ideological belief that a state has certain moral and ethical obligations to its citizenry, distinguishes between state crimes of commission and those inactions of the state referred to as crimes of omission.[5] Thus, we can define state crimes as those acts that bring physical, material, or social harm to its citizens, a subgroup of people, or foreigners resulting from the actions or consequences of government policy mediated through the practice of state agencies, whether these harms are intentional or unintentional.

Other concepts have been applied to state crimes. In some cases, state illegalities are referred to as *state authority occupational crimes*, a term reserved for individuals vested with particular state authority – the legal power to "represent the force of state law in certain decisions" (Green, 1990, p. 149). Such crimes are possible because of the privileges of state authority occupations and the legal force available to those with government-sanctioned power. In other words, state authority occupational crimes involve the misuse of legally vested authority and force, which includes such acts as corruption, bribe taking, police brutality, military crimes, and illegal domestic surveillance activities. Other labels found in the literature for this type of political crime include *elite deviance* (Simon and Eitzen, 1999) and *occupational crime* (Coleman, 1994, pp. 11-12). Friedrichs (1995, pp. 58, 60) uses the much broader term *governmental crime* as an umbrella concept, under which falls "political corruption," which he terms "political white collar crime." Friedrichs reserves the concept of "governmental crime" for those actions carried out by the state and its agents, both for organizational state goals and people's own personal benefits.

Undoubtedly, governmental crime is characterized by conceptual and typological confusion. Clarifying this messiness is an ongoing task. Some recent distinctions include Friedrichs' (1995, p. 54) use of *governmental crime* as a broad term subsuming "the whole range of crimes committed in a governmental context," *state crime* as "activities carried out by the state or on behalf of some state agency," and *political white-collar crime* as "illegal activities carried out by officials and politicians for direct personal benefit" (p. 54).

This treatment of state crime incorporates acts that are *mala in se* and *mala prohibita*, as well as those behaviors that currently are not prohibited by criminal law. While the appropriateness of states' responsibilities can and historically have been debated, crimes of commission and omission, as well as acts labeled governmental crime, state crime, political white-collar crime (Ross, 1995/2000, pp. 4-6), and state-corporate crime (Kramer and Michalowski, 1990) can be included.

Therefore, as mentioned above, state crime includes such actions as cover-ups, disinformation, unaccountability, corruption, and violations of domestic and/or international law. Also embedded are those practices that, although falling short of being officially declared illegal, are considered socially injurious. This definition recognizes that legal systems are slow to enact legislation, are highly normative, and often reflect elite, class, and nonpluralistic interests (Sutherland, 1949b, pp. 511-15; Schwendinger and Schwendinger, 1975; Quinney, 1977; Barak, 1993; Bohm, 1993; Ross, 1995/2000, p. 6).

Activities that are much more egregious in terms of lost dollars, human lives, and injuries – corporate and governmental wrongdoings engaged in by the powerful – typically are not legislated as criminal and are beyond the purview of the crime control industry. For example, these crimes are codified in regulatory, rather than criminal, law. Politically motivated crimes committed by the dispossessed typically are also activities legislated as criminal, whereas politically motivated crimes committed by the powerful acting in corporate or state interests typically are not.

This inclusive treatment of state crime also addresses and mitigates criticisms from the Right, which argues that state crime theory largely rests on semantics, and from the Left, which occasionally uses ambiguous concepts and unrigorous/questionable research methods. Unlike oppositional political crimes, it is hard to differentiate between violent and nonviolent types of state crimes. For example, many human rights violations can have both violent and nonviolent subtypes.

Relevance of state repression

A number of acts of state crime, often labeled state repression, do not easily fit into standard classifications. Repression typically involves intentional or unintentional acts (most of which appear legal) designed to suppress or silence individuals or groups in order to keep them from participating in the political process. For example, it is perfectly legal for the FBI to park a car in front of a particular house or place of business and watch those who enter and exit. And in most advanced industrialized democracies, as long as the authorities do not enter your premise or step foot on your property, they can go through personal garbage.

State agencies have frustrated or disrupted the activities of dissenters by spying; executing warrants to search homes, offices, or vehicles; threatening dissenters or their loved ones with violence or loss of jobs; and arresting them under legally questionable charges (that is, false pretenses) (for example, Goldstein, 1978). When dissenters do spend time in jail, their bail may be purposely set high, and their prosecution may be dragged out in an effort to exhaust their resources and will. This is true for individuals as well as the organizations to which they belong or lead. Although a conviction may not be obtained, this repression has the effect of wearing the individuals and organizations down. US history is replete with examples of this phenomenon (Parenti, 1995, p. 139).

The US criminal justice system, for example, has a number of mechanisms that have been periodically and selectively used to impede the activities of possible and actual dissenters, including the use of the grand jury, the Internal Revenue Service (IRS), US Citizenship and Immigration Services (USCIS), US Immigration and Customs Enforcement (ICE), US Customs and Border Protection (CBP),[6] the State Department, and individual incarceration. According to Parenti (1995), "Supposedly intended to weigh the state's evidence and protect the innocent from unjustifiable prosecution, the grand jury ends up doing whatever the prosecution wants. This procedure is frequently used to conduct 'fishing expeditions' against persons with unconventional views" (p. 139). Most of these proceedings take place without the defendant present, and when defendants are given the opportunity to be present, they are generally denied counsel. Questions are asked by the prosecution, and evidence is presented that typically leads the assembled juries to err on the side of caution. In other words, juries tend to favor the arguments put forward by prosecutors and to vote a "true bill" or indictment.

The IRS has been accused of using its power to audit individuals and organizations selectively. Groups such as the Communist Party, the National Council of Churches, "the Black Panther Party, Students for a Democratic Society, gay rights advocates, environmental groups, journalists, liberal politicians, and many other politically oriented individuals, organizations, and publications" have allegedly been investigated by the IRS (Parenti, 1995, p. 140; see also Burnham, 1991).

The USCIS, ICE and CBP are responsible for monitoring immigrants and visitors to the US. The federal legislation that they are responsible for enforcing allows them the power to deny entry to individuals whom they believe are threats to US national security and civil society. This branch of the US Department of Homeland Security is given the authority "to exclude anyone who might be affiliated with communist, anarchist, or 'terrorist' groups, or engaged in activities 'prejudicial to the public interest' and harmful to 'national security'" (Parenti, 1995, p. 140). Countless professionals, including "prominent authors, artists, performers, journalists, scientists, and labor-union leaders from other countries have been denied the right to visit and address audiences in the United States" (Parenti, 1995, pp. 140-1). This is even more difficult for individuals who have a criminal record. All of these activities have increased in the post-9/11 era. Many of these state practices are given legitimacy with the passage of The USA PATRIOT Act.

Other branches of the government have also discouraged the free flow of visitors. For example, the US State Department, through its Office of Passport Control, has denied travel visas to Americans wishing to visit countries such as Cuba and other communist countries, against which the US has a trade embargo.

Finally, Americans and other citizens have been incarcerated for long periods of time because their activities were at odds with the dominant elite interests of the time, or because judges had the latitude to hand down extended sentences for minor charges. These so-called legal lynchings were imposed on controversial figures such as Eugene Debs, Martin Sostre, Reverend Ben Chavis, and members of the Black Panther Party (Parenti, 1995, pp. 144-5). Even today, those currently incarcerated may be singled out for abuse by correctional institutions because of their political persuasions (Ross and Richards, 2002).

Summary

This chapter has reviewed the conceptual confusion and definitional issues surrounding state crimes. The following five chapters cover the interrelated practices of political corruption, illegal domestic surveillance, human rights violations, state violence, and state-corporate crime. Each qualifies as a widely recognized and practiced type of state illegality. Political corruption is treated primarily as a form of individually motivated state crime made possible by the status and occupational opportunities available to government workers and managers. Illegal domestic surveillance, human rights violations and state-corporate crime are more complex. They are organizational state crimes in which states or their agencies, acting as units, adopt policies that usually are secretive and may employ illegal domestic surveillance and violations of human rights as ongoing standard operating procedures. State violence can be treated as both an organizational and an individual crime, depending on the circumstances of the pertinent events.

Notes

[1] In this context, the state is not limited to the elected government, but also includes opposition political party members and those individuals working in the public administration.

[2] This is consistent with other theorists' conceptualizations of the state (see, for example, Alford and Friedland, 1985).

[3] Nation states develop when nations occupy a particular geographic territory and establish a formal government structure.

[4] Other scholars use subtle variations of this definition (see, for example, Rothe, 2009, p. 6).

[5] A crime of omission is in many respects similar to what is generally considered the crime known as "deliberate indifference."

[6] Formerly the Immigration and Naturalization Service (INS).

SEVEN

Political corruption

Introduction

The term "political corruption," and the related act of bribery, refers not only to unethical activity, but to crimes committed by state agents (that is, bureaucrats, officials, representatives, etc.) primarily for their own personal, political, material, and non-material gain, "rather than on behalf of a state goal" (Friedrichs, 1995, p. 57). Such actions qualify as occupational crimes "since they are obviously not intended to promote the government's organizational goals" (Coleman, 1985, p. 87). Typically, only individual personal gain results from political corruption, although occasionally both state representatives and their organizational units benefit when the criminal activity is mutually compatible with both personal and organizational goals. Although state workers are typically the recipients of the benefits, private sector representatives usually provide the incentives (Ackerman, 1978; Coleman, 1985, p. 86).

Definitional and conceptual issues

Most government agencies operating in advanced industrialized democracies have codes of ethic or standards of conduct that are taught to new employees and reinforced through a variety of mechanisms during the course of an individual's career in public service. When individuals engage in actions that violate the norms of organizations their behavior is typically called "deviance." When public officials violate organizational rules and/or break the law, these acts are often labeled malfeasance, misfeasance, and nonfeasance. One term closely related to deviance is "corruption," also known as "graft." According to McCarthy (1996), this practice includes "the intentional violation of organizational norms (that is, rules and regulations) by public employees for personal material gain" (p. 231). This behavioral category subsumes theft, smuggling contraband, embezzlement, and misuse of authority (p. 232). Corruption, however, is not a synonym for deviance, but rather a subset of this practice.

Corruption typically includes accepting or soliciting bribes (that is, usually money or some other economic benefit, like a gift or service). A bribe is something of value (for example, money, gift, or favors) given or promised to a person who is capable of using his/her position to influence an outcome (Websters, 1996, p. 226). Many observers suggest that corruption should not be considered a political crime, because it most commonly involves personal gain.[1] However, if we subscribe to Friedrichs' (1995) perspective, corruption is definitely a governmental crime through which the citizenry's trust has been violated.

Corruption by state officials mainly takes the form of misuses of political power, primarily motivated by economic gain (Friedrichs, 1995, p. 62). Political crime involves corruption that is committed by individuals for personal political gain. An example of such a crime is former US President Richard Nixon's alleged theft by his "plumbers" of Democratic Party papers during the Watergate break-in (1972) in an effort to help his re-election prospects (Woodward and Bernstein, 1974; Haldeman, 1994). The concept of "political crime" is generally reserved for only those people who violate laws for their own partisan gain rather than for financial benefit to themselves or an organization. Political corruption can provide rewards that are partisan rather than immediately pecuniary, like bribe taking (Friedrichs, 1995, p. 73).

Solicitation and acceptance of gratuities

One of the most frequent problems commonly confused with corruption is the solicitation or acceptance of gratuities by government employees (from bureaucrats to elected politicians). A gratuity is something of minor value – a cup of coffee, for example, or other gift or small reward – offered as a "token of appreciation" in return for favorable behaviors. Accepting gratuities "is a common practice in many police departments, but this practice is considered to be unethical by" influential police organizations, such as the International Association of Chiefs of Police (Roberg and Kuykendall, 1993, p. 187). Even though a police agency may have a written policy against the acceptance of gratuities, a disproportionate number of its rank and file ignore this rule.

There are both positive and negative issues involved in accepting gratuities. On the positive side, for example, business owners/government contractors may believe that offering gratuities, especially alcohol or tickets to entertainment venues, may help to build trust in the relationship. Additionally, in the case of shop owners providing benefits to law enforcement officers, they may believe or know that police presence minimizes the possibility of criminal victimization (such as shoplifting, robbery, etc.). The gratuities may also reflect business owners' and managers' appreciation for police officers' work. The general public may also not be aware of the problematic nature of giving public officials gratuities. Refusal of an offer may sometimes be interpreted as an insult.

On the negative side, gratuities may compromise a government worker's ability to "operate in a democracy in a balanced and fair fashion" (Roberg and Kuykendall, 1993, p. 188). In other words, state employees may be in danger of granting preferential treatment to those who give gratuities and may, thus, apply the law unequally. Acceptance of gratuities may even lead to government employees thinking they are something special (p. 188). Critics of the acceptance of gratuities also believe "it may lead to more serious forms of corruption" (p. 188).

Special case of high crimes and misdemeanors

Closely related to corruption is the notion of high crimes and misdemeanors. This charge has been infrequently levied against high ranking government officials who were believed to have committed severe crimes against the state. This classification includes such acts as misappropriation of public funds, interference in elections, acceptance of bribes, neglect of duty, and various forms of corruption. Although high crimes and misdemeanors has mainly been applied within the context of the UK's Parliament, this charge also exists in the US Constitution (Article II) and can serve as the basis for the impeachment of a public official.

In 1998, the term gained popular media attention when it was used by a number of right-wing/conservative US pundits (see, for example, Coulter, 1998) during the highly visible impeachment proceedings against former President Bill Clinton (1998). In 1994, shortly after the election of Clinton, news surfaced that during his time as Governor of Arkansas (1979-81, 1983-92), he, his wife Hillary Clinton, and other business associates were involved in a speculative land sale deal called Whitewater that had negative legal ramifications. This scandal motivated Republican members of Congress to initiate an investigation headed by Conservative Prosecutor Kenneth Starr. During this investigation, a number of charges were levied against Clinton including obstruction of justice (that is, frustrating the work of law enforcement, regulatory agencies, and prosecutors from conducting an investigation). In the midst of this investigation, it was discovered that Clinton had engaged in an "improper relationship" with Monica Lewinsky, a White House intern. In the aftermath of these discoveries, the House of Representatives impeached Clinton, thereby calling into question his legitimacy as president. The Senate, however, did not successfully impeach him. Thus, he remained in office.

How widespread is the problem?

Like most property crimes, political corruption often goes undetected and is veiled by the ongoing daily operations of the office holder (Sykes, 1980, pp. 58-62). Many bureaucratic systems subtly encourage or facilitate corruption. Undoubtedly, the amount of corruption that government employees and political representatives engage in and that the public learns about varies over time and administrations/government agencies. One additional factor is the type of political system in operation. It is generally believed and empirically demonstrated that in democracies with well-developed anti-corruption statutes (Green, 1990, p. 166; Transparency International "Corruption Perceptions Index"),[2] corruption is less of a problem. Thus, in many advanced industrialized countries when corruption is discovered by either the news media or a watchdog organization, like Congress Watch, the Center for Public Integrity, or Transparency International, it has the potential to become a scandal.

History

Bribery and corruption both have long histories (Chambliss, 1971). Because of their unique positions and poor remuneration, the first state officials had something to exchange that others, who were not in their jobs, did not possess. In fact, bribe taking by public officials has been documented over the past four millennia (Noonan, 1984). One of the most recent (1994) estimates of bribe money passed to both public and private officials in the US, for example, ranges from US$3 billion to US$15 billion annually (Coleman, 1995, p. 254).

Effect of political corruption

Political corruption is a betrayal of the public trust, and therefore, the citizenry is the ultimate victim of this type of political crime. This leads the public to become increasingly cynical and apathetic about politics, politicians, and their deeds and misdeeds (Greider, 1992). Political corruption can cause far-reaching social harms, as the public is deceived, lied to, and in some cases, denied the impartial representation due them from state officials. The subsequent distrust can also lead to increased scrutiny of public officials, making their jobs more burdensome, and causing government to function less efficiently, more expensively and consuming additional taxpayer money.

The most serious harms resulting from corruption are symbolic. In advanced industrialized democracies, elected and appointed officials are viewed increasingly with skepticism and cynicism by the citizenry. Politicians have been accused of participating in political corruption, resulting in reduced faith in public institutions and elected and appointed officials. This shift is manifested in declining numbers of voters and growing political apathy and distrust of public officials (Nye et al., 1997).

Social harms also arise from political corruption and have consequences that are sometimes more far-reaching than the other types of crimes. Political corruption is generally uncovered, detailed, exposed and/or alleged by the news media, opposition politicians, watchdog agencies, and whistleblowers. Wealthy public officials accused of political corruption often enjoy the benefit of the doubt and usually have the resources to buy the best legal representation available. Their resources far exceed those available to the vast majority of individuals charged with street crimes. Because of access and the broad use of favors, powerful public figures have the ability to slow down the wheels of justice as investigations, hearings, depositions, and trials are delayed at seemingly every turn (Parenti, 1995, Chapter 8; Reiman, 1998). Such perceptions of lawmakers are widespread and contribute to ongoing public skepticism regarding their ethics (Greider, 1992).

Who are the perpetrators?

A multitude of government officials and agents, at all levels of government (local, state, and federal), engage in political corruption, including but not limited to elected politicians, appointed officials, judges, police officers, and regulatory agency inspectors.

Singling out the dominant types

Three broad types of political corruption – that specific to the legislative process, that connected to the criminal justice system, and that connected to the regulatory process – are arguably the most important manifestations of this form of state crime.[3] These actions occur "through a person's exercise of state authority ... [meaning] powers lawfully vested in persons by a state through which those persons can make or enforce laws or command others" (Green, 1990, p. 149). Individuals who have the opportunity to commit such crimes have particular powers with which they can "represent the force of state law in certain decisions" (Green, 1990, p. 149). These three forms of political corruption are the focus of the remainder of this chapter.

Political corruption usually appears in the form of bribe taking. This typically involves the acceptance of money by public employees in exchange for their exercise of authority and influence in the business of the state (Green, 1990, p. 165). Even though politically motivated bribe taking can involve various state occupations and professions, the three most frequent acceptors of bribes are legislators, the police, and regulatory inspectors due largely to the frequency and nature of their contacts with the public.

Corruption by lawmakers

Political corruption among elected and appointed officials is typically manifested in bribe taking, which includes receiving money and favors in return for supporting or frustrating legislation to benefit the person or organization offering the bribe. And between the two perpetrators, bribes accepted or solicited by government officials is far more consequential in the long run (Coleman, 1995, p. 255) as it "diffuses its harm throughout an entire populace" (Green, 1990, p. 165).

Although the acceptance of bribes by lawmakers may be less common than the more subtle forms of influence peddling (see, for example, campaign contributions and lobbyists' perks), it is "the offense that is most likely to lead to the criminal prosecution of elected officials" (Coleman, 1994, p. 50). About 42 percent of criminal indictments of members of Congress have been for accepting some type of bribe. The most sought-after favors in return for a bribe are the introduction of special bills and the casting of votes in a way that benefits the person offering the bribe. About 30 percent of charges filed against members of Congress have been for such violations of public trust. In addition, about 27 percent of indictments have been for helping private companies win government contracts (Coleman, 1994, p. 50).

Laws against bribe taking by members of the US Congress have existed since 1852, although the first conviction for such unlawful behavior did not occur until the 20th century. As recently as 1970, "only ten members of Congress had been convicted of crimes involving bribery" (Green, 1990, p. 172). Although politicians may have engaged in corruption early in their careers, these actions may not come to public attention until much later (see, for example, Barlow and Kauzlarich, 2002). Such was the case with former Vice President Spiro Agnew (p. 126). In 1973, Agnew was charged with a number of crimes including bribery in connection with his work as county executive, Governor of Maryland and Vice President. He pleaded no contest to a tax related charge.

Also during the 1970s several Congressmen were convicted of accepting bribes in what was called the Abscam case. In 1978, the bribe takers were unknowingly filmed while accepting bribes from undercover FBI agents. Federal agents posed as wealthy Arab businessmen desiring political and business favors from Congressional members in exchange for bribes, some of which were as high as US$100,000. In all, five Congressmen were convicted and sentenced to prison terms ranging from 18 months to 3 years. Not only have federal politicians been indicted and convicted of corruption charges, but so too have state and local officials. In addition to Abscam, some of the more prominent investigations included the FBI's "Greylord Operation," "Operation Lost Trout" (also known as "Bubba Gate"), and Azcam (in Arizona; see Sykes and Cullen, 1992, p. 269).

In Canada, over the past three decades, there have been a number of similar cases (see, for example, Langford and Tupper, 1994). The so-called Sky Shops Affair (1972-1976) involved the participation of prominent businessmen and a senator (see Malvern, 1985):

> Gordon Brown and Clarence Campbell, ... offered $95,000 to Liberal Senator Louis Giguere in exchange for his assistance in reversing the federal transport ministry decision not to extend Sky Shop Export Limited's lease to operate a duty-free shop at the government-owned Dorval Airport in Montreal. [...] Conspiracy charges were subsequently brought against the [participants]. Although Brown and Campbell were charged and convicted, Giguere was unexpectedly adjudicated not guilty of conspiring to accept a benefit. (Corrado and Davies, 2000, pp. 63-4)

In 1989, in a seemingly more complicated instance of corruption, Oliver North, a Marine Corps colonel and a national security adviser to then President Ronald Reagan, gained public attention because of his activities, that were later part of what was called the Iran-Contra Scandal or Irangate (Woodward, 1987). In sum, North was responsible for managing and (depending on the source) orchestrating a deal whereby Nicaraguan Contras were provided financial aid and allowed to secretly sell and/or transport illegal drugs, the profits from which were channeled to Israel to pay for anti-aircraft missiles to be later shipped to Iran. During this time, the Congressionally mandated Boland Amendment placed an embargo not only on the types of aid that the Contras could receive, but also on the goods that the US could supply to Iran. North was charged with lying under oath, obstructing a Congressional inquiry, taking money without claiming it on his taxes, and destroying government documents. He had also accepted an illegal gratuity: a home security system worth US$13,800 (Marshall et al., 1987; Woodward, 1987). North was convicted in 1989, but this was overturned because his testimony at the trial had been "immunized." This outcome was predictable because the appellate panel was composed mainly of Republican appointees, the political party of the president under which he conducted these activities. Similar outcomes (that is, light sentences) befell North's accomplices who held high ranking posts in the Reagan administration, including Elliott Abrams, Claire E. George, Robert McFarlane, Richard R. Miller, John M. Poindexter, and Carl (Spitz) Channel (Shank, 1980 pp iii–iv). Charges were dropped or reversed on appeals, and the individuals were acquitted. Some of the accused were later pardoned (and their sentences were nullified) by President George H. W. Bush.

During the 1990s numerous instances of corruption came to public attention including that of Congressman Dan Rostenkowski (Democrat). In 1994, Rostenkowski, who represented a district in Chicago, and held prominent leadership positions in Congress, was charged with several instances of corruption (including having nonexistent employees on his payroll). In 1996, he pleaded guilty for mail fraud and sentenced to 17 months in federal prison. He ended serving 15 months behind bars and two in a halfway house. In 2000 President Bill Clinton pardoned Rostenkowski.

Other prominent instances of corruption in the US occurred in the past decade including the 2005 conviction of House of Representatives member Randy "Duke" Cunningham for accepting US$2.4 million in bribes. Duke, a former highly decorated navy jet pilot, who served the 50th District 9 (that is, San Diego County) (1990-2005) was charged and convicted of numerous federal charges (conspiracy to accept bribes, under-reporting his income, and wire and mail fraud). Cunningham was sentenced to eight years in federal prison and required to pay US$1.8 million in restitution.

In 2006, Jack Abramoff, former businessman and lobbyist, was convicted of mail fraud and conspiracy. Along with various White House officials, he had engaged in corruption by selling political influence to a number of individuals and organizations, including selected American Indian tribes who were trying to obtain concessions for their gambling operations.

In Canada, it is routinely believed that political corruption is rampant in the maritime provinces of Newfoundland, Nova Scotia, and New Brunswick. One of the most colorful episodes concerned former New Brunswick Premier Richard Hatfield, who "rose to prominence in 1970, largely on a platform that emphasized honest government, untainted by the corruption that had characterized previous administrations" (Corrado and Davies, 2000, p. 65). However, he supposedly:

> ... received special considerations during a police investigation and his subsequent trial on a criminal drug charge relating to the possession of a small amount of marijuana. Hatfield was acquitted at the end of a very strange trial wherein the trial judge, a Hatfield appointee, accused the journalist [who broke the news] of having planted the substantive evidence in Hatfield's luggage. (Corrado and Davies, 2000, p. 65)

Finally, during the mid-1980s, the Progressive Conservative government of Prime Minister Brian Mulroney's numerous "Instances of Tory indiscretion" were brought to public attention. These included "objectionable spending habits, blatant patronage and more widespread and insidious scandals.[...] Mulroney's personal disregard for public funds was perhaps best exemplified by a $300,000 'loan' that he secured in 1987 from the PC Canada fund for custom renovations to his official residence" (Corrado and Davies, 2000, p. 66).

Corruption by law enforcement officers

Police occupational deviance can be divided into two subcategories: police misconduct and police corruption (Ross, 2012, Chapter 9). Police misconduct involves violations of organizational policies, procedures, rules, and other standards, whereas police corruption covers any criminal act in the commission of one's job that benefits either the officer in question or someone else.

In this context, one must take into consideration the fact that deviance is situational; in one police department, a behavior might be interpreted as normative, while in another it is perceived as deviant. This relativity is especially pronounced in the use of profanity, sleeping (that is, "cooping") on the job, and engaging in personal business (for example, going to the bank) while on duty.

As stated earlier, "police corruption, the second subcategory of occupational deviancy, involves overt criminal activity by police officers. This includes committing crimes like theft or robbery, selling drugs, or taking money or something of value to not enforce the law" (Roberg and Kuykendall, 1993, p. 190). These types of actions are known among police officers as "going on the pad, collecting a steady note, or collecting the rent" (Barker, 1977). Police officers may receive money or other items of value, both legal and illegal, in exchange for not citing or arresting an individual for prostitution, illegal gambling, or drug possession or dealing.

Situations for corruption have existed for a long time. As Fogelson (1977) observes, during the political era, "the police did not suppress vice; they licensed it" (p. 32). Throughout the country, "they permitted gamblers, prostitutes, and saloon keepers to do business under certain well understood conditions. These entrepreneurs were required to make regular payoffs to the police" (Roberg and

Kuykendall, 1993, p. 192). Some jurisdictions, like New York City, have a long history of police corruption. Over the history of the NYPD, at least nine major corruption investigations have been exposed and investigated.[4]

What is the difference between corruption and bribery? In short, bribery specifically involves the acceptance or solicitation of bribes and gratuities (which usually involve money or some sort of economic benefit, gift, or favor) in exchange for past, current, or future actions that will benefit the individual or organization that gives the bribe. Corruption incorporates a wider array of actions, as discussed below.

Types of police corruption

Police corruption is a broad and varied problem. Examples include: corruption of authority (see, for example, through the offering of free meals and drinks – especially alcohol – services, or discounts); kickbacks (money, goods, and services); opportunistic threats (victims, burglary, or unlocked buildings); shakedowns of criminals; protection of illegal activities (vice operators, business people); traffic citation fixes; misdemeanor or felony charge fixes; direct criminal activities (burglary, robbery); and internal payoffs (off-days, work assignments). Some experts have rank-ordered the seriousness of different kinds of corruption (Caplan and Murphy, 1991).

In general, corrupt officers can be divided into two types. On the one hand, so-called "grass eaters" are officers who engage in minor (that is, low-level) corruption. These kinds of actions are usually reactive and are generally not frowned upon by other officers. On the other hand, "meat eaters" are police officers who actively engage in crimes, including burglary and drug dealing, on a regular basis. These officers are proactive in their endeavors. Police departments commonly protect reactive grafters but not proactive grafters, and "meat eaters" are usually ostracized by other officers.

Many police officers may accept low-level bribes, which they call "clean graft," but they usually refuse to take drugs or money from drug dealers, which they consider "dirty graft." Clean graft includes taking money found on the street or valuables left behind in public places by drunken, distracted, or belligerent middle- or high-class individuals. For example, an honest citizen may find a wallet, flag down a police officer to report the discovery, and then turn over the wallet to the officer. Perhaps, the police officer then looks through the wallet, finds US$100, and decides to pocket a US$20 bill before logging the property in with the department. On the other hand, dirty graft involves actively taking items of value from drug dealers, cop killers, and other serious criminals.

Box 7.1: *Prince of the City* (1981)

This movie, based on the Richard Daley book with the same title (1978), and directed by Sidney Lumet, chronicles the activities of Robert (Bob) Leuci, who during the 1970s was part of the Special Investigations Unit of the NYPD. Leuci's unit had a stellar track record of arrests and convictions of drug users and dealers. During the process, however, Leuci was known to take both drugs and money for personal use and to give drugs as incentives to his informants. In order to accomplish his unit's goals, Leuci established an elaborate web of informers. He rationalized his actions as the cost of doing business. As a police officer, he argued that many people treat police officers as the lowest rung on the socioeconomic ladder, and moving up the police ladder commanded a certain amount of respect. Under scrutiny, Leuci agreed to participate in a federal investigation and wore a wire on his former associates. This led to additional convictions.

Causes

The problems linked to misconduct and corruption are plagued with numerous misconceptions. The issues are commonly interpreted through two basic perspectives: popular and scholarly.

Popular conceptions

Police chief commissioners and their directors of public information traditionally suggest that deviance and corruption are the result of the "bad or rotten apples" in their ranks. "The 'rotten or bad apples' are either weak individuals who have slipped through the elaborate screening process of most police departments and succumbed to the temptations inherent in police work, or deviant individuals who continue their deviant practices in an environment which provides them ample opportunity" (Barker, 1977, p. 354). Despite the logic that seems to support this conclusion, this explanation can be easily discounted.

The "bad or rotten apple" explanation suggests that despite the elaborate screening mechanisms that police departments use, one or more corrupt police officers may, nonetheless, be hired. Alternatively, political and community activists and some pundits typically offer a "bad barrel" explanation. This is the claim that an entire police department can be deviant or corrupt. In most cases, this perspective is a vast overgeneralization.

Scholarly/expert conceptions

Over the past five decades, numerous dominant causal explanations for police corruption have been offered: irresistible opportunities for corruption presented to police officers; low pay rates; cynicism surrounding the pay and promotion mechanisms; socialization and reinforcement; extent of corruption in the community and broader society; tolerance among citizens and the police; and inadequate leadership (Barker, 1977; Roberg and Kuykendall, 1993; White, 2007).

Opportunity: first, police officers "are constantly exposed to situations in which the decisions they make can have a positive or negative impact on an individual's freedom and well-being. Citizens may try to influence this discretion by offering … any item of value that will result in a favorable decision" (Roberg and Kuykendall, 1993, p. 192). Because of the way that policing is designed, including a lack of direct supervision and the clientele police must deal with on a daily basis, multiple opportunities for corruption may present themselves during any given week (Barker, 1977).

In the area of so-called "victimless crimes" (for example, gambling, prostitution, drug possession and dealing), police officers are placed in an untenable position. They have a great deal of discretionary power to invoke criminal sanctions (Barker, 1977). Because the police regulate vice activities, they face numerous opportunities to collect graft on a regular basis.

If, for example, officers respond to a burglary at a store or a residence, they might take items of value that do not belong to them. They may rationalize that the goods are insured, thus the rightful owner will be reimbursed for the loss (Barker, 1977). Occasionally, officers will lie on the stand (commit perjury) during a criminal trial in exchange for some sort of benefit. Some police officers believe in personal entitlement. They argue that because they work hard or because they put their lives on the line, they should receive extra perks from their job situations.

Pay rates and cynicism surrounding remuneration and upward career mobility: another cause for corruption may be the belief of some police officers that they are not paid enough (Barker, 1977). They may believe that the risks they take deserve more compensation than what they are paid, and thus, they may feel entitled to more money than their standard pay and benefits. Additionally, the career advancement model in most police departments may serve as a cause for corruption, as suggested by White (2007):

> Opportunities for advancement in police department … is limited, yet the only way to get a significant pay increase is through promotion. [...] Structural elements of the promotion process can also frustrate officers.[...] The lack of opportunity for promotion clearly limits officers … who are unhappy with their pay may be tempted to seek illegitimate means to add to their salary, particularly if they believe that their performance has not been evaluated fairly. (p. 245)

Socialization and reinforcement: police officers share both their history and their identity. By interacting with other officers and being exposed to similar situations (for example, boredom, fear, and excitement), officers can form deep and often hidden emotional bonds. Through this process, norms and values are transmitted and shared (Barker, 1977).

Many officers may view the world as a "us versus them" environment (Becker, 1963). "Police tend to see the world as being composed of insiders and outsiders – police and persons who are not police officers are considered outsiders and are viewed with suspicion" (Kappeler et al., 1994, p. 60).

Despite individual convictions, the work group of police officers remains a powerful influence on each officer (Barker, 1977). In the police academy context, the building of communal officer identity begins, and is further developed once work on the force starts. Shortly after graduating from the academy, through a combined process of working on the streets, plus through interactions with senior police personnel, officers soon became cynical and have a higher proclivity to engage in deviance. Specifically, this cynicism may pave the way to corruption.

Extent of corruption in society: the community and political environment are influential in establishing attitudes toward corrupt activities. When corruption is found in other government agencies, among judges, prosecutors, and politicians, and in the business world, it contributes to the ability of the police officer to rationalize his or her own behavior (Newfield and Barret, 1988; Roberg and Kuykendall, 1993). The officer may believe that if the community in which they serve and protect is not honest, why should I?

Tolerance by citizens and the police department: this rationalization can lead to tolerance of abuses. Because of apathy and/or a belief that "as long as police get the job done," then the public may believe that a little bit of corruption is okay. Alternatively, as Roberg and Kuykendall (1993, p. 194) argue: "Many officers even come to believe that if they are to be good police officers, they have to violate some of the standards they are supposed to follow." Thus, administrators are willing to disregard many acts of corruption.

Inadequate leadership: an environment in which many officers either accept the existence of corruption or participate in corrupt activities calls into question the quality of leadership. Roberg and Kuykendall (1993) describe this phenomenon:

> Even nondeviant officers are both tolerant and tolerated because few will break the code of silence among officers. This belief can even carry over to the chief executive and managers in the organization, particularly if they have, or are, participating in the deviant behavior themselves. In addition, executives and managers may be 'blamed' and lose their jobs if the deviancy is exposed, even if they are not involved. (p. 194)

In the aftermath of the 1972 Commission to Investigate Alleged Police Corruption (also known as the Knapp Commission), the frequency and pervasiveness of corruption in US police departments decreased.

In the end, a variety of reasons may motivate police officers to engage in corrupt acts. Officers may lose respect for their superior officers, and they may see corruption in other parts of the criminal justice system (including among judges and prosecutors). They may abuse drugs and alcohol, which can impair their judgment. Meanwhile, the pressures to perform well in their duties are high. All too frequently, their contributions to the mission of the police department are not appreciated. Thus, officers may end up believing that engaging in corruption is an acceptable decision.

Controlling police corruption:[5] police corruption has numerous effects, including an attrition of public trust, the possibility that corruption will seep into other government organizations, the lessening of police morale, and the loosening of controls. Most of the arguments pertaining to the control of police deviance, including corruption, have their origins in the study of large bureaucratic organizations. Additionally, those mechanisms established to control various police practices, such as illegal surveillance and police violence, are broadly applicable to the bigger problem of police corruption. Nevertheless, formidable obstacles mitigate the implementation of the control mechanisms, most significantly the lack of sufficient resources, information, discretion, and sanctions (Sherman, 1978). In addition, in many police departments, the kinds of officers' behaviors/actions that could be considered corrupt change over time. Furthermore, the networks that engage in corruption continuously shift their activities, whenever they sense they are under the watchful eye of Internal Affairs officers or the news media.

Box 7.2: Frank Serpico

Frank Serpico is a retired NYPD detective who was instrumental in providing information about incidents of police corruption to the Knapp Commission. Serpico revealed information about the corruption to the *New York Times*. His story was the focus of a bestselling book written by Peter Maas (1973), a Hollywood movie starring Al Pacino (1973), and an A&E-televised *Biography* episode (2000). Serpico grew up in a working-class Italian family in which police officers were respected. During the 1960s corruption was rampant at all ranks throughout the NYPD. In his testimony, Serpico suggested that police corruption is part of the police socialization process. Rookie police officers learn early on how to break the rules and cut corners in order to survive in the police organization. Because Serpico did not accept graft, he was ostracized by his fellow officers. As a result of officer apprehension, Serpico was shot while on a drug bust. He survived and shortly after testifying in front of the Knapp Commission, he moved to Switzerland out of fear of police-related retaliation. He has since returned to the United States.

Admittedly, allegations of corruption have existed since the establishment of the first police department. Some of these episodes led to high-profile corruption scandals. Better controls on police officers and their departments have been advocated by members of the public, government officials, and honest police officers and administrators. Prominent anti-corruption policies and practices have been implemented in most big city police departments. Some of these recommendations are proactive, while others are reactive.

One should not forget that police officers are under constant scrutiny. Recently, supervision has been facilitated by the introduction of police vehicles with dashboard video capability, cell phones, and internet-based technology. Most cell phones and personal data assistants (PDAs) now come equipped with photographic and video capabilities. It is now much easier for citizens to record conversations between themselves and police officers, which can be used as evidence in departmental or legal proceedings. As can be seen, a combination of internal and external controls can be effective in the control of police deviance and corruption.

Potential solutions include the following:

> ... improved pay scales; teaching ethics to police officers; routine transfers of police officers; internal affairs bureaus/departments; accreditation; integrity officers; corruption investigations/commissions; and hiring police administrators from outside departments. (Ross, 2012, pp. 138-42)

Police deviancy and corruption is an everyday problem for most police departments. Law enforcement officers have an extremely important duty to serve and protect society. They hold the public's trust, but the legitimacy of that trust can erode quickly if an officer or group engages in corruption. When evidence of corruption emerges, police departments must make bold steps to fairly investigate and eradicate it as soon as possible. Anything short of this will perpetuate fear and distrust among the public.

Regulatory inspectors

Local ordinances (including health and safety, food, and occupancy), often complex and voluminous, particularly in the case of regulatory laws, allow government agents, who are responsible for monitoring, ample opportunities for discriminately deciding how to proceed with violations. Building ordinances, laws governing surface coal mining, and local fire codes, for example, are often too numerous and dynamic for builders, mine operators, and night club managers, among others, to obey (Gardiner and Lyman, 1978). By simply doing business, most business owners are more than likely in violation of one or more local ordinances. As a result, individuals may willingly abide by the more serious laws and perhaps pay off police officers and regulatory inspectors for ignoring other less serious violations (see Damania et al., 2004). Some building contractors or construction companies are happy to pay off inspectors, believing that bribes are much less costly than abiding by the letter of the law (Coleman, 1994). These particular forms of political corruption are considered occupational crimes since they are not intended to benefit or promote a government's organizational goals (Coleman, 1994, p. 45).

Regulatory inspectors who are responsible for ensuring workers' and consumers' safety have been known to accept bribes for instrumental rather than organizational agendas. They accept bribes in exchange for ignoring infractions; falsifying governmental reports regarding work-site conditions; and issuing citations for minor infractions rather than major, perhaps life-threatening, violations of law.

But, from the evidence available, it appears that bribery and other forms of corruption are not nearly as prevalent among regulatory inspectors as they are among police officers (Coleman, 1994). Several factors may account for these differences. First, among regulatory agencies, unlike police departments, a generations-old culture of corruption typically does not exist into which individual employees are socialized. Second, police officers working in vice are presented with numerous opportunities to accept bribes and can rationalize their unwillingness to enforce the law because they believe that no one is being harmed because vice participants almost always voluntarily participate in their vice. This supplies the rationale and notion of "victimless crimes." For this reason, it is safe to assume that regulatory inspectors responsible for the safety of workers and consumers cannot rationalize their unwillingness to enforce the law as easily as, say, vice patrol officers. Third, regulatory inspectors do not deal on a daily basis with actively known violators of the law, unlike, for example, vice officers. As a result, regulatory inspectors are exposed to far fewer opportunities and are less likely to be approached by individuals willing to bribe them than police officers on the street. However, since regulatory inspectors monitor the more lucrative forms of deviance, such as those that qualify as white-collar crimes, they have the opportunity to pocket far greater sums of money from a single bribe than most street police officers.

Summary

Politicians, police officers, and regulatory inspectors do not necessarily resemble criminals on the surface, yet it is well known that some of them engage in a variety of crimes, including political corruption. Political corruption remains a fundamental problem for advanced industrialized democracies. Within the cultures of politics and policing, there remains a veil of secrecy and a distrust of outsiders encouraging corruption to take place undefeated. In some cases, the violation of laws is fundamental to the occupational cultural norms and values of politics and policing. Thus, quite often both the public and the state expect these corrupt activities to go hand in hand.

Notes

[1] A similar response is given regarding smuggling. Over history, countries have embargoed the sales of scarce commodities, especially military weapons, to those states they believe are national security risks. Since the 1970s, this has happened with increasing frequency against individuals, organizations and businesses supplying Libya, Iran, and Iraq with weaponry.

[2] Since 1995, Transparency International (TI) has conducted an annual "Corruptions Perceptions Index" that ranks 90 countries "in terms of the degree to which corruption is perceived to exist among public officials and politicians." Advanced industrialized countries are regularly ranked as the least corrupt.

[3] During the Reagan administration, the Justice Department, under the direction of Attorney General Ed Meese, allegedly stole software from a company called INSLAW, and tried to force the company out of business. This product was allegedly given to friends of the Reagan administration (Fricker and Pizzo, 1992).

[4] In 1895 (by the Lexow Committee); in 1900 (by the Mazet Committee); in 1913 (as a result of the Curran investigations); in 1932 (by the Seabury Committee); in 1942 (as a result of the Amen investigation); in 1952 (by the Brooklyn Grand Jury); in the 1970s by the Knapp Commission (as a result of the Serpico revelations) (Mass, 1973); in the late 1970s (as a result of the "Prince of the City" investigations); in 1986 (as a result of the Buddy Boys investigation); and in 1993 (by the Mollen Commission) (McAlary, 1987).

[5] This section builds on Ross (2012). Other authors (see, for example, Stevens, 2009) have created other lists. Stevens, for example, under internal monitoring, singles out supervision, close supervision, performance evaluations, early warning/intervention systems, internal affairs, and professional standards. Under external monitoring, he includes monitoring committees, the courts (especially through Supreme Court cases), and civil liability.

EIGHT

Illegal domestic surveillance

Introduction

Domestic surveillance consists of a variety of information-gathering activities, conducted primarily by the state's coercive agencies (that is, police, national security, and the military). These actions are carried out against citizens, foreigners, organizations (for example, businesses, political parties, etc.), and foreign governments. Such operations usually include opening mail, listening to telephone conversations (eavesdropping and wiretapping), reading electronic communications, and infiltrating groups (whether they are legal, illegal, or deviant).

Although a legitimate law enforcement/intelligence-gathering technique, surveillance is often considered unpalatable to the public in general and civil libertarians in particular. This is especially true when state agents break the law by conducting searches without warrants, collecting evidence that is beyond the scope of a warrant, or harassing and/or destabilizing their targets.[1] These activities are illegal (because the Constitution, statutes, regulations, and ordinances specify the conditions under which surveillance may be conducted), and they violate individual rights to privacy.

Not only should legitimate surveillance be distinguished from illegal domestic surveillance, but the latter practice should also be separated from espionage/spying.[2] In short, spying/espionage, covered in chapter four, is conducted against a foreign government, its businesses, and/or its citizens, and illegal domestic surveillance takes place inside a specific individual's country.

Definitional and conceptual issues

Although domestic surveillance is crucial for particular types of legitimate law enforcement/national security investigations, and is often a useful information-gathering tactic, relevant state agencies and their employees frequently collect information on individuals and groups in an illegal fashion. This unlawful activity takes place largely because state agents have defined the target's political ideologies, affiliations, and strategies as being deviant and/or a threat to homeland/national security. Illegal domestic surveillance may also be used for coercive leverage. J. Edgar Hoover, former director of the FBI, for example, used his agency to closely monitor the activities of rising politicians and the President, as a means to retain his position of power.

Needless to say, the majority of legitimate intelligence is collected from open sources (available to the general public). Skilled intelligence/national security officers are very adept at using publicly available sources to obtain the kinds of information they need to do their jobs. In most cases, there is no need to use a surreptitious listening device (or "bug," as it is colloquially called). Often, skilled intelligence officers are as adept, if not better, at finding information than seasoned reference librarians. Intelligence personnel also have the option of using human sources. It is not illegal to observe or ask people questions, nor is it necessary to have a warrant to carry on an information-probing conversation. Then again, those questioned by an intelligence officer are not under any legal obligation to speak or to tell the truth. However, if someone does fabricate information, he or she may later be charged with impeding a criminal investigation.

Increasingly, intelligence agencies are moving from human sources (HUMINT) to signals intelligence (SIGINT) that includes the interception of most forms of electronic communications (Laqueur, 1985). Intelligence agencies also make it a priority to keep up with changes in technology, as do some political criminals.

How widespread is the problem?

Even though the intensity and pervasiveness of a country's surveillance of citizens waxes and wanes over time, it is the stock-in-trade activity of domestic law enforcement (Marx, 1988). Domestic surveillance has been a part of law enforcement practices since the birth of policing, although it has become much more widespread since the 1930s. It has mainly been used in connection with a growing number of people defined as threats to "national order," including dissident groups, labor unions, and political activists (see, for example, Quinney, 1974, Chapter 4; Theoharis, 1978; Harring, 1983; Coleman, 1985, Chapter 2; Tunnell, 1995a, 1995b).

Illegal domestic surveillance has been conducted by numerous law enforcement, national security, and military agencies. It has often been an official, yet covert, organizational policy; these actions have been standard operating procedures supported by numerous field offices, agents, and headquarters, and have been approved and directed by administrators and, in some cases, presidents.

Causes of illegal domestic surveillance

There are six interrelated causes of illegal domestic surveillance: a person and/ or group is defined as a threat; the inability or difficulty that individuals and/ or organizations encounter in attempts to convince the public that they are not dangerous; the political climate; practitioners' belief that illegal domestic surveillance is necessary; overzealous state agents; and poorly trained state officials.

First, one of the most important elements in understanding why someone has been targeted for illegal domestic surveillance relates to the characteristics of the individuals and entities that are identified and labeled as threatening. Those identified as potential and actual dissenters are identified by both subtle and not so subtle clues that are detectable by those in positions of power. These clues might involve deviant political opinions, speeches, or actions that fail to conform to perceptions of normative standards. State agencies in democratic countries typically spy because individuals and groups come to be defined as security risks or threats to national order. Whether the entities are or are not actual threats is often irrelevant; the telling concern is that they are defined as such by those with the power and authority to set in motion the state's surveillance machinery.

Second, because of the inordinate resource differentials between the state and dissidents, governments, through various channels of communication and networks, can easily label certain people and groups as criminal or as threats to national security. Compared to private entities, the state can more easily justify its actions as necessary in order to persuade the public to believe that certain individuals and groups (for example, the Students for a Democratic Society [SDS], an organization committed to advancing civil rights and ending the war in Vietnam, or Parti Québécois [PQ], a political party that wanted the province of Québec to separate from the rest of Canada) are inappropriate, extreme, radical, subversive, or that they are armed terrorists capable of destabilizing "our democratic way of life." Thus, it is very difficult for people and organizations that have been labeled as subversive to demonstrate successfully to the public and the media that governments and their agents that they are not threats.

Third, although the state typically has a legitimate monopoly on force and law, it tends to rely heavily on illegal domestic surveillance during crises (Torrance, 1977, 1995). This was evident in the US, for example, during the political disturbances of the 1960s and 1970s, when the SDS and the Black Panther Party (BPP) were politically active, and again during the 1980s, when critical questions were raised regarding US policies toward Central America. Not only was the SDS placed under surveillance by the FBI, but local (particularly big city) municipal police departments also spied on the group (Churchill and Vander Wall, 1988). The FBI determined that the group's activities were threatening to the status quo and that the SDS ideology embraced communism. Soon, every FBI field office in the country became involved in the ongoing surveillance of the SDS (Donner, 1990). Although politically rightist groups have been monitored due to state officials' perceptions that they are well armed and potentially violent, historically leftist groups have regularly been victims of domestic surveillance operations (Zwerman, 1988; Coleman, 1995, p. 258). Since the September 11, 2001, attacks on the World Trade Center and the Pentagon, and because of the enabling aspects of The USA PATRIOT Act, a greater number of US citizens have been put under surveillance. The majority of this attention has been directed towards individuals of Muslim descent and those with origins or citizenship in the Middle Eastern countries.

Fourth, little consensus exists among the public on the legality and necessity of domestic surveillance. The organizational mind-set of law enforcement agencies, national security agencies, and the military, on the other hand, supports the use of domestic surveillance as an essential element in the protection of national security, the prevention of disruptions to social order, and in some instances, the preservation of capitalism, power, and privilege as the dominant economic order.

Fifth, illegal domestic surveillance is often blamed on young, inexperienced, and overzealous officers. They may also be frustrated with the typical burdens of proof that are necessary in order to conduct a successful investigation.

Finally, poorly trained officers are commonly the cause of illegal domestic surveillance. This is a regular finding in many official investigations. It is not simply a matter of cutting corners. Usually, the individual in question was either not trained or was not trained well with respect to the kinds of situations that may be encountered in his or her career.

In short, efforts to affix blame occur in a political context with those in the higher echelons of a domestic or national security organization, in an effort to minimize damage to their careers, reputation, and to avoid criminal sanction/s, try to distance themselves from the foot soldiers, who they may have ordered to conduct the illegal actions. This is often done through the context of plausible deniability (that is, it protects the administration by opening up the possibility that subordinates did not follow rules that were communicated orally).

Box 8.1: *The Conversation* (1974)

This movie, directed and produced by Francis Ford Coppola, stars Gene Hackman as Harry Caul, a contractor who specializes in eavesdropping. Caul runs a crew of individuals whose job is to eavesdrop on the conversations of people identified by his clients. He is in enamored with his technological gadgets and his ability. The movie begins with Caul completing some work that involves eavesdropping on the conversation of a young couple. The audience really does not know the substance of the wrong this couple has committed, but there is a belief that the man is cheating on his wife. Caul eventually discovers that the information that he obtains may be used to kill the man. This causes Caul to question his ethics. As the movie progresses, during an impromptu meeting with some other professionals in the field, we learn that Caul's previous work in New York City had resulted in someone's death. He is also a highly religious man who goes to confession.

Although the movie is dated, for its time, it shows the basics of the ethical conflicts that can occur with specialists in this line of work. The film raises one major question: was Caul's work illegal? The question hinges on the reasonable expectation of privacy.

Effects of illegal domestic surveillance

Through domestic surveillance, it is possible to gather useful information to combat oppositional political crime. Many people, however, are opposed to this state activity because they value their right to privacy and because domestic surveillance tests constitutional guarantees (especially privacy and civil rights). In addition, the public believes that government agencies have no right to spy on citizens except under the most unusual of circumstances. Domestic spying operations have been criticized by opponents who claim that a government's spying operations against its citizens is criminal.

The negative effects of illegal surveillance are broad. It can expand the number of state enemies, increase state expenditures, and produce psychological and economic damage to the innocent individual who is placed under scrutiny. More generally, illegal surveillance can injure the trust and faith of ordinary citizens in the integrity of their government.

Even if an individual is innocent, damage or harm can come to his or her reputation and employability (Churchill and Vander Wall, 1988). For example, during the 1950s, many individuals who were falsely accused of being communists, or holding communist sympathies, appeared in front of the House Committee on Un-American Activities (1938-75), and through the work of Senator Joseph McCarthy, as chair of the Senate Committee on Government Operations (1952-54), suffered considerable psychological and financial damage (Navansky, 1991). Many, either due to economic reasons or disgust, left the US. Once accused of being disloyal, a person may hire an attorney to pay legal fees to put on a spirited defense. This is an added expense that the individual must incur.

Illegal surveillance and the corresponding possibilities for misuse of increasingly sophisticated surveillance technologies available in the contemporary information age are the "negative features" of law enforcement surveillance (Marx, 1988, p. 222). The sheer number of new surveillance technologies available to agents within the crime control industry (Christie, 1993) is disturbing, as they are extended to and used against people and organizations who are not involved in or suspected of committing crimes, but rather are defined as potentially threatening to the dominant political and economic order.

Undoubtedly, some constituencies (for example, governmental agents and apologists) may explain away such activities as anomalies or as the actions of a few deviant or rogue governmental employees. However, many domestic surveillance operations were simply too complex, involved too many state agents and offices, and were either directed by or had the blessings of top-level administrators to have resulted from a few misguided, front-line employees. These activities were organizational in nature, meaning that the spy programs became a standard operating procedure for certain government agencies (for example, Hoover's COINTELPRO) (Coleman, 1985, Chapter 2).

Historical perspective

Federal and local law enforcement from all three countries featured in this book have periodically engaged in illegal domestic surveillance. A multitude of government agencies that collect intelligence operate in the US, including the CIA, the FBI, the National Reconnaissance Office, the National Security Agency, the Defense Intelligence Agency, the State Department Bureau of Intelligence and Research, the Drug Enforcement Agency, and a number of Pentagon organizations. The FBI and the CIA, in particular, are the most well-known government organizations for which we have the most evidence of illegal domestic surveillance operations (Ranelagh, 1987). In Canada, the former Royal Canadian Mounted Police-Security Service (RCMP-SS) and the Canadian Security Intelligence Service (CSIS) have played similar questionable roles (Brown and Brown, 1978; Sawatsky, 1980; Dion, 1982). And in the UK, surveillance and other questionable techniques are usually carried out by MI5 or MI6. The FBI and RCMP are national police forces with the responsibility of policing domestically (although FBI field offices now exist in several countries, including the former "nemesis," Russia, and the RCMP has officers in many embassies throughout the world). The CIA, on the other hand, concentrates its activities abroad. And, although many Americans disagree with its operations, such work is largely accepted as necessary for "national security."

Research on these agencies has been produced by reporters, scholars and government inquiries, which takes place at the national and local level. These endeavors are often supported by organizations, like the Canadian Association for Security and Intelligence Studies (CASIS) and the Intelligence Studies Section of the International Studies Association.

The US experience

One of the most widely used spying techniques is wiretapping, which was declared illegal in the US in 1934. Although the FBI continued using this technology despite the ban, agents did discontinue its use briefly after a 1937 Supreme Court ruling that specifically applied the law to the FBI and its operations. Two years later, President Franklin Roosevelt claimed the FBI had the authority and right to wiretap in "national security" cases (Coleman, 1985, p. 59). Wiretapping remained illegal until 1968 when it was ruled legal if authorized by a court order based on sufficient probable cause. Despite this judicial intervention, illegal domestic surveillance continued unabated. Even today, criminal justice personnel often have to go "judge shopping" in order to gain the trust or confidence of a sympathetic judge. Illegally planting listening devices (bugs) is possible mainly through burglaries. Over the past decade, technology has advanced far enough to allow such devices to be set up without a physical entry. While the rate of using these devices has varied, former FBI Director J. Edgar Hoover condoned illegal burglaries and the planting of listening devices (Coleman, 1985, p. 60).

Even though a federal court order is necessary for any law enforcement agency to open private mail, between 1959 and 1966, the FBI examined 42 million pieces of mail in New York City alone. Furthermore, the CIA, prohibited by legislation from engaging in domestic surveillance, read private mail sent between the US and the former USSR during the height of the Cold War. Scholars have determined that the CIA opened 216,000 pieces of mail and compiled a list of 1.5 million names of individuals from these mailings alone (CIA's Mail Intercept, 1975; Halperin et al., 1977; Coleman, 1985). During the 1960s, the CIA "investigate[d] and determine[d] whether foreign elements had infiltrated protest activity. This program, Operation Chaos, involved the surveillance activities of domestic groups and violated the CIA's initial charter, the National Security Act, which clearly excluded its activities from the domestic arenas" (Hagan, 1997, p. 33).

Break-in of the Democratic National Committee headquarters

The FBI and CIA are not the only agencies that have been accused of illegal domestic surveillance. Although he denied it, in 1971, former President Richard M. Nixon assembled a group dubbed "the Plumbers," "an investigation team organized under the aegis of the President and his staff," to engage in political sabotage. The Plumbers apparently "coordinated the congressional investigations into the leaking of the Pentagon Papers.[...] The administration hoped to secure prosecution of the individual who released the papers on grounds of espionage" (Roebuck and Weeber, 1978, p. 23).

In 1972, the Plumbers also burglarized and bugged the Democratic National Committee (DNC) headquarters, located in the Watergate Building in Washington, DC, in an attempt to steal secret DNC materials (Woodward and Bernstein, 1974; Haldeman, 1994). When investigations into the Plumbers were conducted, it was found that they "ultimately handled such tasks as forging diplomatic cables and hiring thugs to disrupt peace rallies" (Roebuck and Weeber, 1978, p. 24). Immediately there were calls for the impeachment of Nixon. He left office before Congress was able to successfully impeach him, and various members of the Plumbers received prison sentences.

COINTELPRO

Even though dissident groups in the US had suspected for some time that they were being watched, infiltrated, and, to some extent, de-stabilized by the FBI, it was not until March 8, 1971, that their suspicions were confirmed. On that date, a group identifying itself as the Citizens' Commission burgled a regional FBI office in Media, Pennsylvania (Davis, 1992, Chapter 1). The Citizens' Commission stole about 1,000 Counter-Intelligence Program (COINTELPRO) documents that indicated that the FBI had, for years, operated a national, organizational, and illegal surveillance operation against several dissident groups in the US. The spying focused primarily on the New Left, which was composed of disparate but like-minded groups. FBI files also revealed that the Black Panther Party (BPP), the American Indian Movement (AIM), Students for a Democratic Society (SDS), and the Communist Party of the US (CPUSA) had all been extensively spied on and infiltrated, and their activities had been disrupted (Blackstock, 1975; Churchill and Vander Wall, 1990, Chapter 7; Davis, 1992, Chapter 6).[3] Civil Rights leader Martin Luther King was not spared from this kind of activity either.

Later, "court records in 1977 revealed that the FBI paid $2.5 million in Chicago to recruit an army of more than 5,000 spies who informed on Chicago-area residents and organizations between 1966 and 1976. During the same period, the

FBI opened files on about 27,900 individuals and organizations in Chicago who were regarded as possible security risks or extremists" (Roebuck and Weeber, 1978).

After photocopying the FBI's files, the Citizens' Commission mailed them to various journalists, academics, and members of Congress (Davis, 1992, p. 7). The resulting Congressional investigation of the FBI revealed that COINTELPRO was illegal and unconstitutional. Furthermore, the investigation showed that the operation, which had existed since 1956, involved 12 separate counterintelligence programs (each involving a different citizens' group). Everyone involved had been initiated on Hoover's directives and every FBI field office in the US was complicit in the operation. The FBI and Hoover assured Congress that COINTELPRO and similar domestic surveillance operations were discontinued on April 28, 1971 (Churchill and Vander Wall, 1990). Yet just a few years later, another FBI spy program was in place to target the citizens' group Committee in Solidarity with the People of El Salvador (CISPES).

In an attempt to monitor dissent, local, state, and federal law enforcement agencies increased their domestic surveillance activities. Most major urban police agencies (for example, Chicago, New York, Los Angeles, and Philadelphia) spied on US citizens during this time (Donner, 1990). Each police department had special units whose responsibilities focused on information gathering and the infiltration and destabilization of citizens' groups suspected to be threats to the social order (Donner, 1990). While engaging in their own surveillance operations, the city police departments often acted in tandem with national law enforcement agencies, most typically the FBI.

In 1978, the US government passed the Foreign Intelligence Surveillance Act (FISA). Its passage was a response to the perceived excesses of the Nixon administration in connection with spying against political groups that engaged in legitimate political dissent. The Act also arose because of the revelations of the Church committee (United States Senate Select Committee to Study Governmental Operations with Respect to Intelligence Activities) that investigated illegal domestic surveillance engaged in by both the FBI and the CIA. FISA was designed to monitor communications between foreigners outside of the US and was not intended to record domestic communications.

CISPES (1983)

The FBI's investigation of CISPES began in March 1983 and ultimately involved 52 FBI field offices (Davis, 1992, Chapter 7). As in earlier surveillance programs, people were covertly investigated because of their political, rather than criminal, activities. Also, this spy operation, like earlier COINTELPRO activities, was not the product of "rogue" FBI agents operating without proper authorization. Directives concerning this operation came from FBI headquarters, as indicated by an FBI memo from March 30, 1983, which instructed 11 field offices to begin surveillance specifically on individuals involved in CISPES (Davis, 1992, p. 178).

CISPES was founded because many US citizens were concerned with the continued financial support and military training of the El Salvadoran government, a regime that most human rights watch groups considered repressive (Power, 1981, pp. 44-61). Because of its commitment to the government of El Salvador, the US labeled groups opposing its capital and foreign policy toward El Salvador as sympathetic to leftists in Central America and as threatening to ongoing relationships and stability in that region. Thus, CISPES found itself under surveillance; its offices were mysteriously burgled, and its activities were infiltrated and disrupted by the FBI.

The FBI's operations were uncovered through a search using the Freedom of Information Act. As a response to the adverse publicity this garnered, William Sessions, the new FBI director, ignored the organizational nature of this surveillance program and imposed disciplinary sanctions against six agents. Nonetheless, a Senate Select Committee criticized the FBI and its continuing surveillance of people and groups involved in dissident political activities, acts that contradicted the FBI's claim that domestic surveillance had been discontinued.[4]

Carnivore (1997)

Between 1997 and 2000, the FBI utilized a computer program called Carnivore, to intercept all email traffic coming in and out of the US. In 2001 this system was relabelled DCS-1000 and in 2005 replaced with software called NarusInsight. Reflecting a less serious but probably more pervasive accusation, news reports periodically allege real or purported bugging incidents. For example, in February 2002, it was revealed that the CIA had planted listening devices in the rooms of Japanese officials during the most recent round of trade negotiations between the US and Japan. FISA was amended in 2001 because of The USA PATRIOT Act. The legislation was once again changed in 2007 through the Protect America Act. This new Act expired one year after its implementation and was seriously flawed, thus a new FISA bill was passed in 2008.

The USA PATRIOT Act (2001)

In the middle of October 2001, Congress passed sweeping legislation against terrorism in what is now referred to as The USA PATRIOT Act. Some of the more important highlights include so-called roving wiretaps (tied to certain people rather than to particular telephone lines); nationwide search warrants, instead of those limited to specific jurisdictions; searches of electronic mail; and the power to detain foreigners for extended periods of time. The bill gives "authorities the ability to hold immigrants suspected of terrorist acts for 7 days without filing charges."[5] Part of The USA PATRIOT Act also includes longer and more severe sentences, and the extension of the "statute of limitations on terrorism cases."[6] Few literate Americans, including some congressmen and women who passed the bill, have read this rather draconian anti-terrorism legislation.

As of early 2005, Congress was considering very comprehensive anti-terror legislation, dubbed Patriot II Act. Both the House and the Senate developed separate terrorism bills that would "enhance domestic surveillance powers, stiffen penalties for terrorism and make it easier for law enforcement and intelligence agencies to share information" (Lancaster, 2001). Increased monitoring and regulation of financial institutions was also considered, as it was recognized that in order to mount a successful campaign, a terrorist organization needs financing (Adams, 1986). Without new legislation, banks are only required to report to the federal government transfers and withdrawals that are over US$100,000. Closer monitoring of financial transactions would undoubtedly slow down the pace of international capitalism.

Finally, The USA PATRIOT Act allows law enforcement to enter a premise and explore parts of it and if anything may appear incriminating, to enter this into evidence. These so-called "sneak and peak" searches go beyond the typical procedures involved in typical search warrants (www.aclu.org/national-security/surveillance-under-patriot-act). In general, The USA PATRIOT Act embodies a lower standard than probable cause.

The Canadian experience

Canadian citizens also have been subject to illegal surveillance by their law enforcement communities. The RCMP-SS, in particular, has engaged in activities similar to those of the FBI. It has periodically engaged in illegal surveillance against dissident, labor, and leftist groups and people.[7] For example, during the 1960s, the Agency Presse Libre du Québec (APLQ) and the Movement for the Defense of Political Prisoners of Québec (MDPPQ) were both spied on by the RCMP-SS, sometimes in cooperation with the Montreal Urban Community Police Department (MUCPD) and Sureté (the Québec Police Force) (Sawatsky, 1980). APLQ and the MDPPQ were perceived to be threatening to Québec and Canada's social order since, according to law enforcement officials, they had as their goals "to publish political bulletins about events in Québec and to transform society" (Dion, 1982, p. 52). Furthermore, the police described the general ideology and ongoing objectives of APLQ as expressing "the grievances and the interests of workers and of progressive organizations struggling against the present economic and political system" (Dion, 1982, p. 53). When these groups were defined as threatening to existing order, programs designed to monitor, contain, sabotage, and destabilize these activists were initiated.

In October 1972, in Montreal, RCMP-SS, along with MUCPD and Sureté, burgled the offices of the APLQ. About a ton of documents was stolen – all believed to be relevant to the APLQ's ongoing political agenda to work against the dominant political and economic order (Dion, 1982, Chapter 1). This particular crime was not the first for the RCMP, as other police officers had broken into the APLQ offices a year earlier to plant listening devices and had re-entered at times to repair those electronics. Eventually the police photocopied, analyzed, hid, and finally destroyed the stolen documents.

The RCMP also investigated alleged homosexuals working for the government. If someone was found to be gay, he or she was than asked to resign or were fired (Sawatsky, 1980, Chapter 10). Similarly, the leftist Partisan Party of Vancouver, later amalgamated into the Canadian Communist Party, was spied on and had files stolen by the RCMP. These were disruptive rather than intelligence-gathering tactics (Sawatsky, 1980, Chapter 20).

The British experience

The security service and police intelligence agencies of the United Kingdom include MI5, the Secret Intelligence Branch (SIB) (or MI6 as it is commonly called), Special Branch, and the Anti-Terrorist Branch.[8] According to Thurlow (1994), there have been "three main targets of political surveillance, the Communist Party of Great Britain, the British Union of Fascists, and the Sinn Fein and its links with the Irish Republican Army" (p. 3). Stemming from the "Northern Ireland problem" (also known as "The Troubles"), British intelligence has repeatedly been accused of illegal surveillance in what were later called the Stalker Affair, the trials of the Birmingham Six, and the Guildford Four (Ross, 2000c).

Also in Britain, the National Security Agency and the General Command Headquarters illegally undertook massive surveillance of activists, trade unionists, and British businesses through a microwave network set up in the 1960s for such purposes. The extent of the activities of this apparatus first came to light in the mid-1970s when *New Statesman* journalist Duncan Campbell revealed the level and sophistication of Signals Intelligence (SIGINT), later referred to as the ABC Affair (Thurlow, 1994).

After 9/11, "sweeping anti-terrorism laws were adopted in Britain, providing for lengthy imprisonment for politically-motivated acts classified as 'terrorist,' not to mention long term detention without charging. The Civil Contingencies Act of 2004 also empowered the government to issue sweeping emergency regulations in any event that 'threatens serious damage to human welfare' or 'war on terrorism,' which threatens serious damage to the security of the United Kingdom" (Head, 2011, p. 31).

Joint operations

One of the most pervasive contemporary intelligence operations bears the name ECHELON (Hagan, 1997). Although its existence was originally denied by the US National Security Agency, the operation monitors every electronic transmission related to US interests, including cell phone calls and email messages. Not only does ECHELON work on behalf of the US, but it is jointly managed and operated by Australia, Canada, New Zealand and the United Kingdom. A scandal broke out in Europe in February 2001 when it was discovered that the CIA was spying on behalf of US businesses (Redden, 2000).

Illegal domestic surveillance by local police forces

Historical analyses of the rise of police surveillance beginning in the days of intense labor struggles and violence (for example, the Haymarket tragedy of May 1886) shows that it increased in frequency from the 1930s through the 1960s (Donner, 1990). Most big-city police agencies (for example, Chicago, New York City, Los Angeles, and Philadelphia) have spied on US citizens (Donner, 1990). Each had special units whose sole responsibilities included information gathering, infiltrating, and destabilizing citizens' groups defined as threatening to social order (Donner, 1990). While engaging in their own surveillance operations, city police departments often acted in tandem with national law enforcement agencies, most typically the FBI and the RCMP.

For example, the Chicago Police Department's (CPD) political surveillance operation claimed in 1960 that it "had accumulated information on some 117,000 local individuals, 141,000 out-of-town subjects, and 14,000 organizations" (Donner, 1990, p. 92). Until 1968, most of its spying had been limited to ideologically threatening groups – the Communist Party and the Socialist Workers Party. However, with the DNC scheduled for Chicago in 1968, surveillance increased and included a wide variety of "civic groups and prominent citizens," linking them, as best the authorities could, to communism and communist subversion, although next to no substantiation ever materialized (Donner, 1990, p. 93). Groups spied on by CPD included the American Civil Liberties Union (ACLU), the National Association for the Advancement of Colored Peoples (NAACP), People United to Save Humanity, the National Lawyers' Guild, the League of Women Voters, the World Council of Churches, universities, and churches.

Finally, in March 1975, a Cook County (Chicago) grand jury heard testimony about the intelligence unit within the CPD and subsequently issued a report strongly condemning its activities. Intelligence unit officers who were ordered to testify before the grand jury told of the division's illegalities. "In addition to illegal electronic surveillance, police officers admittedly engaged in burglaries, thefts, incitements to violence, destruction of mailing lists, and other criminal acts

Table 8.1: Countries, national security/intelligence agencies and well-known acts of illegal domestic surveillance

Country	Most prominent national security/intelligence agency	Well-known acts of domestic surveillance
United States	FBI CIA	COINTELPRO CISPES investigation Operation Chaos
Canada	RCMP-SS (now CSIS)	Numerous actions during the 1960s and 1970s against pro-separatist individuals and groups
United Kingdom	MI5 MI6 Special Branch	Stalker Affair Birmingham Six Guildford Four

because 'they believed it their duty'" (Donner, 1990, p. 104).[9] Although allegedly dissolved in 1975, six years later the CPD admitted in federal court that since then its intelligence unit had engaged in a widespread surveillance operation against "77 civic, religious, antiwar, civil rights, and political organizations" (Donner, 1990, p. 153).

New York City had its own spy unit, the Bureau of Special Services (BOSS), and Philadelphia, under former mayor Frank Rizzo, the son of a police sergeant and a career police officer himself, established its own surveillance unit known as the Civil Defense Squad. The New York, Philadelphia, and later the Los Angeles Police Departments operated similar surveillance squads, clearly violating laws and spying on their cities' own citizens. During the 1990s, shortly after former Los Angeles Police Chief Darryl Gates retired in 1993, evidence emerged indicating that he had used a special LAPD surveillance force for spying on various leftist sympathizers and political enemies, including the actor Robert Redford and former mayor Tom Bradley (Rothmiller and Goldman, 1992). As part of the post 911 War on Terror, in 2012 the NYPD came under intense criticism for its infiltration of Muslim student groups on college campuses in and around New York City.

Summary

This chapter has argued that illegal domestic surveillance is not an isolated phenomenon. Rather, it has been an ongoing organizational policy and practice in democratic states and has been sanctioned by, in some cases, heads of state. Furthermore, illegal surveillance operations have been launched against both violators of criminal law and individuals involved in legal political dissident.

Critical questions are raised regarding domestic surveillance as political crime. For example, at what point is spying elevated to an illegitimate form of political policing and becomes criminal? And how are politics and political ideology relevant to a government's surveillance of its own citizens? These questions are fundamentally important for understanding the subtle nuances of the illegal spying that threatens those legal and constitutional guarantees enjoyed by citizens of democracies. And, as Sykes (1980, pp. 57-8) has made clear about the US experience with domestic surveillance and other political crimes of the state, these activities may be the dirty work that people abhor but nonetheless consider necessary. Given the history of illegal domestic surveillance in industrialized democracies, it is reasonable to expect such programs to continue at varying levels.

Notes

[1] This kind of action violates generally accepted standards of civil rights. In the US, in particular, the Constitution, through the Fourth Amendment, guarantees everyone to be safe from unreasonable searches of their homes.

[2] Foreign surveillance was reviewed earlier in the book, in the discussion concerning espionage (Chapter 4).

[3] Immediately after the break-in, then-FBI director J. Edgar Hoover closed 100 FBI offices and ordered in 100 special agents with a single objective – to find the Citizens' Commission. The group was never located, and the case remains unsolved today (Davis, 1992).

[4] Beyond this condemnation from the Senate Committee, in a federal lawsuit, the Socialist Workers Party was awarded damages resulting from the FBI's ongoing surveillance, infiltration, and disruption of its political activities. It was discovered that between 1960 and 1966, the FBI had burglarized the Socialist Workers Party's offices at least 94 times, an average of once every three weeks for six-and-a-half years, in order to photograph and steal various documents (Coleman, 1985; Davis, 1992).

[5] See note 4.

[6] "House committee approves anti-terrorism measure," *USA Today*, 4 October 2001.

[7] The RCMP-SS has been replaced by the CSIS.

[8] For an in-depth review of domestic intelligence in the United Kingdom, see, for example, Bunyan (1976).

[9] The grand jury concluded that primary surveillance targets were almost entirely groups opposing Chicago's former Mayor Richard Daley and his policies. Furthermore, the jury stated that, "groups which received the most intensive scrutiny had also been openly critical of some policies of the Chicago Police Department" (Donner, 1990, p. 104).

NINE

Human rights violations

Introduction

One of the most well publicized and accepted state crimes is the category of human rights abuses and violations. With increasing frequency, the media are reporting on human rights violations and on recent efforts to bring to justice the individuals and states committing these crimes.

Definitional and conceptual issues

Human rights abuses include both violent and nonviolent actions. Examples of the former infringements include the beating, torturing, or executing of dissidents, and genocide. Instances of nonviolent responses encompass restrictions on political participation, including infringements on individual rights to vote for representative government; interference with dissident political activities and organizations; restrictions on the freedom of expression, association, assembly, and religion; violations of due process; discrimination based on racial, gender, ethnic, and religious grounds; and institutionalized sexism and racism. Somewhere in the middle of these two types (that is, violent and nonviolent) falls the actions linked to arbitrary detention of political dissidents in correctional facilities or mental hospitals. In other words, these two outcomes are not exclusive but may exist in combined forms. Regardless of the degree of violence in connection with these actions, human rights violations are usually carried out by or involve a variety of state criminogenic agencies, including the armed forces, national security agencies, police, and government-sponsored militias.

Only recently have human rights issues been treated as political crimes primarily by a small yet vocal group of criminologists. Previously, these actions were simply considered social problems and beyond the legitimate study of criminology. Many progressive criminologists, activists, and organizations, however, have interpreted commissive and omissive behaviors of states as human rights abuses (see, for example, Cohen, 1993).

Thus, some of these actions include homelessness (see, for example, Barak, 1991), poverty, the "grossly inequitable distribution of wealth," hunger (Bohm, 1993, p. 8), the high numbers of incarcerated prisoners, and the selective incarceration of individual "political prisoners" as violations of basic human rights.

Part of the problem in both identifying and responding to human rights violations is tied to the concepts of ideology, cultural relativism, and *raison d'état*. First, the protection of human rights at home and abroad is seen as a cornerstone of left-wing ideology. Second, although many practices and policies that occur in other countries and among other cultures may appear brutal or repressive compared to Western society (see, for example, Pollis and Schwab, 1979), those in the West must be careful about intervening in ways that could be construed as cultural insensitivity. Moreover, many controversial practices that America does (that is, Gitmo, death penalty, water-boarding) seem brutal, and repressive to those in other countries, but are justified in terms of national security in the United States. Third, some observers have suggested that in order to protect state sovereignty, the West should not or only rarely meddle in the affairs of other countries, thus protecting the independence of all states. Some semblance of these actions has been the tendency of the United States and other countries to opt out of treaties, conventions, and international bodies (for example, International Criminal Court) that would expose their negative actions to greater scrutiny.

Human rights versus civil rights

Human rights are typically minimal conditions or rights granted to all living humans in the world. Typically, this refers to freedom to not be physically harmed or killed and freedom from repression. These rights are typically protected by international agreements, such as the Universal Declaration of Human Rights.

Civil rights are given to people who are part of a community (for example, city, state, country). They are guaranteed in the form of an agreement (typically protected by a constitution) between individuals and their government (for example, speech, press, religion, due process). Civil rights are non-transferable from place to place. In other words, if a person goes to a different jurisdiction, there is no guarantee that they will be granted the same civil rights that they were given in their home country. The distinction between human rights and civil rights are frequently blurred.

How widespread is the problem?

The pervasiveness of human rights violations is difficult to determine due to governmental secrecy, the reluctance of victims and perpetrators to come forward, and the unwillingness of repressive governments to make such information accessible. It is also impossible to determine the number of political prisoners, although some human rights organizations produce relatively reliable data (for example, Amnesty International and Human Rights Watch). Although human rights violations occur in Western democracies (especially against minorities, illegal immigrants, etc.), the frequency of this activity is higher in lesser developed countries that have totalitarian or authoritarian regimes. Ironically, many oppressive countries are either periodically supported or tolerated by Anglo-American democracies (for example, Panama under Geneva/Manuel Noriega, Egypt under Hosnei Mubarak, Iran under Shah Pahlavi).

Human rights violations in the United States

Human rights violations occur in all countries. The following is a brief review of notable human rights violations in the US. Although the scholarly community and jurists did not have the language of human rights back then, it is instructive to note that reading back in history will innumerate numerous examples of these practices.

The War of 1812

During the War of 1812, the US government, as a security precaution, arrested numerous British citizens who were living in East Coast cities. Some were deported back to England, while others voluntarily relocated to Canada (and became known as the Upper Canada Loyalists).

The Seminole Wars

The First Seminole War (1814–19), instigated and led by the then General, and later President, Andrew Jackson, included numerous instances of what today's experts would unquestionably consider as human rights violations and genocide against the indigenous people of Florida. Until recently (see, for example, Meacham, 2008/09), few history books would have described Jackson as "slaveholder, land speculator, executioner of dissident solders, exterminator of Indians" (Zinn, 1980/2010, p. 129).

First World War

In 1918, in an effort to shore up support for the entrance of the US into the First World War (1914–18) and to reduce criticism of the war, the Sedition Act of 1786 was amended. The Act was made more specific and was popularly referred to as the Sedition Act. During this time, close to a thousand individuals were incarcerated under state or federal sedition laws because they opposed US involvement in the First World War or because of their "controversial" union activities or religious or political beliefs (Kohn, 1994). During the US involvement in the First World War (1917–18), the Department of Justice also interned 6,000 German and other European-born civilians and merchant seamen in military barracks in Georgia and Utah. These seizures were motivated by both justifiable and unfounded suspicions of espionage and subterfuge in North America (Krammer, 1997).

Second World War

During the Second World War (1941–45), 120,000 Japanese-American citizens (born in the US) and 8,000 Japanese nationals were interned in prison camps located in Utah, Colorado, Idaho, and Washington. Besides these individuals, 3,500

Germans and 1,000 Italians (US citizens and foreign nationals) were incarcerated. The internment included women and children, and lasted through the declaration of peace. These innocent people lost their jobs and homes, and suffered great hardships that continued into the years that followed the war (Goldstein, 1978).

1960s

Post-war examples of human rights violations in the US include the behavior modification "high security units" at the federal penitentiaries in Marion, Illinois, and Lexington, Kentucky, where once politically active individuals were imprisoned until Amnesty International investigated and condemned the ongoing practices of the US Bureau of Prisons (Zwerman, 1988).

Beyond these special units, prisons across the US house "political prisoners," that is, people who have received very lengthy prison sentences and whose incapacitation is qualitatively different from other inmates because of their former or current political participation (see, for example, Deutsch and Susler, 1991). Furthermore, the US government, through the Attorney General's office and the Immigration and Naturalization Service, violated the human rights of many of the Mariel Cubans who emigrated to the US in 1980. These immigrants quickly found themselves imprisoned in maximum security facilities without having been accused of committing crimes, without trial, and without any due process proceedings (Hamm, 1995).

Another noteworthy incident which called into question civil rights issues was the beating of African-American motorist Rodney King. On March 3, 1991, King and two passengers were pulled over by Los Angeles Police Department (LAPD) officers. King was slow in heeding the officers' commands, and during the subsequent interaction, he was beaten. The entire event was videotaped, and a select portion of which quickly aired on local and national television stations. The episode created considerable public outrage and led to a criminal trial against the officers. In May 1992, officers Stacey Koon and Laurence Powell were acquitted of the charges. The verdict prompted devastating riots in Los Angeles and in several other cities across the country. The federal government, through the US Department of Justice, quickly filed charges against the officers, alleging that they had violated King's civil rights. In 1993, a conviction was achieved, and Koon and Powell went to federal prison (Ross, 2000a).

The most recent human rights violations in the US are linked to the prison in Guantanamo.[1]

Enemy combatants at Guantanamo

At the southeastern end of Cuba is a naval base that is owned and operated by the US government. This installation, which sits on Guantanamo Bay, consists of a number of camps and is now generally referred to as Guantanamo (or "Gitmo," for short). In 1903, based on the Platt Amendment (a treaty between Cuba and the US), the US government was supposedly granted a perpetual lease on the 45 square miles that comprise the base. Although the communist regime of Fidel Castro, which came to power in 1959, cashed one of the cheques made in payment for this property, the Cuban government was virulently opposed to US presence on the island.

Background

Shortly after the 9/11 attacks (September 11, 2001) and before the US bombings of Afghanistan (October 7, 2001), the US government formulated plans to detain captured members of the Taliban and al-Qaeda terrorist organizations. In the end, the Bush administration determined that Guantanamo would serve as the ideal destination for these prisoners. More fundamentally, US officials had decided not to treat the suspected terrorists either as criminal defendants or as prisoners of war: "Because either option could preclude interrogation to learn of impending attacks. One consequence has been to land detainees in a legal netherworld with no obvious exit" (Shane, 2006).

Gitmo offered several benefits: it was technically "outside the jurisdiction of the US legal system, safe from attack, [and] quiet enough for focused interrogations" – plus, it was relatively close to the US (Higham, Stephens and Williams, 2004). Approximately 9,500 US troops are stationed on Gitmo. The camp is almost totally self-sufficient, producing its own water and electricity. What makes this situation all the more anomalous is the fact that Guantanamo is the only US base on communist soil.

Prisoners detained on US soil would arguably pose a large threat to national security. The military did not want to move the detainees to US soil because any escaped prisoners would only be closer to potential targets. Most importantly, keeping the detainees in military prisons qualified the prisoners as "enemy combatants," a term that falls within a grey area of the law.

The first prisoners arrived at Gitmo on January 11, 2002. "The prisoners included some people picked up outside of the so-called war zone of Afghanistan and Pakistan, in places like Bosnia, Zambia, and Gambia" (Ratner and Ray, 2004, p. 10). The detainees were of varying nationalities and origins, hailing from Saudi Arabia, Yemen, Pakistan, and Afghanistan among others.

Much of what we know about the conditions at Guantanamo and the treatment of the detainees has been obtained through visits by US politicians, monitoring by delegations from international nongovernmental and human rights organizations, reports from individuals who have been released, statements by lawyers defending those who have been detained, and information from reporters representing selected newspapers (for example, *The New York Times* and *The Washington Post*). There have also been a handful of written accounts by former guards; another publication was produced by the US Muslim chaplain who was detained for 76 days on charges of espionage that were subsequently dismissed. In addition, a number of websites have been developed to inform the public about Gitmo's history and the current state of affairs with the detentions.

The base contains a number of smaller camps that have been given alphabetic military names. Detainees were originally housed at Camp X-Ray, but this location was closed in April 2002. Prisoners were relocated to Camps Delta, Echo, and Iguana, each of which contained a series of detention camps. The original conditions at Camp X-Ray were described as "cages, each 8 feet by 8 feet. Constructed on slabs of concrete and covered with sheets of metal and wood, the collection of cages looked like an oversized dog kennel" (Higham, Stephens and Williams, 2004).

The conditions of confinement at Guantanamo range from sparse chain-link cages to buildings with dormitory or communal living spaces. At one extreme are small, mesh-sided cells with no privacy and lights that are on 24 hours a day. Here, detainees are subjected to a regime not that different from what US prisoners receive in the various Supermax prisons. Prisoners are interrogated at all hours of the day and night, and there have been allegations that prisoners have been abused, tortured, and intimidated. Others have reported witnessing the desecration of religious items, such as copies of the Koran (the Muslim holy book).

During the initial year of operation, the detainees were not allowed access to legal counsel, nor were they permitted visits by friends or family. Moreover, in a Kafkaesque fashion, these prisoners were not informed about the formal legal charges against them. Most importantly, the detainees were denied the right of habeas corpus (the notion of innocent until proven guilty), arguably the bedrock of Anglo-American jurisprudence, "In the case brought forward by the Center for Constitutional Rights, the lower courts ruled that the detainees had no right to file a writ of habeas corpus" (Ratner and Ray, 2004, p. 4).

Some detainees have alleged that their US captors were not opposed to torture. Reports have mentioned such tactics as withholding food, depriving prisoners of sleep, forcing them to kneel for hours while being chained to the floor, subjecting them to loud noise, music or extreme temperatures, and beatings. This kind of treatment usually relied on the assumption that it would break the detainee's will, who would then provide useful intelligence in the war against terror. "The government has admitted that it conducts three hundred interrogations a week. In mid 2004, it had 2,800 soldiers and civilians (including interrogators) among a camp with somewhat more than seven hundred prisoners for two years" (Ratner and Ray, 2004, p. 41). Among the prisoners released some claimed being "interrogated as many as two hundred times," with all kinds of different techniques.

A number of different policing and/or intelligence agencies have interrogated the detainees at Guantanamo, including members of the FBI and the CIA. Similarly, members of MI5 (a British intelligence agency) questioned British detainees, and Mossad (an Israeli intelligence agency) interviewed Moroccan detainees.

The detainees

At its peak, there were approximately 700 "enemy combatants," most of whom are members of al-Qaeda and the Taliban, detained at the Guantanamo detention facility; some 290 Gitmo prisoners have been released or sent back to their home countries, according to the US Pentagon. Regardless of country where these individuals were picked up, they have been subjected to a litany of interrogations by different individuals working for various national security-related government agencies.

In sum, particularly since the US invasion of Afghanistan, numerous individuals have been arrested, detained, tortured, or killed. After release from Gitmo, some detainees were presumably sent to third countries in a process called rendition. It is commonly assumed that these detainees are being tortured by those countries.

Prisoners are frequently given psychotropic medications for depression, despondency, and psychosis. Meanwhile, in an attempt to deal with the hunger strikers, the military has resorted to the force-feeding of detainees. Numerous hunger strikes have been staged, and over 41 suicide attempts have occurred among the prisoners. In June 2006, three detainees died, and their deaths were ruled suicides. This was the first time since the camp opened that the administration confirmed this method of death by someone in US custody at Gitmo. Whether the detainees committed suicide because of depression or as a political act is unknown.

Legal status of the detainees

In January 2002, Alberto R. Gonzalez, former White House counsel and US Attorney General, advised President George W. Bush that the Geneva Convention should not be used with the detainees. In 1949, in the aftermath of the Second World War, the countries of the world assembled and produced the Third Geneva Convention:

> [It] requires that any dispute about a prisoner's status be decided by a 'competent tribunal.' American forces provided many such tribunals for prisoners taken in the Persian Gulf War in 1991. But President Bush has refused to comply with the Geneva Convention. He decided that all the Guantanamo prisoners were 'unlawful combatants' – that is, not regular soldiers, but spies, terrorists and the like. (Lewis, 2004, p. ix)

In the case of Gitmo, if the Geneva Conventions had been followed, the prisoners would have been considered prisoners of war to be held in POW camps and not subjected to interrogation and torture. "If there is any doubt as to whether they are POWs, there is a special hearing procedure in which a 'competent tribunal' makes individualized determination as whether a detained person is a POW. Until that tribunal meets a detained person must be treated as a POW" (Ratner and Ray, 2004, p. 11).

Most likely, the government "doesn't really want to apply the laws of war across the board.... The United States will not call the people held at Guantánamo prisoners of war, or even prisoners, the official designation being 'detained personnel' or simply detainees. The Pentagon has made up a new term 'enemy combatant'" (Ratner and Ray, 2004, p. 18) Many jurists argue that the term does not have any legal significance.

In July 2004, after several legal challenges, the US Department of Defense allowed Combatant Status Review Tribunals so that the detainees could formally contest their enemy combatant status. The process involved three "neutral officers," including a judge advocate. Despite criticisms from US and foreign jurists, Amnesty International, Human Rights Watch, and the United Nations, that the procedure was a sham, the military finished its reviews by March 2005, and 38 civilians were released.

Controversies over US policies and practices at Gitmo

The decision to house al-Qaeda and Taliban suspects at Guantanamo has been routinely criticized by Americans and foreigners alike. "The violation of the Geneva Convention and that refusal to let the courts consider the issue have cost the United States dearly in the world legal community – the judges and lawyers in societies that, historically, have looked to the United States as the exemplar of a country committed to Law" (Lewis, 2004, p. ix).

Many observers dislike the fact that detainees are held in an offshore prison and that their legal status is unclear. Some argue that if the "enemy combatants" were held on US soil, then they would be afforded the same civil liberties as those who reside on US soil. Others say that this, in fact, is a moot point because the military base is a US possession. Critics object to the effect the detentions will have on public opinion toward the US. Some suggest it will only foster the impression of the US as a big, bad bully on the world stage.

A number of individuals and organizations have visited Guantanamo. A handful of congressional delegations have inspected the premises and followed up on allegations of abuse. Simultaneously, human rights organizations (for example, Human Rights Watch and Amnesty International) have inspected Guantanamo and/or have issued reports highly critical of the conditions and reasons for confinement.

It has been argued that many of the detainees had no association with either the Taliban or al-Qaeda. When the US military went to Afghanistan, the troops rounded up 10,000 people in the first six months on suspicion of engaging in terrorism or fire-fights with the coalition forces.

> Those were not necessarily people found on the battlefield. Many were from Pakistan and the surrounding areas; many were ... taken in midnight raids that had nothing to do with the Taliban or with al-Qaeda.... Villagers and warlords, including members of the Northern

Alliance, started turning over their enemies or anyone they didn't like, or finally, anyone they could pick up (Ratner and Ray, 2004, p. 9).

This story calls into question whether or not the detainees were actually involved in any acts of terrorism. According to a Los Angeles Times article based on a classified document and cited by Ratner and Ray (2004, p. 14), "as many as 10 percent of the Guantanamo prisoners were 'taxi drivers, farmers, cobblers, and laborers' that some were 'low-level figures conscripted by the Taliban in the weeks before the collapse of the ruling Afghanistan regime'" (Ratner and Ray, 2004, p. 14). Ratner and Ray add, "of the 147 prisoners who had been released two years later, only 13 were then sent to jails. The other 134 were guilty of absolutely nothing.... It is certainly conceivable that the majority ... of the people in Guantanamo had nothing to do with any kind of terrorism" (Ratner and Ray, 2004, p. 14). To date, approximately 23 have been released to Afghanistan, five to the United Kingdom, four to Saudi Arabia, and three to Pakistan. On their release, some of the detainees were treated like heroes. Most have said that they were victims of circumstance, simply being in the wrong place at the wrong time.

The future

Many experts, foreign countries, and respected international nongovernmental organizations (INGOs) believe that the US is functioning in violation of the Geneva Convention, which specified the appropriate treatment of prisoners during wartime. The Third Geneva Convention did not specify a difference between "prisoners of war" and "enemy combatants." In short, the Bush administration refused to bring the detainees to trial, effectively ignoring international legal precedents and standards.

As a compromise, the US implemented the concept of Combatant Status Review Tribunals. This process, however, has been criticized as simply being a "rubber stamp" (in other words, the outcome of what to do with the detainee has been decided in advance), and the detainees are relatively powerless to defend themselves regarding the claims made against them.

About five years after the detainees were captured, the US advocated military-style tribunals for the 595 detainees being held at Guantanamo. This was made amid requests by national and international human rights monitoring organizations for better conditions and for the speedy processing of prisoners using the US criminal justice system rather than military-style tribunals.

In 2004, the Supreme Court ruled that individuals, regardless of their citizenship, who are in the custody of the US, must be granted a lawyer and a hearing before a neutral judge. Not only does this apply to those detained in the US, but it also pertains to the Guantanamo detainees. On June 30, 2006, the Supreme Court ruled in Hamdam vs Rumsfeld that the tribunals that the US government wished to use to try the detainees violated both US military law and the Geneva Convention. Despite this ruling, the justices did not provide a course of action to be taken, other than a recommendation that something should be worked out by the President and Congress.

The USA PATRIOT Act

Since 9/11, the US has significantly revamped the ways and means used to provide and insure national security against terrorist attacks. The passage of key legislation, including The USA PATRIOT Act (signed October 2001) and its revision, the US Patriot Improvement and Reauthorization Act of 2005 (passed March 2006), created new rules on domestic surveillance and detention. The Act gives the government increased powers to detain suspects. It has a lower threshold of proof than the previous legislation, and since its passage, there have been a limited number of incidents where it has been used on ordinary criminals to ensure the likelihood of conviction or longer sentences. One of the most egregious applications of this Act was a 2003 case through which telemarketers, who tricked individuals into believing that they had won a lottery in Canada, were tried. Although the connection to human rights violations is distant, the misuse of the Act is an example of how a law has an ominous quality. One of the most profound effects of The USA PATRIOT Act has been "the indefinite detention, without trial, of hundreds, if not thousands, of foreign citizens in military camps at Guantanamo Bay and elsewhere, including secret locations in allied countries, where detainees were 'rendered' for torture" (Head, p. 61).

Human rights violations in the United Kingdom

The detention of citizens and the use of highly questionable interrogation methods, including allegations of torture, by the British Army in Northern Ireland have led to several human rights complaints and official investigations (Ross, 2000c). In 1971, for example, the British Army detained and interrogated 14 alleged members of the Irish Republican Army (IRA) Provisionals, using a number of questionable interrogation techniques and sensory deprivation such as "prolonged wall standing, loud noises, hooding, and deprivation of food, water, and sleep" (Roberts, 1976, p. 16; Hurwitz, 1995, p. 301).

Consequently, that same year, the Republic of Ireland sent a petition of complaint to the European Court of Human Rights. "Although the Irish petition contained a series of charges and demands, the most important and significant component of the Irish petition was the allegation that the British security forces …'tortured' suspected Irish Republican Army (IRA) internees" (Hurwitz, 1995, p. 301).

> These methods were termed 'sensory-deprivation' … and they were designed to elicit information from the internees … one of the major issues was not whether these occurred, but rather, whether such

behavior and additional actions by the British government constituted
a violation of the European Convention. (Hurwitz, 1995, p. 301)

The United Kingdom eventually "admitted fault, stopped the practice of sensory
deprivation," and made financial compensation to the victims (p. 301).

In February 1972, in Londonderry (Northern Ireland), following a civil rights
demonstration, British soldiers shot and killed 13 people and wounded 16 unarmed
civilians. This incident, generally referred to as "Bloody Sunday," was the subject
of a highly publicized inquiry that culminated in the Widgery Report. This report
was perceived as a whitewash of British Army activities during this incident. In
1997, new material emerged in connection with Bloody Sunday that further
implicated the British Army in a planned act of murder (Ross, 2000c).

Human rights violations in Canada

Canada, which has an international reputation of being a peace-loving country
(Ross, 1995/2004), is rarely accused of human rights violations. Nonetheless,
over the past two decades, the country has been scrutinized by the worldwide
community with respect to police use of excessive force and "degrading treatment
or punishment of its indigenous peoples" (called First Nations in Canada) (www.
state.gov/g/drl/rls/hrrpt/2000/wha/index.cfm?docid=729).

The history of human rights violations against the First Nations can be traced
back to the original founding of Canada by both the French and the British. One
of the first rights violations was carried out in law enforcement-militia actions
(that is, Royal Northwest Mounted Police) against the people living in the lands
west of Manitoba. One example of this was provided by the Indian Residential
Schools – children of Native Canadians were forcefully removed from their parents
to attend schools run by Christian denominational ministries (for example, the
Jesuits), where numerous abuses were reported. As Canada matured, gained relative
independence from the United Kingdom, and took its place in the world, other
human rights violations were committed and came to public attention.

Certain kinds of legislation, in hindsight, have been identified as violating the
human rights of Canadians. One of the earliest was the Chinese Immigration Act
of 1885, which subjected foreigners from China who came to Canada to work
a high fee. It was amended in 1923; however, the Chinese were still singled out
in the legislation. Like the US, during the First World War Canada treated many
foreigners as enemy aliens and confined them to 24 concentration camps in the
country's interior. Singled out were Ukrainian Canadians, most of whom lost their
wealth and possessions. During the Second World War, the Canadian government
confiscated the possessions of Japanese Canadians and relocated them from the
provinces of British Columbia and Alberta to work camps.

Similar relocations of the Inuit (indigenous peoples of the High Arctic) occurred
during the 1950s, during the height of the Cold War. The Inuits were promised

that they would be returned to their homes, but the Canadian government failed to comply with this agreement (Canada, 1994).

In the last two decades, Canada has been under the global human rights spotlight for two issues. In 1993, Quebec's controversial Bill 101, which attempts to protect the use of the French language and curtail the use of English, came to the attention of the UN Human Rights Committee. This committee chastised the province for breaking the Covenant on Civil and Political Rights, arguing that a country may choose one or more languages but may not curtail public expression in any language. In 1999, the longstanding separate school system, that allows both religious (typically, Protestant and Roman Catholic) and public schools to operate concurrently, was rebuked through a ruling by the UN Human Rights Committee. The ruling accused the Canadian government of discriminating against religious-based private schools.

Safeguarding human rights

In general, there have been six areas where the protection of human rights has been expressed or implemented: philosophy, treaties, state-level documents and bodies, regional bodies, international agencies, documents, policies, processes, and nongovernmental organizations that protect human rights.

Philosophical background

Human rights doctrines can be traced back to the Code of Hammurabi, through religious laws, and finally through the Magna Carta. The notion of human rights, as a concept, originated during the period of Enlightenment in Western society (18th century), especially through the scholarship of English philosophers like Hobbes and Locke. Well-known US statesmen, such as Thomas Jefferson and Thomas Paine, also contributed to the formulation of human rights law. This concept has also been expressed in various legal documents, including the English Bill of Rights, the American Declaration of Independence, the US Constitution and Bill of Rights, and the French Declaration of the Rights of Man and of the Citizen.

Treaties

The history of attempts at safeguarding against human rights abuses begins around the time of the Treaty of Westphalia (1648). At this time, John Locke and Hugo Grotius, among others, began promoting the Natural Law principles of inalienable human rights to life, liberty, and property. Although these basic principles were eventually adopted by many countries, blatant violations continued to exist in the form of slavery and genocide (Bennett, 1991, p. 372). As a result, in 1815, Great Britain urged states where slaves were shipped to develop treaties suppressing the slave trade. During the 19th century, agreements were enacted protecting individuals from various injustices. A significant advance culminated, after the First

World War, in the peace treaties of 1919, which sought to guarantee fair treatment for inhabitants of the captured territories and for particular racial minorities in Eastern and Central Europe. At the end of the First World War, the League of Nations established the International Labor Organization (ILO), which was responsible for improving working conditions throughout the world's ongoing industrialization and for promoting workers' rights (Akehurst, 1987, p. 76).

Why would a country want to monitor human rights violations in other states? A number of reasons have been suggested. Perhaps a country genuinely cares about the welfare of others. During the late 1990s and early 2000s, for example, the United Kingdom's Prime Minister Tony Blair and Robin Cook, the Foreign Secretary, articulated an "ethical foreign policy" which justified military engagement in Kosovo. It was also used by Blair, against Cook's wishes, in connection with the UK's involvement in Iraq. Blair and his Labour party used the "Hussein killed his own people" argument.

Alternatively, a state may worry about the economic climate for doing business in another country. It may not want to damage its reputation by conducting business with a particular country. For example, during the 1980s, it was discovered that US actress Kathy Lee Gifford, who co-hosted a popular television morning show with Regis Philbin, was promoting a clothing line manufactured in a lesser developed country, where workers' conditions and pay were akin to sweatshops. Needless to say, a country may criticize another for human rights abuses but, for economic benefit, still trades with them (for example, the US re PRC, or Britain re Libya, or US re Israel). In most cases, however, countries often sidestep the issue. They don't criticize, but tend to justify and defend the actions of their trading partner. For example, many scholars and activists have pointed out that Israel frequently cites human rights abuses in the Middle East states and hopes that it distracts attention away from itself. Furthermore, countries might worry about a refugee or immigrant problem in their own country that might be caused by the exodus of individuals from the states where abuse is taking place.

Additionally states that monitor the human rights violations of other countries may use this practice as a form of public relations in the world arena, a way to gain favorable exposure for their work. Moreover, the monitoring may serve as a rationale for invasion. And finally, it may be a way of nonviolent payback in the court of world opinion.

Country-level departments

Attempts at safeguarding human rights have occurred primarily at four levels: national, regional, international, and nongovernmental. At the national level, states monitor civil rights abuses through such governmental bodies as federal, provincial, or state civil rights commissions. Many countries' constitutions contain statements on human rights, and commissions have been created to investigate alleged abuses, although states often cannot and do not monitor human rights abuses that they themselves have generated (see, for example, Hurwitz, 1995, p. 284). Some states delegate the monitoring of human rights abuses to their State Department or Ministry of External or Foreign Affairs. The US State Department, for example, investigates and publicizes human rights violators. And during treaty negotiations, trade and official missions make official visits to countries where human rights violations may become an issue.

Regional efforts

Gaining widespread agreement on human rights violations and solutions is difficult. For example, because of diverse ideologies and interests, and a general lack of trust, making human rights agreements are difficult in the context of the UN. Regional organizations also contribute to the protection of human rights, most notably the Council of Europe, which has existed since 1950 (Bennett, 1991, p. 374; Hurwitz, 1995). Regional levels of agreement, however, have proven easier to obtain when greater amounts of trust exist among participating states and where common values and interests are shared regionally (Akehurst, 1987, pp. 78-9).

The Council of Europe, for example, investigates complaints and works toward conciliatory solutions to disputes. If that proves unsuccessful, the case is referred to the Committee of Ministers, which may rule that the violating state must rectify the abuses. In extreme cases, expulsion from the organization may occur (Akehurst, 1987, p. 80).

In Europe, the Helsinki Accords of 1975, which was the culmination of the Conference on Security and Cooperation in Europe, provided another gain in regional efforts at controlling human rights abuses. Although not a treaty and lacking adequate mechanisms for enforcement, the Accords include respect for human rights and fundamental freedoms, "including freedom of thought, conscience, religion, or belief" (Bennett, 1991, p. 375).

The atrocities of mass murder and concentration camps as official state policy during the Second World War provided the impetus for the universalization and internationalization of human rights (Bennett, 1991, p. 372). The UN Charter, declaring the promotion of human rights, was "the watershed document that marked the beginning of ... expansion of human rights as an appropriate area for international concern" (Bennett, 1991, p. 372).

International bodies

Undoubtedly, the founding of the UN (1945) was a pivotal event. Its "Charter pledges on human rights were circumscribed; the duty was to promote human rights, not to guarantee them as a matter of law for all citizens" (Robertson, 2000, p. 26). The most important (and controversial) document has been the UN Declaration on Human Rights. Although each of the statements contained in this document varies, collectively they support the ideal of inalienable rights and freedoms that supersede policies and practices of specific states and governments (Hagan, 1990, p. 423). Article 55 of the UN Charter mandates that the UN shall promote "universal respect for, and observance of, human rights and fundamental freedoms for all without distinction as to race, sex, language or religion" (Akehurst, 1987, p. 76). Buttressing the language of this article, UN members pledged to act independently and cooperatively for the promotion of human rights. Even though gains have been made, the Charter's language undoubtedly leaves some discretion to states about fulfilling their obligations, and in some countries, few human rights advances have occurred (Akehurst, 1987, p. 76). Regardless, the UN General Assembly and Trusteeship Council are obligated to promote human rights, and through the Economic and Social Council, the rights of women and minorities in particular have been addressed, although, as with most attempts at promoting human rights, with mixed results (Bennett, 1991, p. 373).

The Universal Declaration of Human Rights, a resolution passed by the UN General Assembly on December 10, 1948, provides first for civil and political rights and second for economic, social, and cultural rights, including "the right to social security, to full employment and fair conditions of work, to an adequate standard of living, to education and to participation in the cultural life of the community" (Akehurst, 1987, pp. 77-8).

Although General Assembly resolutions are legally nonbinding, the Declaration of Human Rights has had a major impact on human rights standards worldwide. Today it is widely known and serves in advancing a "common standard or conduct for the protection and expansion of individual rights" (Bennett, 1991, p. 373). Furthermore, the Declaration has been cited in various court opinions.

> [It] has been partially incorporated into at least forty-five national constitutional documents (including the [former] Soviet and Chinese), has influenced national legislation, has been referred to in international treaties, and is constantly alluded to in the United Nations debates and documents. It may be reasonably argued that the Universal Declaration, through this usage and as an explication of Charter purposes and obligations, has progressively attained the status of international law. (Bennett, 1991, p. 373)

Immediately after its adoption, a movement was initiated to rewrite the Declaration into treaties or conventions that would bind those states subscribing to the UN Declaration of Human Rights. Even though many differences emerged across the years of effort, finally, on December 16, 1966, after 12 years of discussion, the UN completed the drafting of two treaties designed to transform the principles of the Universal Declaration of Human Rights into binding and detailed rules of law: the International Covenant on Civil and Political Rights and the International Covenant on Economic, Social and Cultural Rights (Akehurst, 1987, p. 81; Bennett, 1991).

The Covenants became effective in 1976 (Akehurst, 1987). Since that time, the Covenants on Human Rights have been extended to more specialized treaties on various aspects of rights, including protecting women's rights and refugees' status, and denouncing slavery, forced labor, torture, South Africa's apartheid, and discrimination in employment and education (Bennett, 1991, p. 374).

Despite the establishing and signing of numerous treaties, conventions, and declarations on human rights, not one individual was convicted of abuses until 1977. This is not because there were not numerous examples of human rights violations taking place during this time period. Essentially, "the Human Rights Commission remained tight-lipped about breaches of the Universal Declaration, or the Genocide and Geneva Conventions, by any government that was a member of the UN" (Robertson, 2000, pp. 39-40), especially about abuses committed by the CIA or the Soviet Union. One of the setbacks has traditionally been that some political leaders invoke the problems connected with insensitivity to local customs, Western imperialism, and cultural relativism as reasons for inaction. In 1975, because of Pinochet's regime, the UN signed the Declaration Against Torture (Robertson, 2000, Chapter 2).

Beyond these public national, regional, and international agencies, private groups have also been active in promoting and safeguarding human rights. Indeed, the UN Commission on Human Rights sessions typically include the participation of several INGOs in the proceedings (Bennett, 1991, p. 375). Representatives of these private organizations not only attend the meetings, but frequently "invoke their privilege of addressing the sessions on such subjects as apartheid in South Africa, violations of human rights in Israeli-occupied territories, the use of torture in several countries, or the problem of missing persons in Latin American states" (Bennett, 1991, p. 376). Among these private participants, the most respected, but also one of the most vilified by the regimes accused of gross human rights violations, is Amnesty International and Human Rights.

Although it is difficult to identify human rights violations in advanced industrialized democracies (Ross, 2000b), several well-publicized examples have taken place. During the Cold War, in the US in particular, several "mind control" experiments were sponsored by prominent state criminogenic agencies involving unsuspecting individuals, both citizens and employees of various agencies.

> Using code names such as Bluebird, Artichoke, and MKULTRA, the CIA, FBI, and military in the 1950s experimented with various behavioral control devices and interrogation techniques including ... drugs, polygraphs, hypnosis, shock therapy, surgery, and radiation. This involved secret experiments on unknowing citizens and, when harm took place, a cover-up. (Hagan, 1997, p. 36)

These tests were not restricted to the US:

> A Canadian teenager seeking medical treatment for an arthritic leg
> was subjected to LSD, electroshock therapy, and forced to listen to
> hours of taped messages ... as part of a series of bizarre experiments
> financed by the CIA and conducted by a former president of the
> American Psychiatric Association. Over 100 Canadians from 1957 to
> 1961 were unknowing guinea pigs, causing them much psychiatric
> harm. (Hagan, 1997, p. 36)

Starting in the mid-1940s, various federal departments involved in nuclear research "conducted experiments on US citizens, including injecting them with plutonium, radium, and uranium" (Hagan, 1997, p. 360). These findings were revealed in a 1986 House Energy and Commerce Subcommittee hearing, documented that this practice continued for a 30-year period (Kauzlarich and Kramer, 1998).

Nongovernmental organizations that protect human rights

There are a number of NGOs that monitor and campaign on behalf of human rights. During the past three decades, grassroots progressive organizations, activists, and progressive-minded lawyers have taken up the cause of human rights. Two prominent NGOs (in danger of becoming over-bureaucratized and distant from their membership and constituency have worked in this area over the years: Amnesty International and Human Rights Watch.

Amnesty International

Amnesty International "is a worldwide campaigning movement that works to promote all the human rights enshrined in the Universal Declaration of Human Rights and other international standards".[2] Originally established in 1960 in London, the organization slowly expanded until it became a worldwide entity. AI's initial focus was on "prisoners of conscience," those incarcerated for their political beliefs. Later, Amnesty International sent observers to countries where political detainees were being tried for their political offenses. In particular, Amnesty International "campaigns to free all prisoners of conscience; ensure fair and prompt trials for political prisoners; abolish the death penalty, torture and other cruel treatment of prisoners; end political killings and 'disappearances'; and oppose human rights abuses by opposition groups" (www.amnesty.org).

Amnesty International "has around a million members and supporters in 162 countries and territories. Activities range from public demonstrations to letter-writing, from human rights education to fund-raising concerts, from individual appeals on a particular case to global campaigns on a particular issue" (www.amnesty.org). The backbone of Amnesty International's lobbying efforts are letter-writing campaigns to highly placed officials in the countries where detainees are being held. Amnesty International also issues annual reports on the state of human rights throughout the world.

During the 1980s, Amnesty International groups met once a month at universities and places of worship. Each group adopted a "prisoner of conscience" (an individual who was incarcerated because of his or her political beliefs and/or sexual preference) and initiated a massive, focused letter-writing campaign. The goal was that a dictator, after receiving bags of mail from average citizens, would be motivated by guilt or negative international publicity to eventually release the imprisoned individual.

Amnesty International "is impartial and independent of any government, political persuasion or religious creed. Amnesty International is financed largely by subscriptions and donations from its worldwide membership" (www.amnesty. org). The organization has earned the respect of many international bodies and now has what is called consultative status at many world bodies (for example, the UN, UNESCO, etc.). It even won the Nobel Peace Prize in 1977.

Human Rights Watch

Human Rights Watch is dedicated "to protecting the human rights of people around the world." The organization works "with victims and activists to prevent discrimination, to uphold political freedom, to protect people from inhumane conduct in wartime, and to bring offenders to justice." Human Rights Watch "investigate[s] and expose[s] human rights violations and hold[s] abusers accountable." Members "challenge governments and those who hold power to end abusive practices and respect international human rights law" (all quotes in this paragraph are taken from www.hrw.org/about/about.html).

Originally founded in 1978 as Human Rights Watch/Helsinki, in response to a call for support from embattled local protest groups in Moscow, Warsaw, and Prague, it

> … had been set up to monitor compliance with the human rights provisions of the landmark Helsinki accords. A few years later, when the Reagan administration argued that human rights abuses by right-wing 'authoritarian' governments were more tolerable than those of left-wing 'totalitarian' governments, HRW formed Americas Watch … to counter this double standard.[3]

By 1987, the organization had "honed a powerful set of techniques – painstaking documentation of abuses and hard-hitting advocacy in the press and with governments – and put them to use all over the world as Human Rights Watch." Currently, Human Rights Watch is "the largest US-based human rights organization."

"Through its reports and advocacy efforts, Human Rights Watch works to stop abuses." In order to accomplish its mission, Human Rights Watch's "staff of over 100 regional experts, lawyers and linguists helps explain why abuses break out and – most important – what must be done to stop them." Human Rights Watch seeks to damage their "reputation and legitimacy if they violate the rights of their people."[4]

Human Rights Watch "seek[s] to curb abuses regardless of whether the victims are well-known political activists or those of lesser visibility such as factory workers, peasants, farmers, undocumented migrants, women forced into prostitution, street children, or domestic workers." The organization "also address[es] such war-related abuses as indiscriminate shelling or the use of rape or starvation as weapons of war – no matter which side in a conflict is responsible."[5]

Human Rights Watch "also presses for withdrawal of military, economic and diplomatic support from governments that are regularly abusive." It:

> ... conduct[s] frequent investigations in countries where abuses take place. In a number of hot spots, [it] maintains offices to gather information on an ongoing basis ... interview victims and witnesses of human rights abuse ... meet with government officials, opposition leaders, local human rights groups, church officials, labor leaders, journalists, lawyers, relief groups, doctors, and others with reliable first-hand information on the current human rights situation. If a country refuses to allow us to enter, ... we find other ways of obtaining information to compile as complete and accurate a picture as we can. (www.hrw.org/about/info/qna.html)

Civil liberties organizations

Finally, almost every advanced industrialized democracy has a major civil liberties organization. In the context of this chapter, the most important organizations are the American Civil Liberties Union, the Canadian Civil Liberties Association, and the National Association of Civil Liberties in the United Kingdom.

Undoubtedly, there are problems with these organizations. For example, the longer an organization is in existence, the more distant the leadership gets from its membership and the more bureaucratic it becomes.

War crime

"International law has sought to regulate wars in two ways: initially, by restricting the justifications for waging them, and (when that failed) by prescribing rules for conducting them humanely" (Robertson, 2000, p. 167). Unfortunately, these laws contain numerous contradictions and are selective because some parties benefit from them while others do not, especially in the context of "low intensity civil war or internecine struggle in which one state seeks to suppress rebel militias or armed dissidents" (Robertson, 2000, p. 168).

After the Second World War, both high-ranking Nazi (German) and Japanese commanders were subjected to war crimes trials. Arguably, the most famous of these were the Nuremberg trials held between 1945 and 1949.

Since 1993, the UN International Criminal Tribunal for the former Yugoslavia has been investigating war crimes in connection with the Srebrenica massacre in Kosovo. Beginning in 1994, a similar process, conducted by the International Criminal Tribunal for Rwanda, addressed the abuses and genocide in Rwanda.

Although the issue of war crimes affects most advanced industrialized countries because they take responsibility for conducting the affairs and for marshaling the resources in order for the tribunals to take place, rarely have these countries been charged with similar kinds of offenses.

Changes in human rights practice

During the 1970s, disappearances, torture, and death squads operated in several South American countries (Berman and Clarke, 1982). Unfortunately, many of the perpetrators (that is, torturers, killers, and their supervisors) were granted amnesties or pardons. A similar fate can be observed in the so-called Truth Commissions, which have taken place in a handful of countries (Robertson, 2000, Chapter 8). Alternatively, formerly war torn countries have increasingly relied on the International Court of Justice in The Hague to seek justice against perpetrators of human rights violations.

Truth Commissions

Because of the genocides in Yugoslavia, the Hague Tribunal was established to prosecute those charged with war crimes:"many argued it would demonstrate how war crimes were committed only by a handful of evil individuals, thus relieving their countrymen from the stigma of 'collective responsibility' for crimes against humanity" (Robertson, 2000, p. 417). In the context of Yugoslavia and the genocide against the Croatians, the UN Security Council was and is practically ineffectual in matters of international human rights. The North Atlantic Treaty Organization (NATO) also had considerable difficulties in forcing the surrender of Milosevic and highly-placed Serbian generals. Courts are severely circumscribed in what they can do in the matter of human rights violations. "There is no court as yet to stop a state which murders and extirpates its own people; for them, if the Security Council fails to reach superpower agreement, the only salvation can come through other states exercising the right of humanitarian intervention" (Robertson, 2000, p. 420).

Another recent example of human rights violations was provided by the case of East Timor, which "was important because an invasion force was mustered which was prepared not only to kill but to be killed in the cause of human rights" (Robertson, 2000, p. 425). Despite its intent, this force was not allowed entrance until after countless East Timorese were slaughtered by the Indonesian army and the militias it backed. The problem of East Timor demonstrates the futility of the

International Court of Justice. In 1975, the case came before the Court, which reviewed the atrocities that had occurred because of the Indonesian referendum on independence. The UN failed in its oversight of East Timor, but acted properly both before and after the atrocities were under way (Robertson, 2000).

International Court of Justice

In 2001, the British government attempted to deport former Chilean dictator Augusto Pinochet from Chile to Spain, and there were rumblings among the Western leftist community over the possibility of arresting and trying Henry Kissinger, former US Secretary of State under President Richard Nixon, as a war criminal (see, for example, Hitchens, 2001). During the summer of 2001, Slobodan Milosevic, the former President of Yugoslavia, was finally handed over by Serbian authorities to the International Court of Justice.

Summary

Safeguarding and promoting human rights create a paradox of sorts. On the one hand, lessons from history inform us that the need to protect human rights is apparent. On the other hand, the state – that entity with the power, force, and law to protect human rights – is usually the perpetrator or silent partner in infringements on those rights. Furthermore, countries are protective of their own sovereignty, which complicates matters because guaranteeing a protection of human rights has traditionally fallen solely to domestic jurisdictions.

International efforts are likely perceived as external threats or even revolutionary, and typically are resisted by managers and agents of sovereign states. "The international community and regional organizations are ill-equipped to enforce uniform standards of human rights on individual countries. Their methods fall short of compulsion and involve primarily persuasion, publicity, and the pressure of public opinion" (Bennett, 1991, p. 379). States accused of violating human rights often respond by ignoring the charges or by blaming their accusers of human rights atrocities in their own countries. And as long as differences persist in basic values, definitions, and value systems, the adoption of universally accepted standards of human rights will remain difficult to achieve and implement.

Notes

[1] This discussion builds on Ross (2007).

[2] This information is taken from the Amnesty International website, but no longer exists.

[3] This information was retrieved from www.hrw.com in 1992.

[4] See note 3.

[5] See note 3.

TEN

State violence

Introduction[1]

State violence, as a form of political crime, generally consists of illegal, physically harmful actions committed by a country's coercive organizations (that is, the police, national security agencies, and the military) against individuals and groups.[2] Regardless of the political system, victims of state violence generally are actual or suspected criminals, political opponents (dissidents) of the government or regime in power (for example, activists, trade unionists, and peasants), members of various racial, ethnic or religious groups, or immigrants. Such violence can be domestic or foreign in nature (for example, against another country, especially during war).[3] Here, however, our discussion is limited to what takes place in the US, Canada, and the UK.

Since the 1960s, numerous well-publicized incidents of state violence have occurred in Anglo-American democracies. During the 1960s, student protests against US involvement in Vietnam, and later Cambodia and Laos, led in many instances to police overreaction. The police beating of African-American motorist Rodney King in Los Angeles (1991), the FBI shooting of white supremacist Randy Weaver's wife and child (1992) in Idaho, and the ATF/FBI standoff and siege in Waco, Texas, against David Koresh and his followers (1993) were examples of how excessive state violence in the US could violate the civil rights of individuals and their loved ones, and could call into question governmental use of force in confrontations with citizens.

Nine principal interrelated actions are subsumed under the category of state violence: disappearances or kidnappings, death squad activity, torture, deaths in custody, police violence or excessive force, police riots, police use of deadly force, terrorism, and genocide. Even though state violence has occurred in all types of political systems and has been perpetrated by all kinds of state coercive organizations, the relative frequency of each subtype varies across political systems. For example, and directly germane to this discussion, disappearances/kidnappings, death squad activity, genocide, and state terrorism rarely occur within advanced industrialized democracies. They are more likely to be present in less developed countries with authoritarian or totalitarian leadership. In short, richer democratic countries typically find nonviolent ways to sanction or harass their dissidents, but poorer authoritarian countries commit murder because they cannot afford internment, to deter citizens, or because of the expedience of this action.

When state violence becomes public, it often is interpreted, and sometimes appropriately labeled, as a human rights violation (see Chapter Nine, this volume).

Thus, much of the literature, theory, and controls that are applicable to human rights are pertinent to the problem of state violence.

Our knowledge of state violence is limited. Much information about this type of crime is not public, thus few people ever learn about these actions. Data tend to be unreliable and are collected in an unsystematic fashion. This minimizes our ability to take appropriate actions to prevent, minimize, or stop this behavior. In fact, it appears as if the media's focus is usually on oppositional, rather than state, violence as a form of political crime.

Most information about state violence comes from eyewitnesses or victims of this political illegality. Their stories may be or may appear exaggerated and biased because of the physical or psychological trauma they have experienced or due to their own political agendas. The appearance of bias may also result from media sensationalism.

How widespread is the problem?

Incidents of state violence have been exposed and documented in popular and alternative media accounts, governmental commission reports, coroners' inquests, autopsy reports, academic treatments, and the reports of nongovernmental bodies (for example, international monitoring agencies like Amnesty International and Human Rights Watch).

Four principal organizations produce relevant data on state violence: Amnesty International, Freedom House, Human Rights Watch, and the US Department of State. Other organizations, such as Freedom Now, have made important contributions by examining "prisoners of conscience" (www.freedom-now. org). Although all of these sources report on a variety of state violence activities, each suffers from a number of problems, including access to data, a lack of comprehensiveness due to the unsystematic use of different time periods, data that are difficult to disaggregate by year, the complexities tied to systematically comparing countries, and decisions that often are guided by organizational imperatives and ideological constraints that depart from the strict dissemination of information on state violence (Mitchell et al., 1986). In order to better comprehend this type of political crime, the definitions, history, and some causes of torture, deaths in custody, police riots, police use of deadly force, and genocide are reviewed.

Evidence concerning the incidence of violence at the hands of state employees is mixed. Because of its controversial and hidden nature, it is impossible to determine with any degree of reliability the amount, types, and frequency of state violence in any jurisdiction.

One of the most recent attempts to address this shortcoming in connection with police use of excessive force is Section 210402 of the Violent Crime Control and Law Enforcement Act 1994 that states, "The Attorney General shall, through appropriate means, acquire data about the use of excessive force by law enforcement officers." The wording of this act reflects Congress and the

Attorney General's concern about allegations of police brutality and the use of excessive force.

Thus, in general, events that come to public attention are available for intense scrutiny. Some recent data bears directly on this subject. According to the relatively recent report on *Contacts between police and the public, 2005*, which was produced and published by the Bureau of Justice Statistics of the US Department of Justice:

> … an estimated 707,520 persons age 16 or older had force used against them during their most recent contact with the police in 2005.[...] This estimate is about 1.6% of the 43.5 million people reporting face-to-face police contact during 2005. The percentage of contacts involving police use of force was relatively unchanged from 2002 to 2005. (Durose et al., 2007, p. 7)

If we are to believe this self-reported statistic, at least in recent history and contrary to popular belief, very few people in the US are recorded as victims of police violence. But this is not to say that there have not been periods of considerable police use of excessive force. Moreover, when we deconstruct what police violence really signifies, the comparison between actual and perceived levels of police violence becomes extremely important.

Different types of state violence

Numerous types of state violence occur. However, ten distinct actions are discussed most frequently in scholarly literature: genocide, law enforcement SWAT teams, police vehicle chases/pursuits, dog bites, death squad activity, torture, deaths in custody, police riots, correctional office violence, and police use of deadly force. The following are brief reviews of these actions.

Genocide

Genocide is the systematic killing of an ethnic, racial, religious, or cultural group (Kuper, 1985). Historically, one of the most salient genocides was that of the Holocaust:

> At its peak, Nazi Germany and its allies occupied virtually all of Europe, except for Britain and part of Russia. Under its fanatical policies of racial purity, Germany rounded up and exterminated six million Jews and millions of others, including homosexuals, Gypsies, Communists, and others. These mass murders, now known as the Holocaust, along with the sheer scale of war unleashed by Nazi aggression, are considered among the greatest crimes against humanity in history. Responsible

> German officers faced justice in the Nuremberg Tribunal after the war. (Goldstein, 1996, p. 39)

This famous trial "established that participants can be held accountable for war crimes they commit. German officers defended their actions as 'just following orders' but this justification was rejected; the officers were punished, some executed for their war crimes" (Goldstein, 1996, p. 299). The trials led to the establishment of genocide and torture conventions, and the placement of human rights issues within international jurisdiction. Nevertheless "the pledges of world leaders after that experience to 'never again' allow genocide ... have been found wanting as genocide recurred in the post-Cold War era in Bosnia and Rwanda" (Goldstein, 1996, p. 39). Similar genocides have occurred throughout more recent human history, including the recent troubles in Indonesia and Kosovo (Fein, 1993). However, in the context of advanced industrialized countries and during the period of investigation, genocides, in the strictest use of the term, have not occurred.[4]

Box 10.1: *The Killing Fields* (1984)

Directed by Roland Joffé, and based on real life events, this movie begins in 1973 when *New York Times* reporter Sidney Schanberg arrived in Phnom Penn, Cambodia. He eventually meets Dith Pran who acts as Schanberg's interpreter. During this time a civil war, similar to the one occurring in Vietnam, is taking place in Cambodia between the communist led Khmer Rouge and the South (that is the Cambodian National Army). Despite the United States militarily supporting the south, the Khmer Rouge are making significant gains. Schanberg hears about the bombing of a city by a US B52 bomber that allegedly strayed for Vietnamese airspace. He is initially incensed by the amount of deaths, injuries and destruction and later by the activities of the international press corps who seem to be easily cowed by the American. The story begins again in 1975 when the communists are taking over Phnom Phen. Schanberg manages to get Pran's family a US passport, but has difficulties securing one for Pran. Pran, who is branded as an intellectual, is eventually arrested by the Khmer Rouge and taken to into a forced labor camp. He escapes and during his journey passes through "the killing fields," one of several locations where Cambodians were executed. Schanberg leaves Cambodia and lobbies different humanitarian organizations in order to detect and secure the release of Pran. Pran eventually escapes to a Red Cross camp located just over the border in Thailand.

Law enforcement SWAT teams

Over the past three decades, police departments in most advanced industrialized democracies have developed specialized teams of police officers who respond to crisis events. Known as Special Weapons and Tactical (SWAT) teams or units, they have helped in complex negotiations with kidnappers and hostage takers (particularly in the context of bank robberies). In recent times, SWAT teams have come under intense scrutiny after a series of incidents during which innocent people were injured or killed.

Police vehicle chases/pursuits

For better or for worse, the police are inextricably linked to chasing motorists suspected of moving violations (i.e., speeding, running a stop sign or red light, etc.), individuals who fail to yield to commands to pull over while driving, and people who the police believe to have committed a crime. In many instances, the suspects, innocent civilians, and sometimes the officers are injured or killed, and the extent of the property damage can be high (Alpert and Fridell, 1992; Alpert et al., 2000).

> The National Law Enforcement and Corrections Technology Center reports that more than 70 percent of pursuits end with the successful apprehension of suspects, yet collisions occur in 32 percent of pursuits, property damage occurs in 20 percent, personal injury in 13 percent, and fatalities in 1.2 percent.[...] Police departments have been under increasing pressure to control officers' discretion in hot pursuits.[...] PERF [Police Executive Research Foundation] found that 91 percent of departments have a written policy governing pursuits, and nearly half have modified their policy within the last two years. (White, 2007, p. 251)

Dog bites

A number of police departments have used dogs in their departments, not simply for search and rescue, but also to chase and intimidate suspects. Not only have suspects been bitten by dogs, but so have officers. "During a foot chase, it is not uncommon for ... officers to be bitten if they do not heed the handler's instructions to stay behind him or her" (White, 2007, p. 250). In some jurisdictions (for example, Prince George's County, Maryland, during the 1990s), the police came under intense security because of their use of dogs during chase and arrest situations involving African-American males.

Death squad activity

The activities and methods of death squads (also known as hit squads), particularly assassinations, have been documented in popular and alternative media accounts, in the reports of international monitoring agencies, and in various academic publications. These types of incidents are forms of state violence and crime, and they fall within an array of other types of violence, such as kidnapping, rape, and torture, all of which might result in murder as a final act. These actions occur primarily in less developed countries, at various levels of the police hierarchy, and in both rural and urban locales. Victims are generally actual and suspected criminals and political opponents (including activists, trades union leaders and members, and peasants) to the regime in power.

In general, death squad activity consists of military, paramilitary, and irregular units engaging in violent acts against citizens to deter them from lending support to opposition groups. Death squad violence exemplifies is intended to induce compliance through fear. It may be employed reactively or proactively. The most critical distinguishing feature of this kind of violence is that it is usually sanctioned by the governmental regime in power, either explicitly through policy pronouncements or implicitly through a lack of effort to curtail such acts (Mason and Krane, 1989).

Sometimes, the offenders are police officers; many times, they are vigilantes who are led, trained, or directed by the law enforcement or the military. According to Mason and Krane (1989), "Death squads are most prevalent in societies where an authoritarian alliance between the military and powerful economic elite is faced with a serious challenge to its legitimacy and authority" (p. 178).

Jakubs (1977) suggests four reasons, albeit at the organizational level, to explain the death squads in Brazil: they reflect "a conscious resolution on the part of the police delegates to take justice into their own hands, to do away with as many common criminals as possible"; "revenge"; "attempts to hide the extent to which the Brazilian police are involved in illegal drug traffic"; and "the expansion of the boundaries of public and official tolerance for police violence in times of acute political tension and social disruption" (pp. 100–101). The extent to which these findings may be generalizable beyond the Brazilian context is uncertain (for example, Argentina during the so-called Dirty War (1976-83), and Chile during the Pinochet regime (1973-90)).

Torture

Over the past decade, particularly because of the US detention of terrorist suspects in Guantanamo Bay, Cuba, what counts as torture has been heavily discussed and debated. Nevertheless, for purposes of simplicity, torture can be defined as any act by which severe pain or suffering, whether physical or mental, is intentionally inflicted by or at the instigation of a public official on a person for purposes of obtaining information or a confession, to inflict punishment for an act or a suspected act, or to create intimidation.

Torture involves such physical techniques as beatings, burnings, dry submarining,[5] water boarding, and electroshock. Authorities may use torture as both a specific and a general deterrent. Furthermore, torture is used as "punishment for undetermined guilt," to "extract money from the victim or because somebody has given the police money to thrash him/her," and as revenge (Balagopal, 1986, p. 2029). Torture is used to gain information, as retaliation, and intimidation. It assumes "particularly vicious forms when the suspect has done injury to the police themselves" (Balagopal, 1986, p. 2029). The scholarly literature on torture has ascertained three dominant causes (albeit at the individual level): psychoanalytic processes (Daraki-Mallet, 1976), obedience to authority (Miligram, 1974, 1977), and finally, obedience to the authority of violence (Haritos-Fatouros, 1988).

The literature on torture is problematic because it is difficult to distinguish which government agencies are responsible and to generalize from one situation of torture to another; dominant causal explanations have focused on individuals and avoided structural issues. There is a paucity of reliable data because many reports of torture are based on victim and witness accounts of questionable reliability. Several prominent cases of torture have come to the public's attention during the contemporary period, and one major example from an advanced industrialized country is provided by the British military's treatment of real or alleged members of the IRA (Hurwitz, 1995; Ross, 2000b).

Deaths in custody

Death in custody involves a person who has been detained by the criminal justice system, immigration, or the military and who is subsequently killed because of excessive violence by police/military/correctional officers or by inmates. This kind of death may also involve a failure to provide adequate or proper medical care. This is especially true if the detained individual experiences a medical problem (for example, a heart attack or an epileptic seizure), and the criminal justice agency neglects to transport the individual to the appropriate hospital or to allow medical personnel to provide treatment. Numerous incidents of death sin custody have occurred in Australia (primarily Aboriginal deaths in custody), Canada (First Nations people), Northern Ireland (members of the Irish Republican Army), and England (African-Caribbeans during 1986-2006).

The deaths of citizens while in custody have been exposed in popular and alternative media accounts, governmental commission reports, coroners' inquests, autopsy reports, nongovernmental reports, and academic research. Although deaths in custody may be the result of suicide (for example, hanging), they may also be caused by a violent struggle between a citizen and a police officer before arrest, conflict with law enforcement officers during an arrest and while in custody, a struggle with other prisoners or correctional officers, or torture by police officers or other criminal justice officials. Death in custody occurs in all types of political systems, at different jurisdictional levels of government agencies, and in both large and small cities.

Investigations of deaths in custody are complicated by the state officials' common but questionable explanation that the victim(s) died because of "misadventure" or had committed suicide; these claims disregard the state's obligation to secure the safety and security of an individual's life while in custody (see, for example, Home Affairs Committee, 1980; Scraton and Chadwick, 1985; Hazelhurst, 1991). Balagopal (1986, p. 2028) suggests a mono-causal explanation that police torture is used arbitrarily and results in fatalities, not because a rational use of torture leads to serious and even fatal excesses, but because the normal methods and intensity of torture naturally and necessarily lead to death in a given combination of circumstances: "the lock-up is exceptionally insanitary [sic], the victim is of weak bodily health, does not get adequate food while in lock-up, is dispirited and demoralized by a false or morally unjust accusation, is deprived of proper medical attention, etc" (p. 2028).

Official reports of deaths in custody are based on autopsy evidence and commissions of inquiry, whose reliability is often debatable. The medical examiners gather their evidence in highly politicized environments, usually with the threat of a lawsuit motivating the respective parties. Moreover, explanations rely on many of the same factors as torture and do not explore a variety of other possible causes. In the contemporary period, there has been an overabundance of deaths in custody of Aboriginal peoples in Australia and of native peoples in the US and Canada (Hazelhurst, 1991; Correctional Services of Canada, 1992). Quite often the official ruling is "Death by Misadventure," which places the responsibility on the individual or victim who engaged in risky behavior, rather than the state's duty to protect those who are under its control.

Police riots

Police riots involve the use of excessive violence, primarily by riot squads, in response to public demonstrations, protests, and labor strikes. They take place in both large and small cities (Hahn and Feagin, 1970; Marx, 1970a, 1970b; Stark, 1972; Reiner, 1980). Victims of police riots have traditionally been students, political activists, and striking workers.

Despite the volume of reports and studies, researchers of police riots have not specified causes for their commission beyond the following issues: lower-ranking police following the orders of superiors; poor training; and the stress experienced by officers in tense situations. Mass behavior and collective action explanations have rarely been used in this context.

During the 1960s and 1970s in the US, for example, several police riots occurred as responses to student demonstrations against the Vietnam War and to civil rights protests. Others were reactions to public protests against police brutality. These were mainly centered in large cities, like New York, Chicago, and Los Angeles (Richards and Avey, 2000; Ross, 2000b). In Canada (Ross, 1995b), police riots are rare events. The majority of incidents have surrounded large-scale protests in which the police were deployed and then overreacted. Many police riots have been the subjects of government inquiries/royal commissions.

Since the early 1960s, the UK has experienced many police–citizen confrontations, some of which resulted in considerable worldwide attention. In cases where police violence in the UK has been the focus of study, they are usually addressed in the context of riots, strikes, and deaths in custody. For example, the literature commonly covers the police role in the 1980s 'race' riots (see, for example, Fowler, 1979; Cowell and Young, 1982; Kettle and Hodges, 1982; Benyon, 1984), the 1984 miners' strike (see, for example, Coulter et al., 1984; Fine and

Millar, 1985), other labor disputes (see, for example, Geary, 1985; Scraton, 1985), and deaths in custody (see, for example, Scraton and Chadwick, 1985).

Research aimed at determining explanations for police violence as a form of political crime is hampered by limited data. Furthermore, most research is descriptive and seems not to have progressed beyond case study analyses. Anecdotal evidence suggests that at least in the US, police riots are no longer as frequent as they were during the 1960s.

Correctional officer violence

Prison staff members periodically use physical violence, including less than lethal force (for example, pepper spray and Taser guns) against convicts (Pratt et al., 1999). Correctional officers are allowed by law to use force when life and property are in peril. Additionally, most correctional systems require their officers to be trained in and to follow the "continuum of force" model from which they are taught that there is a range of appropriate responses to inmates who are uncooperative and disobedient, including physical presence, verbal commands, and show of force by having several officers present. This means that violence should be the last resort rather the method of first choice.

When officers do beat convicts, it is often out of retaliation, because the latter have attacked officers or have instigated or participated in work strikes, riots, or escape attempts. Occasionally, correctional officers have been accused and convicted of torture (Kerness and Ehehosi, 2001). Also, if staff violence occurs, then the violence is usually done discretely in ways to minimize witnesses. It often takes place when the correctional offices have power in numbers. In the Federal Bureau of Prisons (FBOP), for example, each institution has a Special Operations Response Team (SORT) (pejoratively referred to by inmates as the goon squad or Ninja Turtles). This group typically consists of five officers and one lieutenant. A SORT is mobilized when inmates refuse to get out of their cells. This is typically called a cell extraction. The most important question with respect to violence by correctional officers is: how frequently is it used, and is it done in an indiscriminate manner? Unfortunately, empirical research on this issue does not exist.

Correctional officers do not need to use violence to get convicts to follow orders, rules, procedures, and policies. They typically achieve their authority through five bases of power. The two most important types of power are categorized as legitimate and informational (see, for example, Hepburn, 1985). If inmates complain about the correctional officers or talk about their acts of deviance or crimes, they may expect some sort of retribution by a correctional officer.

Most often, correctional officers avoid using violence if they can. After all, most prisoners are in better physical condition than most correctional officers (Ross, 2008, p. 87). Additionally, there is a strong likelihood that other inmates will come to the assistance of an inmate being beaten. Moreover, beatings create so much ill will that it is often remembered for a long time. Instead, correctional officers commonly rely on threats and other nonphysical shows of power. Unlike the violence inflicted by the convicts on each other, most correctional officer violence is more subtle. If an officer dislikes an inmate, either alone or in a group, they may engage in a variety of disrespectful actions against the convict (Ross, 2008, Chapter 3).

Police use of deadly force

The majority of people in advanced industrialized countries who are killed by law enforcement officers die because of police use of deadly force. This practice refers to a situation in which a law enforcement officer kills an individual using a weapon or technique that is designed to result in death. Typically, this is done by gun, but it may also involve a baton or other blunt force instrument, choke holds, or other methods. These incidents have been discussed in popular and alternative media accounts, reports of governmental inquiries, and academic research. This focus on deadly force is directly related to the relative ease of documenting these acts. Victims of police use of deadly force are typically minorities and males. A plethora of variables and levels of analysis have been examined as plausible causes of police use of deadly force. The major finding is that a particular police department's policy on the use of deadly force is the most important determinant of the number of citizens shot and killed by the police (Fyfe, 1978, 1979; Sherman, 1980a).

Nevertheless, research on the causes of police use of deadly force has produced its share of criticisms. These studies commonly lack internal validity, and disagreements exist about the precise nature of the dependent variables used in the research process (that is, justifiable homicides versus shots fired) (Binder and Scharf, 1980; Sherman, 1980b; Fyfe, 1988; Geller, 1982; Scharf and Binder, 1983; Binder and Fridell, 1984; Fridell, 1985). Based on a review of 20 articles, Horvath (1987) concludes, "most research has been carried out only in large cities and large urban areas" and "has involved only incidents in which fatalities of citizens occurred" (p. 226). Horvath also points out that, "there are substantial methodological differences between studies making it difficult to draw meaningful comparisons or to generalize from any one group of apparently similar findings" (p. 266). Moreover, some police techniques that can cause death are rarely included in deadly force statistics (for example, choke holds, death by baton). Finally, most studies are confined to the US context.

The US is not the only country with incidents of police violence. In the UK during the late 1970s, several African-Caribbean and white individuals (for example, Blair Peach) died under questionable circumstances allegedly at the hands of the police (for example, London Metropolitan Police Special Patrol Group [SPG]). A subsequent internal police investigation, although exonerating the SPG, discovered that it had in its possession several restricted weapons.

Summary

Of the different types of state violence reviewed above, deaths in custody and police use of deadly force are the most prominent in the advanced industrialized countries. In short, police violence depends on many of the factors articulated in more general studies of police behavior, misconduct, deviance, organizational tolerance, and complaints against the police. These causes can be classified into individual, situational, organizational, community, and legal attributes. Many of these factors interact with each other to create complicated, but highly nuanced, explanations for police violence.

The bulk of work on police violence deals with its causes (see, for example, Reiss, 1968; Worden, 1995). This research can be divided into two categories: studies examining a broad range of police use of excessive force and work focusing on particular forms. Although some scholars have examined the causes of police violence in general (see, for example, Westley, 1953, 1970; Feld, 1971; Manning, 1980), most focused on single factors. Concurrently, causes for police violence are often broken down into internal and external factors (see, for example, Stark, 1972). The former includes influences such as a patrol officer's personality, attitudes and values, working environment, police culture, relationship to the courts, and professionalization (see, for example, Kania and Mackay, 1977).

The latter usually includes community structure and social polarization (see, for example, Feld, 1971). General studies have not demarcated the contribution of different influences in causing police violence. Often ignored is the fact that police violence is indirectly connected to the frequency of street stops, the level of crime in a community, the number of police deployed in a particular area, and the amount and type of arrests. In short, the greater the number of these indirect factors, the more opportunities available to the police to engage in violence.

Several individual, situational, organizational, community, and legal attributes have been posited and/or tested as causes that could lead a police officer to use violence. All said, there are several problems with the general literature dealing with the causes of police violence. Because the literature primarily focuses on the US context, it remains unknown whether the studies' conclusions can be generalized. The data are limited in scope, usually collected in the context of observational studies and are often not comparable between jurisdictions. Furthermore, the work does not examine attempts to remove the presumed causes of such political crimes.

Nevertheless, building on the previous theoretical discussions, there are organizational norms that reinforce the use of violence against certain types of individuals. People who come from certain social classes or religious, ethnic, or racial groups are often selected, and rationalizations are developed to support abuse against them. This type of behavior was disclosed in the trial of US sports figure O.J. Simpson during the testimony and scandal surrounding Mark Fuhrman, the LAPD detective who testified in the case (Barak, 1996).

In addition, there are strong structural arguments that support the idea that state coercive organizations exist to maintain the dominant political order (Ross,

1998/2009). For example, the first modern municipal police force was established due to the influence of the wealthy class of London who wanted their lives and property to be protected against "rogues." There is a long history in the United States, United Kingdom and Canada of using the police to contain labor unrest; force was employed to suppress working-class interests all the while supporting ongoing capitalist industrialization and growth (see, for example, Center for Research on Criminal Justice, 1977; Harring, 1983; Ross, 2012, Chapter 2).

Notes

[1] This chapter builds on Ross (2001).

[2] In most instances, there are three possible perpetrators of state violence: individuals possessing the force of law through their occupations as state agents and who abuse their lawful positions; organizations within the state, such as the police, the military, and national security units; and states advancing an official, yet more than likely unspoken policy of violence and repression. The relative contribution of each of these state apparatuses varies depending on the country and its political system.

[3] This discussion avoids the thorny issue of the illegal use of war that is waged in violation of the UN Charter, which states when and under what conditions a country may engage in war.

[4] Although some writers have suggested that the policies and practices directed against African Americans (Johnson and Leighton, 1999) and Native Americans (Churchill, 1997) are tantamount to genocide, this argument stretches the boundaries of what is meant by the term.

[5] Placing an individual's head under water for a short period, like in a bucket of water or in a toilet bowl.

ELEVEN

State-corporate crime

Introduction

There are three typical legal forms of business organization: sole proprietorships, partnerships, and corporations. First, a sole proprietorship is a type of business in which only one individual is the owner of that business, and if that individual is successfully sued, the plaintiff is entitled access to the owner's personal assets. Second, a partnership is a type of arrangement where more than one individual is the owner of that business, and if the partnership is successfully sued, the plaintiff is allowed access to all owners' personal assets. Third, a corporation is a type of business where numerous entities (for example, individuals or organizations) are part owners of that business (that is, typically through shares in the corporation), and if the corporation is successfully sued, the plaintiff is only entitled to the assets of the corporation. In short, what typically distinguishes these entities is their financial liability.

In an effort to better understand these arrangements, some examples are provided below. For instance, perhaps you establish a sole proprietor business through which you cut grass in the summer, rake leaves in the fall, and shovel snow in the winter. You could probably run this out of your home, if you so decided. However, one day you run over Mrs. Jones' Pekingese dog, injuring the animal badly enough to require expensive veterinarian care. Mrs. Jones sues you and is successful in court. To what sort of assets is Mrs. Jones entitled? Everything you own. In other words, she could take your beat-up pick-up truck and your house if you own one.

Let's take another scenario. Say, for example, the business is going well, and you and your brother decide to form a partnership. He donates his old snow blower and a couple of rusty old rakes lying in his shed. Once again, the same thing takes place with Mrs. Jones' dog. What kind of damages can Mrs. Jones be awarded? Everything that both you and your brother own.

Finally, your brother speaks to a guy he met in a bar, and he convinces both of you to form a corporation. Your brother and you scrape together enough cash and have one of your long-time customers who happens to run a general services law firm draw up the papers for incorporation. Again, you run over Mrs. Jones' dog, and she sues. What kinds of assets can she get? Only the assets of the corporation.

Before continuing, it might be instructive to understand why individuals, businesses, and corporations form corporations. In general, corporations are vehicles or structures created to raise large sums of money, to gain access to more favorable tax laws (that is, pay lower taxes), and to limit personal liability in case the corporation is ever sued.

Keep in mind that corporations are not as simple as often portrayed. In general, there are two basic types of corporations: public and private. Shares of the former are traded on a stock exchange and present a way for a corporation to raise money to help finance its expansion plans. Anyone with the assets can purchase stocks from a publicly traded corporation. Shares of the later type of corporation are only sold or traded through a complex process of negotiation among interested parties. Limited liability corporations differ from this arrangement, and are privately held entities that share elements of corporations and partnerships.

Before continuing, we should briefly address terminology. There is often considerable confusion between the concepts of white-collar, occupational, elite, and corporate crime. Although these categories share similarities, are generally referred to as suite crimes, and the terms specify the context in which particular types of crimes occur.

Differences between white-collar, occupational, and corporate crimes

White-collar crime is committed by individuals who are typically in management positions in businesses and corporations. Such actions involve theft, price fixing, and other business-related wrongdoing. Typically, white-collar crimes are executed without the knowledge and/or approval of other members of the corporation. It is a criminal action committed by an employee against his or her employer. It is done for direct, personal gain. This larger concept can be divided into two categories: occupational theft and fraud (Beirne and Messerschmidt, 1991, p. 173). *Occupational crimes* are also committed for direct personal gain, but *corporate crimes* are "illegal and/or socially injurious acts of intent or indifference that occur for the purpose of furthering corporate goals, and that physically and/or economically abuse individuals in the US and/or abroad. Collusion of top executives of utility corporations to fix prices is an example of corporate crime" (Beirne and Messerschmidt, 1991, p. 172). Corporate crime takes many different forms (for example, misstatement of earnings, fraud, price fixing, manufacturing unsafe products, environmental damage, etc.). At their core, corporations are important political actors, and their power is sometimes achieved through illegal practices. This could include polluting the environment by dumping chemicals into lakes and rivers or contaminating a piece of land. Corporate crime is not a new phenomenon. Some people have argued that the invention of the corporate form was actually grounded in attempts to evade taxes, government regulation, and thus to commit crimes.

Recent examples of corporate crime

Numerous types of corporate crime have occurred in the US over the years, including anti-trust cases (that is, when a corporation violates the fair practice of a trade), the manufacture of unsafe products (for example, the Pinto car design, Firestone/Ford tire problems), environmental crimes (Hooker Chemical, General

Electric, etc.), and securities fraud (Enron/Arthur Andersen). Various federal regulatory agencies, including the Securities and Exchange Commission (SEC), are required to police and monitor corporate behavior.

The Enron/Arthur Andersen scandal (2001-02) revealed America's vulnerability and susceptibility to corporate crime. Because of this scandal, many Americans lost their jobs and life savings. When the trial ended and those convicted were sent to prison, confidence in the corporate sector and in the government's ability to control corporate crime was shaken. Also during this same period, well-known corporations came forward almost daily, or it was revealed that they had misstated their earnings. As a result, the SEC announced new and potential targets for their ongoing investigations.

Although Americans have been the victims of these kinds of crimes in the past (for example, the stock market crash of 1929), current recent events may foreshadow some of the corporate crimes that may proliferate over the next decade.

Uniqueness of state-corporate crime

State-corporate crime, on the other hand, is a relatively recent concept in the ongoing understanding of white-collar, occupational, corporate, and governmental crime. It results from interactions between corporate and state policies, practices, and outcomes. Such crimes take place when organizations (in both the private and the public sectors) pursue goals that result in crime including, but not limited to, injury, disease, death, and ecosystem destruction (Kramer, Michalowski, and Kauzlarich, 2000; Tombs and Whyte, 2003; Michalowski and Kramer, 2006a).

State-corporate crimes are committed by individuals who abuse their state authority or who fail to exercise it when working with people and organizations in the private sector. Their actions and inactions, and the resulting social harms, emanate from mutually reinforcing interactions among corporate and state policies, practices, and outcomes. There are many reasons why the state becomes involved with the business community. One of the most important reasons is because the state insures competitiveness and fairness in the market. Businesses are, thus, subjected to all kinds of regulation. When an entity moves from being a sole proprietorship to a corporation, the government becomes increasingly active. In short, when the entity becomes a corporation, it in effect makes a deal with the devil. But the devil must hold up its end of the bargain.

Definitional and conceptual issues[1]

State-corporate crime first was defined as "a form of organizational misconduct that occurs at the interstices of corporations and governments" (Kramer, 1992, p. 215). These "crimes involve ... the participation of two or more organizations, at least one of which is in the civil sector and the other in the state sector" (Kramer, 1992, p. 215). Aulette and Michalowski (1993, p. 175) add,

> State-corporate crimes are illegal or socially injurious actions that result from a mutually reinforcing interaction between (1) policies and/or practices in pursuit of the goals of one or more institutions of political governance and (2) policies and/or practices in pursuit of the goals of one or more institutions of economic production and distribution.

Although first applied to the space shuttle Challenger case, the concept of state-corporate crime has much wider application today, and is used to explain further state actions that are criminal domestically, internationally, and, following Sutherland's lead (1949b), socially injurious, but not defined by the state as criminal. The state's complicitous role in state-corporate transgressions is especially pertinent regarding acts of commission and omission against less powerful forces and groups that traditionally have been victimized by state crimes, namely workers and political dissidents (see, for example, Friedrichs, 1995).

In addition, this conceptualization of state-corporate crime is organizational, recognizing, however, that individual actors and their interactions within the strictures of organizations and organizations' powerful cultures of competition, within which individuals function, has a strong bearing on the propensity for corporations and states to act in a criminal fashion (Kramer, 1982, 1992).

Although the term state-corporate crime has only recently been applied to specific cases where corporate and state policies have interacted to produce criminal consequences, history is replete with examples of this kind of behavior. These situations simply had not previously been analyzed or labeled as state-corporate crimes.

Typology

Because the field of state-corporate crime is relatively new, the opportunity to classify different kinds of these crimes is in its infancy. To date, the only distinction that exists is between state-initiated and state-facilitated corporate crime (Kramer and Michalowski, 1990). In the former, businesses commit "organizational deviance at the direction of, or with the tacit approval of, the government" (p. 191). In the latter, "government regulatory institutions fail to restrain deviant business activities, because of direct collusion between business and government, or because they adhere to shared goals whose attainment would be hampered by aggressive regulation" (Kramer and Michalowski, 1990, p. 6). This distinction should serve as jumping-off point for further classificatory schemes, theory development, and hypothesis testing.

Historical perspective

Old cases

There are many examples from history both in the US and elsewhere that through the dual processes of colonialism and imperialism, in retrospect, might be labeled state-corporate crimes. In the US, these include but are not limited to the genocide of indigenous peoples; the ongoing appropriation of Native American lands; the international slave trade; convict leasing to wealthy land owners in the southern states; the private ownership of everything from the means of production to schools, churches, and stores in mining communities; and the use of armies and law enforcement in containing, and in some cases quashing, labor strikes (see, for example, Brown and Brown, 1978; Taft and Ross, 1979; Matthiessen, 1991; Tunnell, 1995a, 1995b). The connections between governments and corporations have been exposed by the mainstream and alternative news media and through the hard work of consumer and political activists like Ralph Nader and the numerous organizations that he helped establish.

Recent cases

Contemporary cases that have explicitly been labeled as state-corporate crimes include the January 1986 space shuttle explosion (Kramer, 1992); the Exxon Valdez oil spill (1989); the September 1991 deadly Imperial Foods chicken processing plant fire in Hamlet, North Carolina (Aulette and Michalowski, 1993); the National Highway Transportation Safety Association's (NHTSA) failure to adequately respond to the Bridgestone-Firestone/Ford tire problems (2010); the federal government's failure to monitor Enron (1997-2001); the US Invasion of Iraq (2001); the role of Halliburton in Iraq (2001-06); the participation of private military contractors in small wars and insurgencies (see Rothe and Ross, 2010); and the US Department of Energy's role in nuclear weapons production (Kauzlarich and Kramer, 1998). The section below highlights some of these cases.

The explosion of the space shuttle Challenger technically resulted from faulty seals; however, a deeper analysis points to the "hurry-up" agenda of the National Aeronautics and Space Administration (NASA), a state agency, and of the management of Morton Thiokol, the company that manufactured the seals. Although corporate engineers voiced misgivings over the scheduled flight of the shuttle, their concerns were overridden by both NASA and Morton Thiokol's management, which yielded to state-corporate pressures to produce a series of space shuttle flights in a set period of time. The fatal consequences – the death of seven astronauts and the loss of millions of dollars of equipment – were the result of both private producers and state managers whose concerns for production, flight schedules, and a financially self-sufficient space shuttle program overshadowed those for human life (Kramer, 1992; Vaughn, 1996).

In September 1991, an Imperial Foods chicken processing plant fire in Hamlet, North Carolina, killed 25 people. This case is another recent example of the state's omissive behavior, while it at the same time engaged in anticipatory policies to encourage corporations to accumulate increasing wealth. In fact, North Carolina's history of regulatory failure by state and federal agencies contributed to the tragedy in Hamlet. North Carolina failed to fund (and to use available federal funds toward) its own state Occupational Safety and Health Administration program (OSHA) – a program designed to protect workers' safety while on the job. Federal funding for its own OSHA program had decreased in the pro-business, anti-labor political climate of the 1980s. North Carolina had promoted a social climate friendly to business and hostile to labor and corporate regulation. The state's right-to-work laws weakened the little power organized labor held. Workers at Imperial Foods, paid slightly more than minimum wage, were non-union and likely would have remained that way (Shanker, 1992).

Regulatory inspectors (that is, state agents) knew that Imperial Foods kept the plant's fire exit doors locked to prevent workers from stealing chicken parts. Because the doors were locked, 25 workers died in the fire. The state in this case shirked its responsibilities for protecting workers (that is, enforcing the law) and allowed a corporation to engage in illegal and ultimately deadly actions (Aulette and Michalowski, 1993; Wright et al., 1995). Although the company was fined US$800,000 in civil fines (the largest in North Carolina history) for 54 "willful" safety violations and 23 "serious" violations, and the owner of the company was sentenced to prison for manslaughter, the State of North Carolina emerged unblemished. This case is an example of the state playing a role in fostering a climate that solicits business and discourages workers from organizing, while failing to protect its citizens against working in a life-threatening environment.

State-corporate crime, such as that in North Carolina, has been facilitated by the recent rise of conservative governance and politics in the US. For example, guarantees of an individual state's rights can facilitate unchecked power. Relinquishing such power to individual states and provinces while at the same time reducing federal funds available to them for enforcing regulatory law undermines the importance and necessity of worker protection that federal legislation was designed to guarantee.

Kauzlarich and Kramer (1998) apply the concept of state crime to the actions of the US government in three interrelated policy areas: the use and threatened use of nuclear weapons, the production of nuclear weapons, and the involuntary and non-consensual radiation experiments on humans. The authors review many well-known incidents of governmental wrongdoing in the area of nuclear policy and practice.

They argue that, "many of the actions that the United States government has taken with regard to nuclear weapons are illegal under international or domestic law, and therefore, a form of state crime" (Kauzlarich and Kramer, 1998, p. 3). Kauzlarich and Kramer outline the International Court of Justice's stance concerning the use of nuclear weapons and the laws of war. They examine the threat underlying the possible use of atomic weapons during the Korean and Vietnam War, how the production of nuclear weapons has contaminated the environment, the indignity of human radiation experiments, and finally how to "explain and control the crimes of the nuclear state" (Kauzlarich and Kramer, 1998).

In addition, analysis has been done of the Wedtech defense contractor fraud case (late 1980s) (Friedrichs, 1996) and the crash of ValuJet flight 592 in May 1996 (Matthews and Kauzlarich, 2000), both of which fall within the state-corporate crime context. In the former, under the pretense of helping disadvantaged minority businesses, the Small Business Administration, various White House aides, a number of people from Congress, and then Attorney General Edwin Meese III were implicated in corruption charges. In the latter instance, it was discovered that the government inspectors (that is, the Federal Aviation Administration) who were supposed to inspect the safety operations of ValuJet and Sabre Technologies (which had a contract with the airline company) were negligent in their affairs. This omission led to the death of all 109 individuals on board when Flight 592 crashed in the Florida Everglades.

Other transportation cases also fall within the state-corporate crime category. In 2001, the NTHSA released a report indicating that tires manufactured by Bridgestone were responsible for 271 deaths and 800 injuries. Mullins (2006) investigated this corporate crime and indicated that the state's failure to act in a timely fashion to news media attention, court cases, and governmental reports constitutes another example of state-corporate collusion and, thus, a state-corporate crime.

It goes without saying that there are countless examples of state-corporate crime that have been committed by US concerns in foreign countries. The chemical explosion at a Union Carbide plant in Bhopal, India (which occurred on December 23, 1994), is a case in point (Pearce and Tombs, 1998). Because of this tragedy, approximately 400,000 people were permanently injured and as many as 9,000 were killed either by the toxic fumes or when they fled in terror (D'Silva, 2006).

Causes

When tragedies such as those reviewed above occur, the government holds a unique position. On the one hand, the state is established to protect its citizens and to moderate the numerous conflicts that develop in our society, but on the other hand, it is often complicit in various crimes. In the framework of state-corporate crime, the state, as co-conspirator, continues to exercise its authority in its role as investigator of the crime, prosecutor, and fact-finder/adjudicator (judge) of its own involvement in transgressions. The potential for increasing state-corporate crime activities is stunning and is especially detrimental to people and groups who, compared to corporations and states, possess little power (for example, workers, poor land owners, subsistence farmers, and indigenous peoples).

According to Parenti (1995, p. 316),

> On major politico-economic issues, business gets its way with government because there exists no alternative way of organizing investment and production within the existing capitalist structure. Because business controls the very economy of the nation, government perforce enters into a uniquely intimate relationship with it. The health of the economy is treated by policymakers as a necessary condition for the health of the nation, and since it happens that the economy is in the hands of large interests, then presumably government's service to the public is best accomplished by service to these interests. The goals of business (high profits and secure markets) become the goal of government, and the 'national interest' becomes identified with the systematic needs of corporate capitalism.

In all the cases described above, the state had engaged in specific actions in association with the private sector to work towards mutually beneficial material and political objectives. At the same time, the state failed in its obligation to ensure safety as it participated in the creation of a climate that was hostile both to criticism and to specific individuals engaged in progressive politics that were designed to protect the workers' safety.

In the case of the space shuttle *Challenger*, government managers acted in ways that directly affected the explosion and loss of lives. Their actions were exemplified in the pressure they exerted on the private corporation's engineers. Furthermore, state managers' actions in the executive branch of the government pressured NASA's managers to persuade Morton Thiokol's engineers and executives to push on despite doubts. In this state-corporate crime, political officials' actions indict the state in a crime of commission.

On the other hand, the Imperial Foods chicken processing plant fire, another political crime where people lost their lives, resulted from state agents' inactions or omissions.

The State of North Carolina failed to ensure workers' safety from dangers in the workplace. The state and its agents (viz North Carolina's OSHA) did not inspect the hazardous work site; indeed, in the plant's 11 years of operation, it had never been inspected by OSHA. Thus, this state-corporate crime is best explained by the state's failure to act, and is therefore treated as a political crime of omission. This incident also qualifies as a political crime of commission. North Carolina engaged in official and overt policies and practices that culminated in creating an environmental, business, and regulatory climate ripe for just such a tragedy. North Carolina simultaneously attracted low-wage, anti-union businesses and under-staffed its own OSHA regulatory agency. The state's official policies and actions contributed to events that resulted in deaths that are best explained as state-corporate crimes of commission and omission.

There are approximately six reasons why state-corporate crime exists. The first is the attempt by businesses to *cut or minimize expenses and thus increase profitability or protect the corporation from losses.* This has the unintended consequence of either harming workers or producing unsafe products. Second, *close personal relationships* (that is, similar to Mills' 1956 concept of the circulation of elites) mitigate the possibility for checks and balances in the oversight mechanisms in government-corporate behavior. On the contrary, these relationships help illegality to persist. In this scenario, the elites seem to be scratching each other's backs.

Third, *lack of, or poor communication.* In order to understand bottlenecks in the production process, workers and supervisors need to be properly informed. If systematic, regular and open communication does not occur, this can lead to important critical information not making it to the individuals and agencies that can intervene.

Fourth, *nonexistent, ambiguous, or poorly written legislation (including policies and practices)* that controls state-corporate crime can facilitate this action. In this kind of arrangement, short of personal ethics, employees work in a state of ambiguity, never sure if their actions conform to organizational directives that could mitigate problems in the production process or service delivery. Since corporate goals are often vague and done more for public relations purposes, it is difficult for employees to easily interpret.

Fifth, *monitoring bodies may not exist, and/or they may not be properly functioning,* and both of these factors may stem from the fact that the relevant agencies are underfunded, poorly funded, or not funded at all. Although the will and desire might be present among the rank and file in a government bureaucracy, limited funding may result in them not being able to do anything about the corporate intransigence.

Sixth, *failure to fund, or adequately fund, government regulatory agencies* contributes to state-corporate crime. Lack of resources can prevent or hinder an agency from doing its proper job. It cannot provide the appropriate amount of oversight needed to both monitor the compliance of corporations with existing legislation and perform the necessary inspections to enforce the existing law.

Summary

This chapter has described a relatively new category of political crime – state-corporate crime. This unique type of political crime results from interrelationships between the private and public sectors. The "mutually reinforcing interactions" often result in legal violations that are driven by political and private agendas. The potential for further harms resulting from these relationships is alarming, particularly considering that regulatory law aimed at controlling private corporations is currently being scaled back. At the same time, corporations are increasingly transcending national borders both in production and in advancing the consumption of their products. In effect, controls on such political crimes may offer increasingly less protection for workers, consumers, and citizens when compared to those of the past, particularly in comparison to other precarious economic times.

Additionally, with few exceptions (that is, Tombs and Whyte, 2003) the majority of research in this area appears to be in the US context. Clearly, corporations in other countries collude with governments in a criminogenic fashion. Finally, it appears that the majority of state-corporate crimes are crimes of omission. Potential problems are conveniently ignored because they would require an additional outlay of funds, something the corporations or states want to prevent.

Kauzlarich and Matthews (2006) characterize research on state-corporate crime as evolving through three stages: attempts to convince others that state-corporate crime is a legitimate subject for inquiry; outlining the devastating effects of state-corporate crime; and trying to develop theory in this area. As the authors state, "much of this scholarship was organized around empirical examination of cases in which state agencies and corporations caused injuries to workers, transportation passengers, and the natural environment" (pp. 239-40).

Note

[1] For an excellent history of the state-corporate crime literature, see, for example, Michalowski and Kramer (2006a; 2006b).

TWELVE

Conclusion: controlling oppositional and state crime

Introduction

This book's central idea is that political crime is an important subject deserving investigation and explanation. A complete understanding can only be achieved when one appreciates the definitional issues, history, causes, and effects; uses current perspectives; integrates cases; understands theory; and presents and evaluates relevant policy and practices. That being said, in almost any investigation into social phenomena, we must inevitably deal with the thorny issue of control. Compared to scholars of most types of crime, those who study political crime usually do not offer much advice on minimizing this phenomenon: "Part of this reason is that the political crime literature is relatively scant to begin with. Another reason is that political crime is so universal, both historically and cross-nationally, that it almost seems natural and inevitable" (Barkan, 2001, p. 393). Barkan suggests, "political crime is best understood as a function of power, then to reduce political crime we must reduce the disparities of power that characterize many societies. At a minimum, this means moving from authoritarian to democratic rule" (p. 393). Although Barkan has a good point, the countries examined in this book are noted for being the world's most prominent democracies, yet they still have political crime:

> The historical record also indicates that dissenters will turn to civil disobedience and other illegal activities as long as they perceive flawed governmental policies. One way to reduce some political crime, then, would be to reduce poverty, racial discrimination, military adventurism, and other conditions and policies that promote humanitarian dissent. [...] At a minimum, responsible political officials from all sides of the political spectrum must state in no uncertain terms their opposition to these inhumane forms of dissent. (Barkan, 2001, p. 394)

Perhaps through explanation and responsible control measures, we might help create a society that is both more compassionate and reflective of the ideals of human and social justice.

This chapter examines the issue of controlling political crime. Short of eliminating the state (see, for example, Martin, 1995), individuals, organizations, and states have used a variety of methods to combat, minimize, reduce, eliminate, or simply control anti-systemic and state crime. Research and practice to date reveal a series of methods previously used to control both oppositional and state crimes. These techniques are reviewed and critiqued below.

Admittedly, strategies offered here are not exhaustive, and in some instances, they are not very concrete. Because there is such wide variance among advanced industrialized countries and the types of crimes that occur therein, these methods are best understood if presented as suggestions for controlling political crime. Also, strategies for controlling political crimes by or against particular capitalist states may not be applicable to other states.

Distinct cultures and state political structures play significant roles in the development of specific methods for controlling political crime. Undoubtedly, there are similarities in controlling political illegalities that cut across states that share similar economies and political systems, as is the case with advanced, industrialized, capitalist, democratic states. One must also be mindful that traditional controls on oppositional crimes can have the unintended effects of encouraging state crimes.

Controls are exercised by a variety of individuals and by a number of institutions characteristic of democratic societies. Most of these organizations operate under the typical constraints found in bureaucratic organizations. Regardless of the state agency, the controls can be divided into two types: internal and external. Internal controls include such mechanisms as supervisors and chains of command. External controls can be divided between governmental/legislative solutions and nongovernmental/citizen ones. Controls in advanced industrialized democracies are typically exercised through a combination of internal and external mechanisms.

Controlling oppositional crime

Although not willing to use the term state crime, Turk (1982a, Chapter 4), in his discussion of political policing, outlines five controls (including those concerned with maintaining national and public security) used by the police in their capacity of political policing: intelligence, information control, neutralization (specific deterrence), intimidation (general deterrence), and statecraft. Despite Turk's sophisticated and articulate analysis, relationships among these influences remain untested.

Even though it is framed in terms of responses to dissent in Eastern European countries, Braun's (1989, p. 118) outline of five state approaches to dissent can equally be applied to the advanced industrialized countries – incapacitation, deterrence (including specific and general), co-option, containment, and coexistence. Braun suggests that these methods can be "incorporated" into broader strategies of dealing with dissent, which she identifies as pacification through partial inclusion, repressive tolerance, differentiated political justice, and suppression through force. As with earlier attempts, however, the interconnectedness of state responses to political crimes is not articulated. Nevertheless, perhaps an integration of the less objectionable features of both Turk and Braun's categories,[1] and drawing connections between them in an attempt to provide a more informed responsible and progressive approach for controlling anti-systemic political crime, yields an appropriate framework. These categories are consolidated into five types and listed from least to most utilized. This description, however, is not meant to be interpreted as an endorsement of these strategies.

First, *inclusion* in the decision-making process, occurs when the state and its elites involve political dissenters/activists by offering them a true voice in policy making and/or legislation creation, and/or positions in the public administration of a ruling political party. The dissenters may also or otherwise be offered perks associated with elite status (for example, better housing, education for their children, travel opportunities). This may quell the more unsavory types of opposition to state policies and practices by involving them either actually or only superficially in the dominant political and economic system. The activists are treated to the perks and privileges that positions like this afford.

Second, *responsible policing* represents the use of legal and extralegal methods to temporarily terminate the activities of people and organizations that engage in so-called oppositional political crimes.

Third, *deterrence* (including general and specific), combines Turk's (1982a) potentially objectionable categories of neutralization and intimidation: "The aim is to neutralize resistance in ways that ensure that offenders will not repeat (specific deterrence), and [that] contribute to inhibiting any inclinations others may have to resist the authorities (general deterrence)" (Turk, 1982a, p. 137). According to Turk, one of the ways to accomplish this is through terror, and the other is through enclosure. People "may acquiesce out of fear and ignorance.[...] General deterrence is the ultimate goal of political policing; it is the anticipated product of intimidation" (p. 150). The trick here is to implement these methods in a just fashion.

Fourth, a variety of government departments use *legal intelligence collection methods* to "detect potential as well as actual resistance. The more threatened they feel, the greater will be the effort to monitor thoughts and feelings as well as behavior and relationships" (Turk, 1982a, p. 123). Intelligence gathering not only allows authorities to keep abreast of threats to a regime and of acts of political criminality.

Finally, *statecraft* is

> ... the art and science of social control as developed and used in the political organization of social life. Narrowly construed as the operations of political police, political policing may be understood as just the sharpest cutting edge of a more encompassing multidimensional effort to accomplish political dominance. More broadly construed as the total process by which intolerable political opposition is prevented as well as punished, political policing finally becomes synonymous with government. (Turk, 1982a, p. 160)

Turk, building on Gamson (1968), outlines three ways authorities can prohibit political resistance: insulation, sanctions, and persuasion. He distinguishes between internal and foreign control, and examines the problems related to the unintended consequences of controlling oppositional political crimes. For instance, "internal control ... does not itself constitute a solution to the problems created by nature or external social influences" (Turk, 1982a, p. 173). In many countries,

> the reduction or elimination of ordinary legal restraints in dealing with political criminality has been accomplished partly by direct legislation and judicial decision, but largely and more effectively by the creation and operation of special investigative and quasi-judicial bodies ... as well as various counterinsurgency 'intelligence' agencies and programs. Some of the extraordinary measures which have been authorized by the Congress, and generally supported by the courts are: restriction of the right to travel, both outside and within the country; limitation of the right to seek and hold employment, governmental and nongovernmental; electronic and nonelectronic surveillance on a 'possibly relevant' instead of a 'probable cause' basis; compulsory disclosure of self-incriminating evidence; and denial of access to trial courts. It should be noted that such legislation has typically undergone some delimitation in the judicial process, and has in rare cases ultimately been found unconstitutional. (Turk, 1982a, pp. 64-5)[2]

Controlling state crime

Controlling state crime is difficult because much of the government's illegalities are hidden from the public, including the media (Barak, 1990, p. 15; Grabosky, 1989; Ross, 1995/2000). Governments and states conceal their deviant behaviors as prudent measures to prevent public and media scrutiny that would otherwise lead to their loss of power or eventual downfall. Even when a state has engaged in universally despicable behavior, it usually does not admit its wrongdoing but dismisses its activities as necessary for sustaining order. Since the state typically refuses to participate in a critical dialogue or investigation of its misdeeds, there usually is no official recognition of its crimes.

Moreover, when confronted with state transgressions, the public has difficulty constructing informed opinions about them because, typically, media news propagates a state-sanctioned consensus (Herman and Chomsky, 1988) and maintains the assumption that government officials are trustworthy and capable of leading (see, for example, Clinard and Quinney, 1978). Critical queries are rarely heard except in alternative news sources, which lack both a sizable audience and widespread public acceptance.

Ample documentation exists about the biased nature of mainstream news reporting in many capitalist states. The media typically saturate consumers with sensationalized, violent street crimes and rarely touch either corporate or

Box 12.1: Noam Chomsky (1928–)

Born in Philadelphia, Pennsylvania, Noam Chomsky is a retired Professor of Linguistics at the Massachusetts Institute of Technology in Cambridge, Massachusetts. Although he started his academic career as a linguist and has achieved distinction in the field (especially because of his books *Syntactic structures*, 1957, and *Aspects of the theory of syntax*, 1965), he is perhaps better known as a leading intellectual, analyst of power, and one of the most outspoken critics of US foreign policy and the elite media.

Chomsky is the author of numerous articles and books, including *American power and the new mandarins* (1969), *Radical priorities* (1981), *The fateful triangle* (1983), *Pirates and emperors* (1987), *Manufacturing consent* (1988) (with Edward Herman), and *Deterring democracy* (1991). He is a frequent contributor to left liberal and anarchist publications and a speaker at activist functions. He is often interviewed by the alternative press, and his speeches have been broadcast on Amy Goodman's "Democracy Now" show, which is aired on Pacifica Radio. He is the subject of a handful of books, for example, Milan Rai's *Chomksy's politics* (1995), that analyzes his politics.

government illegality (see, for example, Tunnell, 1992; Ferrell and Sanders, 1995). The media's focus on personal crimes also keeps news consumers' attention fixed on street criminals, rather than on state managers' misdeeds (see, for example, Warr, 1995; Reiman, 1998).

Consequently, crimes of all varieties by the powerful typically get little attention, and citizens of capitalist states continue to believe that grave threats to them come from individual predators rather than official governmental policies and practices. As a result, state actions are commonly unquestioned because citizens believe that deviants are individual law violators, rather than government managers and their policies.

A limitation to monitoring and controlling state crime is the strength of the individual's point of view. Whether this is philosophically or ideologically based, once people have adopted or committed themselves to a controversial position, it is often difficult for them to consider information that contradicts their firmly held beliefs (similar to cognitive dissonance). Those who have a blind commitment to the government (such as super-patriots) will persistently argue that the state does not commit crimes. Unwavering adherence to an ideology can prevent individuals from separating their desire to follow an ideology and/or superiors' orders, and make good ethical/moral decisions (for example, the testimony of the accused during Nuremberg Trials).

Apathy, an immense barrier to combating state crimes, often results from state harms being ignored or perhaps dismissed by public or private interests (Ross, 2000b, Chapter 5). Given the state's contradictory involvement as both offender and dispenser of justice, victims of state crime rarely are compensated or satisfied (Barak, 1991). In order for victims to receive some type of justice, the government must first recognize that its agents and policies are socially harmful.

Nevertheless, a range of methods has been developed for controlling state crimes. Various researchers have drafted lists of factors important in the control of particular state criminogenic institutions or state crimes.[3] Moreover, other theorists have outlined potential responses to, if not controls for, state crime. Although brought up in the context of state repression in the US, Wolfe (1973) suggests that the adoption of socialism would lead to a cessation of state crimes. Unfortunately, he does not take into account the historical examples provided by Israel and various Western European socialist countries, where the state committed numerous crimes against its citizens (Ross, 2000b).

Alternatively, Grabosky's (1989) tentative theory of state crime is accompanied by six basic outcomes of state crime: "deterrence," "rehabilitation," "victim compensation," "denouncing the misconduct in question," "reaffirming the rule of law," and "experienc[ing] the threat (or reality) of draconian punishment" (pp. 17-18, 303-8).

Basing his work on the understanding that, given the diversity of official misconduct, no single intervention or control can solve the problem, Grabosky (1989) includes seven methods of controlling state crime: "internal oversight," "organizational redesign," "external oversight," "whistle blowing," "criminal prosecution," "civil litigation," and "participatory democracy" (pp. 308-31).[4] His work is an important starting point in the scholarly effort to understand the control and prevention of state crime, and to secure the proper use of state power.[5]

Before making suggestions, we should briefly explore what has not worked in the past. Usually, changes that are symbolic in nature have no effect. They are simply palliative and may, in fact, contribute to increased dissent. Some of the more popular, relatively low-cost, and ineffective approaches have been little more than name changes and/or the recruiting of new directors or administrators

Box 12.2: Peter Grabosky (1945–)

Trained in political science, Peter Grabosky works for the Regulatory Institutions Network at the Australian National University in Canberra. Born in the US, he later moved to Australia where he became deputy director of the Australian Institute of Criminology. From 1998-2002 he was president of the Australian and New Zealand Society of Criminology; from 2000-05, deputy secretary-general of the International Society of Criminology. He has been vice president of the Asian Criminological Society since 2009. Grabosky received the Sellin-Glueck Award from the American Society of Criminology in 2006, and the Prix Hermann Mannheim from the Centre International de Criminologie Comparée, Université de Montréal, in 2011. His best-known books in the field of political crime include: *The politics of crime and conflict: A comparative history of four cities* (1977) (with Ted Robert Gurr and Richard C. Hula), *Wayward governance: Illegality and its control in the public sector* (1989), and *Crime and terrorism* (2010) with Michael Stohl. He is also the co-author of *Lengthening the arm of the law* (2009) and *Cyber criminals on trial* (2004), which won the 2005 Distinguished Book Award from the American Society of Criminology's Division of International Criminology.

with minimal experience or power. Rarely do they have the ability to change the pervasive effects of organizational culture.

Ross (1995/2000, Chapter 1), on the other hand, develops a structural model of control that seeks to minimize the amount, frequency, and intensity of state crime. The model outlines the principal state criminogenic actors and the main entities that exist to control state crimes. The mechanisms include the following: victims' methods of controlling state crime; controls in context; and internal (state-controlled) and external (both state and non-state controlled) processes for combating state crimes. In a similar vein, Kauzlarich and Kramer (1998) construct an organizational model of the causes and control of state crime that needs to be expanded and integrated. Although Ross specifies a series of propositions for testing, rigorous data collection and testing have not yet been conducted. In the meantime, there are six principal methods that can be used to control state crime in advanced industrialized countries; these should be promoted and given additional attention. They are ranked below from least to most important.

Controlling the perpetrators of state crime[6]

Although states, governments, and their respective agencies were established to benefit the greater good by providing education, public safety, health and welfare benefits, and protection or defense against foreign attack, they can also partake in acts that are unethical, deviant, and occasionally, against the law. The government accomplishes crimes primarily through state criminogenic agencies. Three public agencies that have been routinely identified as perpetrators of state crime are: law enforcement (for example, the police, corrections, and probation and parole), the military, and national security/intelligence organizations.

My point of departure is the first chapter in my book *Controlling state crime* (Ross, 1995/2000). This chapter lays out a conceptualization of the process by which state crimes are controlled. One of the most instructive tools is the figure that appeared in the very beginning of the book. This drawing depicts the integrative model of controlling state crime and spells out the most relevant relationships.

In the center of the process is the state – an organization that comprises subcomponents that periodically engage in crimes. The three most criminogenic sectors – law enforcement, national security/intelligence agencies, and the military – interact with each other as well as with other public and private organizations (for example, corporations). Indeed, other government agencies that have been known to commit state crimes include those entrusted to protect the environment (Zilinskas, 1995/2000), education (Cabrera, 1995/2000), and the economy. Thus, state criminogenic agencies are not simply relegated to the fields of public safety and national security. This chapter organizes the controls on state agencies into several types.

Not only are there mechanisms inside these agencies that provide internal controls (dubbed here internal/internal controls), but external controls also exist within their country of operation (labeled here, the external/internal controls). Some of the controls are outside of both the agency and the country (and are labeled external/external). In short, sometimes the mechanisms operate autonomously, while at other times they interact with each other. The degree to which these entities can respond is dependent on their mandate (that is, what they were established to accomplish). Their major purpose may be as a watchdog agency that can easily marshal resources against state infractions/illegalities, or their work may be conditioned by a prediction of whether or not their actions will be successful. In this latter situation, an entity may pick and choose the issues and cases that it will monitor. Also understood is the fact that controls can be ordered along various continua, including formal versus informal kinds of control. All of these can create some sort of pressure.

In between the state and the controls are typically the victims. Victims can be individuals, groups, organizations, political parties, nations, or states. External controls (for example, organizations and processes) can exist both inside and outside of a country. One need only search the internet to find a plethora of organizations that monitor various issues. This template focuses mainly on structural/sociological factors (that is, organizations or environment attributes). This is not to say that psychological explanations are not important, but it may be easier to understand the controls if presented in this fashion.

Clearly, what works as a control for one state agency may not be as useful for another. Additionally, what is successful in stemming state crime in one country may not necessarily work in another. Because of changes in political ideology and historical contexts, what may work at one period in time may be totally useless in another. In short, several factors militate against a comprehensive explanation or a menu-based explanation of what works to control state criminogenic agencies in all situations. In other words, control is especially context-specific.

Law enforcement and efforts to control it

Law enforcement is a broad term that encompasses not only the police, but also state agencies such as probation and parole, corrections, etc. Law enforcement, particularly the police, dates back to ancient Roman and Greek times. The origins of contemporary modern policing practices can be traced to the turn of the 19th century and the initiatives of Sir Robert Peel in England. Peel proposed a paid (versus voluntary) police force, separate from the military, that could operate during the day and replace the private police forces and private detectives that existed in London during that time. The new police (which eventually became the London Metropolitan Police) would protect citizens and merchants alike. No longer would the public need to rely on private policemen or detectives in order to prevent articles from being stolen, to recover stolen property, or to bring matters of a criminal nature to the attention of magistrates. Peel's idea was questioned by many of the great thinkers of the day, but it eventually passed in the House of Commons. Bobbies, with their distinctive white hats and uniforms, appeared on the street of London in 1829.

The idea of a full-time, non–military police force was replicated across the Atlantic to the US, first to Boston and then to New York City. The New York Police Department was established in 1844 and soon changed from one that operated solely in the day to one that operated 24 hours a day, seven days a week.

The notion of the modern municipal police department was adopted by many cities in the US and other emerging Western democracies. By the late 1870s, cities across the US had established their own police departments. Not only did this concept proliferate in the US, but it also took root in several Anglo–American democracies (those countries that had as their origin the practices of Great Britain) and in many Western European countries during the late 1800s.

Soon after the establishment of the early police departments, they were accused of all kinds of deviant actions, including excessive use of violence, corruption, and illegal surveillance. Much of this had to do with the early political nature of policing. In general, in order to get a job in a police department, an individual had to have connections, such as knowing someone who worked for the police, working for a person who had political connections, or helping an individual win an election. In return, this person would recommend the candidate for a job within the police department. Then, in return for the favor, when it came time for the political party in power to get out the vote, the individual now employed by the police department would be expected to lend a hand. Among other things, police officers were expected to help supportive voters get to the polls and frustrate those who would vote against the candidates in power from being thrown out of office.

Additionally, when the political elite in a city wanted to enforce their will, the police acted as strike breakers, arresting demonstrators and picketers on trumped-up charges or under questionable circumstances. During this period, police officers and their departments were regularly accused of being corrupt, using excessive violence, and engaging in illegal surveillance. This was accepted practice in most police departments in the US, and occurred with even greater frequency in various less developed countries.

Around 1920, several reforms were introduced in federal, state, and municipal governments. These helped to make the civil service and policing more accountable and professional, and reduced political involvement in policing. Police departments became more bureaucratic, relying on scientific processes and borrowing procedures from public administration theories of the day. The era in which one could obtain a job based solely on political connections was ending. It still did not hurt, however, to know someone on the police force who could put in a good word, and certainly this remains an important aspect of being hired by a police department in this day and age. Nonetheless, this is no longer a primary requirement.

In the 1920s, basic changes were made to the ways prospective candidates obtained civil service jobs. This included the beginning of stricter hiring practices that featured such elements as competitive civil service exams, paper-and-pencil exams, physical agility tests, subject matter tests, and specialized training of police officers. More impartiality was introduced when the hiring practices were assumed by the city governments and were no longer the sole purview of the police departments. Joining a police force, thus, became a multi-step process. Police departments also sought and achieved greater autonomy from the mayor and local municipal councils. This period was marked by the creation of internal affairs departments (which would function as a repository for complaints against the police) and often the implementation of proper sanctions against officers who violated either criminal law or departmental policy.

During this time, police unions and associations, like the Fraternal Order of Police and the Police Benevolent Association, were founded or significantly increased in power. In many cases this allowed police an additional mechanism to control their colleagues, ensuring that any "bad apples" among their ranks were disciplined.

Another important change in the past 30 years is the practice of recruiting chiefs of police or police commissioners from outside of departments in order to minimize corruption. This was one of the most important recommendations made because of the Knapp Commission (1972), which was established to investigate allegations of corruption inside the NYPD.

There are advantages and disadvantages to hiring an external candidate. On the whole, however, individuals who have not worked their way up the chain of command and have no history with a department can more easily make tough choices in terms of personnel decisions, particularly in the sanctioning and dismissal of subordinates. They can, with fewer compunctions, fire, transfer, or demote those who have breeched the public's trust and failed to follow orders. Such commissioners have limited loyalty or allegiance to their subordinates. On the other hand, chiefs of police who have risen up through the ranks have loyalty to the people with whom they worked with previously and are often very careful about sanctioning them, especially if they themselves have any skeletons in the closet (for example, engaged in low-level corruption or accepted gratuities).

With respect to corruption in particular, another suggestion has advocated rotating individuals into and out of vice squads. Many street police officers have argued that the longer you stay in a squad that deals with narcotics, prostitution, and large sums of cash, the more tempting it is to become a "dirty cop."

In short, over the past 85 years, we have seen the creation of more checks and balances in police departments, and this has gone a long way in minimizing illegal activities.

The military and efforts to control it

In all countries, the military is a powerful state actor. In some states, the armed forces even run the government and its associated bureaucracies (Fidel, 1975, p. 1; Nordlinger, 1977, Chapter 1). This is especially true if a country is a military dictatorship. In most advanced industrialized countries, the military is subordinate to the government. Here the legislature passes the law and makes decisions about various policies, and the military simply implements those decisions. Spending on the military also influences decisions about what a department of defense can and cannot do.

In most countries, the military has enormous resources that serve to promote and/or enforce its departmental interests. These resources are both a source of power and the means that enable the armed forces to commit state crimes. Often times, the military is substantially funded with the understanding that this money will be used to protect the country from foreign threats. The military is typically used for purposes beyond simply fighting actual and undeclared wars; it may also assist in nation building (for example, planning and building roads, dams, bridges, and water causeways) and in times of crisis (that is, natural disasters and civil disorder) in various civilian relief efforts (for example, building bridges, sandbagging flooded rivers, etc.). In the US, for example, the West was opened up using the cavalry. They were sent, or so legend informs us, to secure the West (against the indigenous population) for settlement and to provide access to raw materials to fuel the rise of capitalism in the US and elsewhere. In Canada, a similar pattern occurred with the North West Mounted Police (later the Royal Canadian Mounted Police) (Brown and Brown, 1978).

In general, the problem of "crime and deviant behavior in the military context," regardless of the state, "has been largely ignored and/or neglected by" academics (Bryant, 1979, p. 6). Where it has been addressed, the general focus of most studies has been on the context of work–deviance relationships or the criminal behavior of soldiers in combat situations (Bryant, 1979, pp. 6, 359). Consequently, it is only natural that literature on controlling crimes by the military is also underdeveloped.

This section reviews crimes by the military (also labeled "khaki-collar crime"). Bryant (1979) examines the mechanisms advocated (some of which have been implemented) to minimize, prevent, and ideally control these crimes, and suggests additional processes to control the military and to prevent or deter it from engaging in state crimes, outlining a model, in general terms, of the control of crimes by the military. This analysis, although broad in scope, will help individuals, groups, and states better understand the variety of methods of control and appreciate the limits of control.

Even though the armed forces throughout the world share similarities, they also differ from one country to another (see, for example, Janowitz, 1977). Thus, the manner by which the armed forces are controlled varies (see, for example, Willimett, 1980, p. 250). Nevertheless, a number of general statements can be made regarding military crimes and their controls.

Even though specific focus on crimes by the military is uncommon, an analogy between war making and organized crime has been made on occasion. Tilly (1985), for example, suggests that "[a]t least in the European experience of the past few centuries, a portrait of war makers and state makers as coercive and self-seeking entrepreneurs bears a far greater resemblance [to organized crimes] than do its chief alternatives" (p. 169). He argues that the army, which he describes as a group of organized criminals, is responsible for the interdependent and complementary acts of war making, state making, protection, and extraction (pp. 181-3). Tilly, however, does not go beyond this distinction to offer solutions for controlling these activities.

In a related interpretive paradigm, the military is guilty of more than injuring and killing soldiers and sometimes civilians; it also perpetrates state crimes against the environment. Indeed, numerous treaties, conventions, and laws have been established to not only make the fighting of war more humane, but also to protect the environment from unnecessary damage. For example, the Geneva Protocol was established in 1925, and the League of Nations was created in 1929. The UN, the current iteration of the League, "bans the use of chemical and bacteriological weapons, and the 1972 Biological and Toxins Weapons Convention (BWC) [...] forbids the development, manufacture, testing, and storage of biological and toxin weapons" (Zilinskas, 1995/2000, p. 235). Additionally, a "third specific arms control treaty, the 1977 Convention on the Prohibition of Military or Any Other Hostile Use of Environmental Modification Techniques (ENMOD)" was created in 1977 (Zilinskas, 1995/2000, p. 235).

Since the creation of the first military, officers and/or concerned citizens and organizations have responded to crimes committed by the military of various states. Several mechanisms have been advocated, many of which have been implemented, to control the armed forces in general and its ability to engage in crime in particular.

Periodically, various scholars discuss controls on crimes by the military. The most common types of controls that have been articulated are conventional civilian criminal codes, military law, and international treaties (Bryant, 1979, p. 6). Within these broad categories, some academics (see, for example, Barnet, 1969; Galbraith, 1969, pp. 52-60; Martin, 1984) have listed a number of alternative mechanisms for controlling the military. Although a necessary beginning, this literature lacks a theoretical framework and primarily focuses on the US. Therefore, these studies may have limited applicability to other countries.

Huntington (1957) and Nordlinger (1977), however, offer more sophisticated treatments, identifying types of controls on the armed forces that citizens can use. Huntington, for instance, offers two broad suggestions: an unstable process called "selective civilian control: maximizing civilian power" and a stable situation labeled "objective civilian control: maximizing military professionalism." Even though Huntington sensitizes his readers to the broad problems and contours of controlling the military, his work has been subjected to a series of critiques (see, for example, Janowitz, 1960; Abrahamsson, 1972; Tilly, 1993) that he was unable to refute.

Alternatively, Nordlinger (1977) outlines three models of civilian control: traditional, liberal, and penetration. In the traditional model:

> Military intervention presupposes a conflict between soldiers and civilian governors; and conflict in turn requires some differentiation between the two groups. [Thus] in the absence of significant differences between civilians and soldiers, the civilians may quite easily retain control because the military has no reason ... to challenge them. (p. 11)

In the liberal model, Nordlinger argues,

> Civilian control is explicitly premised upon the differentiation of elites according to their expertise and responsibilities. Civilians holding the highest governmental offices ... are responsible[for and skilled in determining domestic and foreign goals, overseeing the administration of laws, and resolving conflicts. (p. 12)

Finally, in the penetration model, Nordlinger suggests, "Civilian governors obtain loyalty and obedience by penetrating the armed forces with political ideas (if not fully developed ideologies) and political personnel. Throughout their careers officers (and enlisted men) are intensively imbued with the civilian governor's political ideas" (p. 15).

According to Nordlinger, none of the models of control "can be applied in all types of polities and securely relied upon to ensure civilian supremacy" (pp. 10-11). Therefore, civilian control is problematic and linked to the possibility of frequent coups (p. 19). Even though Nordlinger highlights a variety of different types of civilian control, he neglects other kinds of constraints, and his models of control lack specificity.

If control does take place, it can fall into one of five possible interrelated categories: individual/self-control; control by the military establishment (for example, internal controls); control by government institutions; control by foreign actors; and control by the public. With the exception of individual/self-control, all types of control can lead to either a reduction of crimes by the military or resistance to control. When the latter takes place, a reform of the military is often thwarted. This outcome, however, may motivate concerned actors to once again engage in control efforts.

Moreover, it must be understood that these controls are not mutually exclusive; in other words, some mechanisms may overlap with other strategies. If they are not carefully implemented, they might even increase the number of military crimes.

In general, soldiers are required to obey the commands of their superior officers; thus, they frequently minimize the revelations of crimes committed by their units and organizations. Enlisted personnel, however, can reduce the occurrence of criminal-like actions committed by their organization by disobeying orders given by their superiors. This, however, is particularly difficult for armed forces personnel because there are often severe consequences for insubordination. In an attempt to circumvent this dilemma, Kelman and Hamilton (1989) outline two basic recommendations by which soldiers can "(1) reduc[e] the impact of binding forces by counteracting the effects of rule and role orientation, respectively, and (2) enhanc[e] the impact of opposing forces by buttressing the effects of value orientation" (pp. 321-2). Kelman and Hamilton's specific suggestions, however, would be extremely difficult to implement in traditional military settings where authority is centralized.

Alternatively, in most armies, internal and/or external complaints systems allow soldiers and officers the opportunity to file a grievance. In some armed services, this is an effective process, while in others it is simply a public relations mechanism designed to show outsiders that the organization is fair and just. In the US, for example, the Inspector General of the Army (a staff organization) responds to grievances and "receive[s] complaints of any kind from all personnel. All Army personnel, enlisted men and officers alike ... have a right to register complaints directly with an Inspector General officer instead of taking them up with their immediate superiors" (Evan, 1962, p. 189). Despite the armed forces personnel's use of this process, there are a number of obstacles to due process with this system (pp. 191-4). Unfortunately, self and individual controls do not work very well due to the organizational culture found in the military. Too often, camaraderie and esprit du corps are very important disinhibitors to reporting and engaging in crimes.

Six types of internal controls can be used by military organizations to minimize or prevent crimes by members of their organizations. They are ranked here, from least to most important, in terms of predicted significance: proper training; improving soldiers' general level of education in particular (for example, pro-social) subjects; discipline; professionalism; fostering inter-service rivalry; and threatening or using warnings, counseling, and court martials (Evan, 1962, p. 190; see also Huntington, 1957, 1961; Ujevich, 1969; Abrahamsson, 1972; Lang, 1972, pp. 118-19; Stepan, 1973; Bryant, 1979, pp. 26-7).

Many governments have nonmilitary controls on their armed forces. Seven strategies can be used by governments to control crimes by the military. These mechanisms, ordered from least to most important, include: better regulations on lobbying by the military and their contractors; collecting accurate data on crimes by the military; strengthening human rights organizations; providing selective amnesty for soldiers and officers who commit crimes; reducing military spending; decreasing the size of the military; and abolishing the military (Ross, 2005).

At least five methods exist whereby foreign actors (for example, agencies, institutions, and states) can attempt to reduce crimes by the military. These processes are, from least to most useful: the greater use of war crimes trials; minimizing the number of dependent economies; encouraging a more proactive media; preventing the creation of national security states; and cutting off economic support to countries in which military crimes take place (Ross, 2005).

Most importantly, the public exerts some form of control over the military. This process is generally referred to as "civilian supremacy" (Willimett, 1980, p. 253). The six general means of control by the public are, from least to most important: public protest; draft evasion or desertion; conscientious objection; challenging bureaucratic truth; the support or establishment of public organizations to monitor the military; and self-education (Ross, 2005).

National security/intelligence agencies and efforts to control them

Most countries have one or more national security or intelligence organizations. Typically located in a state department, a ministry of external affairs, or a department of justice, these organizations collect information about threats to domestic, homeland, and/or national security. This is accomplished through both open (that is, publicly available) and classified means (that is, closed sources), and focus is placed on the economic well-being, military resources, strengths, and capabilities of foreign governments. This information is then presented to important government leaders and decision makers (for example, president, prime minister, etc.), who then rely on what they have learned to make decisions that will affect foreign policy and decisions pertaining to relations with those countries. One of the biggest state crimes that an intelligence organization can commit is invasion of privacy by illegally obtaining evidence without an authorized search or court-approved warrant. In the US, both the FBI and the CIA, albeit with different principle missions, are responsible for collecting information that is relevant to national security.

The FBI has many tasks, one of which is the collection of information related to domestic threats such as terrorism and other sorts of oppositional political crimes. The CIA operates not only in the US, but also abroad through the numerous embassies that the US has established. It is perfectly legitimate when the CIA or another US entity collects open-source information in a foreign country. However, when an agency retrieves information in a manner that violates the laws of that country – engaging in illegal surveillance – this is normally regarded as spying. If a CIA or other agent is caught participating in such actions, he or she may be arrested or imprisoned regardless of nationality and affiliation with the US. This even occurs in countries that are allies, such as Canada, France, and the UK. Spying may very well be part of an organization's mission, and its employees may be expected to pursue such activities. If caught, certain protocols are followed.

The FBI was established during prohibition, towards the beginning of the last century. Its original mission was to monitor the illegal sales of alcohol. As prohibition ended, the organization's mission changed; it was eventually tasked with monitoring the threat of communism, anarchism, and Nazism (and their respective sympathizers) in the US. This mission expanded under the leadership of the charismatic former director J. Edgar Hoover to cover almost all kinds of oppositional political crimes (for example, sedition, treason, espionage, terrorism).

Hoover's influence was crucial. He was able to convince Congress to pass legislation that allowed the expansion of the agency's mission. The FBI was soon responsible for monitoring crimes that involved two or more states, kidnapping, embezzlement, federal crimes, etc. It was also briefly responsible for monitoring the sale of illegal drugs like marijuana, until this task was given to the Drug

Enforcement Agency. The state crime in which the FBI was most involved was illegal domestic surveillance. Allegations of this kind of activity have been revealed through numerous media inquiries, the most important of which was the Church Committee (Senate Select Committee on Intelligence, 1989).

The CIA had its origins in the Office of Strategic Services (OSS) that was part of the US military intelligence efforts during the Second World War. The OSS was eventually civilianized and placed under the control of the State Department. In addition to collecting information on foreign threats, the OSS participated in clandestine operations. Over the past half century, the CIA has engaged in all sorts of unsavory actions. This has been documented through news media reports, and a series of Senate investigations, including the most recent 9/11 Commission, which unearthed wrongdoing and malfeasance on the part of the CIA.

General observations and future research

Since the range of controls articulated in this chapter is rather broad in scope, further research and specificity is warranted. To begin with, because it is difficult for investigators to penetrate or conduct ethnographic research on most state criminogenic agencies, perhaps the next and most fruitful step is to dig deeper into the existing histories that have been written on these organizations.

Nevertheless, some preliminary observations can be made. In terms of law enforcement, the controls that have been effective include the reliance on police professionalism, improved hiring requirements, the creation of internal affairs departments, and the hiring of chiefs from outside of departments. With respect to the military, it appears that the greatest controls are tied to the power of the purse (that is, appropriations). In terms of national security/intelligence agencies, the controls that have the greatest effect, although sometimes short-lived, are Senate inquiries.

Citizens, politicians, and various administrative units have an obligation to monitor state crimes and suggest or improve means by which these kinds of crimes can be controlled and resistance be minimized. While labeling abhorrent actions committed by the military as "crimes" may seem like a semantic device, it is an alternative step in the re-conceptualization and control of these unpleasant actions. This approach allows us to move beyond the traditional public administration and policy literature by examining these actions in the context of the critical literature found in other relevant fields such as criminology, criminal justice, law, political science, and sociology. Crimes by the state should not be treated as business "as usual" but as transgressions that need to be legally and morally addressed and, most importantly, to be prevented from reoccurring.

First, an important control is *the development, consultation, and reliance on ethics departments in government.* In advanced industrialized countries, many state agencies at the federal, state, and local levels have departments or units that not only provide some form of internal oversight, but also help to educate and monitor their employees regarding appropriate ethics. To buttress this control, many departments have a unit often called an "inspector general" to investigate real or alleged abuses and recommend appropriate sanctions. Additionally, whistleblower legislation, which allows employees immunity from prosecution if they reveal government illegalities and mismanagement, is present at many, but not all, levels of government.

Second, *empowering victims*. This involves the socialization, education, and training of individuals who may be subject to government abuse so that they can voice their concerns to the proper audiences. It also means the development of an infrastructure to protect victims and to educate victimizers about the distasteful nature of their deeds. A focus on victims also allows us to reward political whistleblowers when appropriate.

Third, *using the free market economic system*. This implies that the power of money is extremely relevant to the process of controlling state crime. People and organizations can boycott companies that do business in countries that engage in state crimes, and they can lobby their elected representatives to pass legislation that reinforces these objectives. Since the 1960s, workers and activists have suggested that to control these types of crime, countries should tightly control trade by banning products manufactured by corporations that are unfair to workers, that use child labor, and that have little regard for the environment (see, for example, Greider, 1992). Such strategies are being implemented today and represent starting points for controlling this type of state crime against labor (Tunnell, 1995a).

Fourth, *fielding social justice candidates in elections*. This is another method for working within the existing democratic system to publicize policies that keep state criminogenic agencies in check. This means that major and fringe political parties should run candidates willing to voice opposition to state policies that are socially harmful and that represent human rights violations.

Fifth, *using the courts*. The democratic freedoms that are constitutionally given should be better protected while minimizing attempts to withdraw those privileges. However, the courts in capitalist states undoubtedly play a significant part in preserving order, enforcing the will of the government, limiting the activities of labor, and adjudicating conflicts between the state and labor. Most democracies have well-conceived procedures that specify how public officials can be kicked out of office. In the US, for example, the right to impeach public officials is outlined by the US Constitution in Article I, Sections 2 and 3, which discuss the procedure, and in Article II, Section 4, which indicates the grounds for impeachment: "the President, Vice President, and all civil officers of the United States shall be removed from office."

Sixth, and most important, is *strong external oversight*. This includes agencies that can monitor the wrongdoing of government agencies and personnel. This category also involves the proper selection and training of managers in techniques to supervise the work of their employees. Other players are watchdog agencies, special prosecutors (with circumscribed powers), and/or an effective system of checks and balances.

There will always be flaws in any potential or actual solution; monitoring state crime is therefore an ongoing reality. One response might entail hiring more people inside the agencies, like integrity officers or inspector generals, who would be on the lookout for crimes. Perhaps sanctions for state employees also need to be harsher. Pessimism abounds on both ideological and structural grounds regarding the possibility of controlling the state (Ross, 1995/2000, 2000b). Although proposing solutions is easy, those that are realistic and practical for minimizing political crime are far from simple. Yet, these crimes are the ones that – due to their devastating effects – most need to be controlled.

Chances are that, as long as states exist, there will always be crime committed by government actors. However, most of those caught receive light sanctions because of the resources they possess or can access. Like the old philosophical question, "If a tree falls in the forest, and no one hears it, did it still make a sound?," in order for a crime to have occurred, someone or some agency needs to know that an illegality has been committed. Governments are reasonably adept at concealing their actions. Meanwhile, state crime occurs at all levels of the government and is widespread, so monitoring and controlling it is extremely difficult. The state has a disproportionate amount of resources, including money and personnel. Typical monitoring entities may be influenced to look the other way or actively participate in cover-ups. As with any type of social problem or crime, there is no absolute or concrete solution. People must become increasingly intolerant of state misconduct, rather than expecting a solution from the state. In addition, incentives must be given to government workers to "snitch" on other workers who commit abuses. Stricter checks and balances must be put into place. If you have the power to commit a state crime, generally you have the power to shift the blame.

In short, a number of traditional and innovative controls have been implemented to minimize, reduce, control, or prevent these types of crimes from occurring again. Determining which ones work best in certain situations is important. Having the will and resources to experiment with new solutions is probably the only way we can develop a more just society.

Summary and conclusion

Although some may question whether it is realistic to simultaneously control oppositional and state crime, we need to be reminded that when the government tries to prevent or minimize threats to its existence, it needs to do so without violating the law. Otherwise, the state engages in a double standard, something the general public finds morally and ethically problematic.

Regardless, political crime will exist as long as the entity we call "the state" exists. In the future, the center of political power may very well shift temporarily or permanently to transnational corporations and organizations. One final question remains: in the future, will political crime increase or decrease? The answer depends on reasoned analysis. What we do know, however, is that most anti-systemic political crime is a barometer of citizen discontent with a government (elected or appointed), including the public administration (bureaucracy). State crime, on the other hand, is too often an indicator of incompetence, lack of training, competition among organizational units, lack of coordination, and overall paranoia on the part of bureaucrats and leaders.

Although human rights violations and state violence (perhaps with the exception of police use of excessive force) are relatively rare in advanced industrialized democracies, state-corporate crime and terrorism will persist and may increase. Especially because of 9/11, citizens of Anglo-American democracies are more cautious and feel more vulnerable about being victimized by terrorism. As the history of this decade is written, we will look back and point to a number of incidents of state repression instituted in the wake of 9/11 and because of the passage of previously reviewed emergency legislation. As long as there are states and power differentials, political crime will exist.

The terrorist incidents of the past decade, both on home soil and abroad, should not force the reader into thinking that either terrorism or incidents of political crime are things of the past. As long as states exist and as long as we have individuals and groups vying for political power, we will have political crime. In order to better appreciate the progression of political crime in advanced industrialized democracies in general, and the United States, Canada and the United Kingdom, in particular, more scholarship needs to be produced. This would include not simply case studies, but also analysis that would place this information into a quantitative format for ease of understanding.

Notes

[1] Where appropriate, the meaning of Braun's categories are inferred.

[2] Turk (1982a) warns that there are changes afoot with respect to monitoring dissent, particularly those in Western democratic nations: "(1) increasing use of field controls, (2) expanding surveillance coupled with more selective targeting for neutralization, (3) more 'subcontracting' of operations, and (4) the internationalization of control policies and programs" (p. 199).

[3] See Ross (1995a) for a review of this literature.

[4] Although Grabosky has sensitized us to the need for more analytical techniques, his factors have received criticism (see, for example, Ross, 1995/2000, p. 9).

[5] Grabosky (1989, p. 4) outlines a series of reasons why studying state crime is important. These can be applied in this situation too, including, "breaches of the law by governments can entail very great cost, in financial as well as in human terms"; "personal embarrassment" of elected officials and governments; violations of rights; and "attacks on the rule of law."

[6] This section builds on Ross (2005).

References

Abbey, E. (1975) *The monkey wrench gang*, Philadelphia: Lippincott Williams & Wilkins

Abrahamsson, B. (1972) *Military professionalism and political power*, London: Sage Publications.

Ackerman, S.R. (1978) *Corruption: A study in political economy*, New York: Academic Press.

Ackerman, S.R. (1999) *Corruption and government: Causes, consequences, and reform*, New York: Cambridge University Press.

Ackroyd, C., Margolis, K., Rosenhead, J. and Shalice, T. (1980) *The technology of political control* (2nd edn), London: Pluto Press.

Ackroyd, P. (2001) *London: The biography*, New York: Doubleday.

Adams, J. (1986) *The financing of terror: The PLO, IRA, Red Brigades and M-19 stand the paymasters: How the groups that are terrorizing the world get the money to do*, New York: Simon & Schuster.

Agee, P. (1975) *Inside the company: CIA diary*, New York: Routledge.

Akehurst, M. (1987) *Introduction to international law*, London: Unwin Hyman.

Akers, R.L. (1994) *Criminological theories: Introduction and evaluation*, Los Angeles, CA: Roxbury.

Alexander, D.W. (1992a) 'Applying Merton's theory of anomie to political criminality', Paper presented to the American Society of Criminology Annual Meetings, New Orleans.

Alexander, D.W. (1992b) 'Political crime: an application of Merton's theory of social structure and anomie', Master's thesis, Virginia Polytechnic Institute and State University.

Alford, R.R. and Friedland, R. (1985) *Powers of theory: Capitalism, the state, and democracy*, New York: Cambridge University Press.

Allen, F.A. (1974) *The crime of politics: Political dimensions of criminal justice*, Cambridge, MA: Harvard University Press.

Alpert, G. and L. Fridell. (1992) *Police vehicles and firearms: instruments of deadly force*, Prospect Heights, IL: Waveland Press.

Alpert, G., D.J. Kenney, R.G. Dunham, and W.C. Smith. (2000) *Police pursuits: What we know*, Washington, DC: Police Executive Research Forum.

Anderson, E.J. (1977) 'A study of industrial espionage, Parts I and II', *Security Management*, vol 21, no 1, January/March, pp. 32, 37-8, 40.

Archer, J. (1971) *Treason in America: Disloyalty versus dissent*, New York: Hawthorn.

Aulette, J.R. and Michalowski, R. (1993) 'Fire in Hamlet: a case study of state-corporate crime', in K.D. Tunnell (ed) *Political crime in contemporary America: A critical approach*, New York: Garland, pp. 171-206.

Bachrach, P. and Baratz, M.S. (1962) 'Two faces of power', *American Political Science Review*, vol 56, pp. 947-52.

Balagopal, K. (1986) 'Deaths in police custody: whom and why do the police kill?', *Economic and Political Weekly*, vol 21, pp. 2028-9.

Barak, G. (1990) 'Crime, criminology and human rights: towards an understanding of state criminality', *The Journal of Human Justice*, vol 2, no 1, pp. 11-28.

Barak, G. (ed) (1991) *Crimes by the capitalist state: An introduction to state criminality*, Albany, NY: State University of New York Press.

Barak, G. (1993) 'Crime, criminology, and human rights: toward an understanding of state criminality', in K.D. Tunnell (ed) *Political crime in contemporary America*, New York: Garland Publishing, Inc, pp. 207-30.

Barak, G. (ed) (1994) *Media, process, and the social construction of crime: Studies in newsmaking criminology*, New York: Garland.

Barak, G. (ed) (1996) *Representing O.J.: Murder, criminal justice, and mass culture*, Albany, NY: Harrow and Heston.

Barak, G. (2000) 'Preface', in J.I. Ross (ed) *Varieties of state crime and its control*, Monsey, NY: Criminal Justice Press, pp vii-ix.

Barkan, S. (2001) *Criminology: A sociological understanding* (2nd edn), Upper Saddle River, NJ: Prentice Hall.

Barker, T. (1977) 'Peer group support for police occupational deviance other than corruption', *Criminology*, vol. 15, no. 3, pp. 353-66.

Barlow, H.D. and Kauzlarich, D. (2002) *Introduction to criminology* (8th edn), Upper Saddle River, NJ: Prentice Hall.

Barnet, R. (1969) *The economy of death*, New York: Atheneum.

Bauman, Z. (2000) *Liquid modernity*, Cambridge: Polity Press.

Bay, C. (1968) 'Civil Disobedience', *International Encyclopedia of the Social Sciences*, Vol II, New York: Macmillan, pp. 473-86.

Becker, H. (1963) *The outsiders: Studies in the sociology of deviance*, London: Free Press.

Beirne, P. and Messerschmidt, J. (1991) *Criminology*, New York: Harcourt Brace Jovanovich.

Bell, J.B. (1978) *A time of terror*, New York: Basic Books.

Bell, J.B. and Gurr, T.R. (1979) 'Terrorism and revolution in America', in H.D. Graham and T. R. Gurr (eds) *Violence in America*, Beverly Hills, CA: Sage Publications, pp. 329-47.

Bennett, A.L. (1991) *International organizations: Principles and issues* (5th edn), Englewood Cliffs, NJ: Prentice Hall.

Benyon, J. (1984) *Scarman and after: Essays reflecting on Lord Scarman's report, the riots and their aftermath*, Elmsford, NY: Pergamon.

Berman, M.R. and Clark, R.S. (1982) 'State terrorism: disappearances', *Rutgers Law Journal*, vol 13, pp. 531-77.

Binder, A. and Fridell, L. (1984) 'Lethal force as a police response', *Criminal Justice Abstracts*, vol 17, June, pp. 25-60.

Binder, A. and Scharf, P. (1980) 'The violent police–citizen encounter', *Annals of American Academy of Political and Social Science*, vol 452, pp. 111-21.

Black's Law Dictionary (1999) St Paul, MN: West Group (6th edn, p. 1335).

Blackstock, N. (1975) *The FBI's secret war against political freedom*, New York: Vintage.

Bohm, R.M. (1982) 'Radical criminology: an explication', *Criminology*, vol 19, pp. 565-89.

Bohm, R.M. (1993) 'Social relationships that arguably should be criminal although they are not: on the political economy of crime', in K.D. Tunnell (ed) *Political crime in contemporary America*, New York: Garland, pp. 2-29.

Bollinger, L. (1981) 'Die Entwicklung zu terroristischem Handeln als psychosozialer Prozess: Begegnungen mit Beteiligten', in H. Jager, G. Schmidtchen and L. Süllwold (eds) *Analysen zum Terrorismus* [*Analyzes of terrorism*], Oplanden: Westdeutscher Verlag, vol 2.

Borovoy, A. (1985) 'Freedom of expression: some recurring impediments', in R. Abella and M.L. Rothman (eds) *Justice beyond Orwell*, Montreal: Les Editions Yvon Blais, pp. 125-60.

Boyle, A. (1979) *The climate of treason: Five who spied for Russia*, London: Hutchinson.

Braun, A. (1989) 'Dissent and the state in Eastern Europe', in C.E.S. Franks (ed) *Dissent and the state*, Toronto: Oxford University Press, pp. 111-37.

Brown, L. and Brown, C. (1978) *An unauthorized history of the RCMP*, Toronto: James Lorimer.

Bryan, G.S. (1943) *The spy in America*, Philadelphia, PA: J.B. Lippincott.

Bryant, C.D. (1979) *Khaki-collar crime: Deviant behavior in the military context*, New York: Free Press.

Bunyan, T. (1976) *The political police in Britain*, New York: St Martin's Press.

Burgess, R.L. and Akers, R.L. (1968) 'A differential association–reinforcement theory of criminal behavior', *Social Problems*, vol 14, pp. 128-47.

Burnham, D. (1991) *A law unto itself: The IRS and the abuse of power*, New York: Vintage Publishing.

Cabrera, N.J. (1995/2000) *Control and prevention of crimes committed by state-supported educational institutions. Controlling state crime: An introduction*, New York: Garland, pp. 163-206

Canada (1946) *The report of the Royal Commission appointed under Order in Council PC 411 of February 5, 1946 to investigate the facts relating to and the circumstances surrounding the communication, by public officials and other persons in positions of trust, of secret and confidential information to agents of a foreign power, June 27, 1946*, Ottawa: E. Cloutier, Printer to the King.

Canada (1986a) *Crimes against the state*, Working Paper 40, Ottawa, ON: Law Reform Commission of Canada.

Canada (1986b) *Crimes against the state*, Working Paper 49, Ottawa, ON: Law Reform Commission of Canada.

Canada, Royal Commission on Aboriginal Peoples (1994) The *High Arctic relocation: A report on the 1953-55 relocation*, Ottawa: Canadian Communications Group.

Caplan, G. (1983) 'On Kelman's incorrect conclusions', *American Psychologist*, vol 38, pp. 1124-6.

Capan, G. and Murphy, P.V. (1991) 'Fostering integrity', in W. Geller and D.W. Stephens (eds) *Local government police management*, Washington, DC: ICMA Press, pp. 239-71.

Carnoy, M. (1984) *The state and political theory*, Princeton, NJ: Princeton University Press.

Center for Research on Criminal Justice (1977) *The iron fist and the velvet glove*, Berkeley, CA: Center for Research on Criminal Justice.

Chambliss, W.J. (1971) 'Vice, corruption, bureaucracy, and power', *Wisconsin Law Review*, vol 4, pp. 1150-73.

Chambliss, W.J. (1976) 'The state and criminal law', in W.J. Chambliss and M. Mankoff (eds) *Whose law, what order?*, New York: John Wiley, pp. 66-106.

Chambliss, W.J. and Seidman, R. (1982) *Law, order, and power* (2nd edn), Reading, MA: Addison-Wesley.

Chapin, B. (1964) *The American law of treason*, Seattle: University of Washington Press.

Chomsky, N. (1973) *For reasons of state*, New York: Pantheon.

Chomsky, N. (1983) *The fateful triangle*, Boston, MA: South End.

Christie, N. (1993) *Crime control as industry*, New York: Routledge.

Churchill, W. (1997) *A little matter of genocide: Holocaust and denial in the Americas, 1492 to the present*, San Francisco, CA: City Lights Books.

Churchill, W. and Vander Wall, J. (1988) *Agents of repression: The FBI's secret wars against the Black Panther Party and the American Indian Movement*, Boston, MA: South End.

Churchill, W. and Vander Wall, J. (1990) *The COINTELPRO papers: Documents from the FBI's secret wars against domestic dissent*, Boston, MA: South End.

CIA's Mail Intercept: Commission on CIA Activities Within the United States (1978) in M.D. Ermann and R.J. Lundman (eds) *Corporate and governmental deviance*, New York: Oxford University Press, pp. 174-85.

Clark, R.P. (1983) 'Patterns in the lives of ETA members', *Terrorism: An International Journal*, vol 6, pp. 423-54.

Clarke, J. (1982) *American assassins: The darker side of politics*, Princeton, NJ: Princeton University Press.

Clarke, R. (1992) *Situational crime prevention: Successful case studies*, Albany, NY: Harrow and Heston.

Clinard, M.B. and Quinney, R. (1978) 'Crime by government', in M.D. Ermann and R.J. Lundman (eds) *Corporate and governmental deviance*, New York: Oxford University Press, pp. 137-50.

Cohen, S. (1993) 'Human rights and the crimes of the state: the culture of denial', *Australian and New Zealand Journal of Criminology*, vol 26, pp. 97-115.

Coleman, J.W. (1985) *The criminal elite*, New York: St Martin's Press.

Coleman, J.W. (1994) *The criminal elite* (3rd edn), New York: St Martin's Press.

Coleman, J.W. (1995) 'Respectable crime', in J.F. Sheley (ed) *Criminology* (2nd edn), Belmont, CA: Wadsworth, pp. 249-73.

Cooper, H.H.A. (1977) 'What is a terrorist? A psychological perspective', *Legal Medical Quarterly*, vol 1, pp. 16-32.

Copeland, M. (1974) *Beyond cloak and dagger: Inside the CIA*, New York: Pinnacle Books.

Cornell, J. (1969) *The trial of Ezra Pound: A documented account of the treason case by the defendant's lawyer*, New York: John Day.

Corrado, R.R. (1981) 'A critique of the mental disorder perspective of political terrorism', *International Journal of Law and Psychiatry*, vol 4, pp. 1-17.

Corrado, R.R. and Davies, G. (2000) 'Controlling state crime in Canada', in J.I. Ross (ed) *Varieties of state crime and its control*, Monsey, NY: Criminal Justice Press, pp. 59-88.

Corrado, R.R., Olivero, A. and Lauderdale, P. (1992) 'Political deviance', in V.F. Sacco (ed) *Deviance: Conformity and control in Canadian society*, Scarborough, ON: Prentice Hall.

Correctional Services of Canada (1992) 'Violence and suicide in Canadian institutions', *Forum on Corrections Research*, vol 4, no 3, pp. 3-5.

Coulter, A. (1998) *High crimes and misdemeanors: The case against Bill Clinton*, Alexandria, VA: Regnery Publishing.

Coulter, J., Miller, S. and Walker, M. (1984) *State of siege: Miner's strike 1984*, London: Canary Press.

Cowell, J. and Young, J. (1982) *Policing the riots*, London: Junction Books.

Crayton, J.W. (1983) 'Terrorism and the psychology of the self', in L.Z. Freedman and Y. Alexander (eds) *Perspectives on terrorism*, Wilmington, DE: Scholarly Resources, pp. 33-41.

Crenshaw, M. (1981) 'The causes of terrorism', *Comparative Politics*, vol 13, pp. 379-99.

Crenshaw, M. (1985) 'An organizational approach to the analysis of political terrorism', *Orbis*, vol 4, pp. 465-89.

Crenshaw, M. (1990a) 'The logic of terrorism: terrorist behavior as a product of strategic choice', in W. Reich (ed) *Origins of terrorism*, Cambridge: Cambridge University Press, pp. 7-24.

Crenshaw, M. (1990b) 'Questions to be answered, research to be done, knowledge to be applied', in W. Reich (ed) *Origins of terrorism*, Cambridge: Cambridge University Press, pp. 247-60.

Crenshaw, M. (1991) 'How terrorism declines', *Terrorism and Political Violence*, vol 3, no 1, pp. 69-87.

Cullen, F., Maakestad, W. and Cavender, G. (1987) *Corporate crime under attack: The Ford Pinto case and beyond*, Cincinnati, OH: Anderson.

Dahl, R. (1961) *Who governs?*, New Haven, CT: Yale University Press.

Damania, R., Fredriksson, P.G. and Mani, M. (2004) 'The persistence of corruption and regulatory compliance failures: theory and evidence', *Public Choice*, vol 21, no 3, pp. 363-90.

Daraki Mallet, M. (1976) *The ESA men*, Athens: Kendros.

Davis, J.K. (1992) *Spying on America: The FBI's Domestic Counterintelligence Program*, New York: Praeger.

Deutsch, M. E., and Susler, J. (1991) 'Political prisoners in the United States: the hidden reality', *Social Justice*, vol 18, no. 3, pp. 92-106.

Dion, R. (1982) *Crimes of the secret police*, Montreal: Black Rose Books.

Dionne, E.J. (1991) *Why Americans hate politics*, New York: Touchstone Books.

Domhoff, G.W. (1983) *Who rules America now?*, New York: Simon & Schuster.

Donner, F.J. (1990) *Protectors of privilege: Red squads and police repression in urban America*, Berkeley, CA: University of California Press.

D'Silva, T. (2006) *The Black Box of Bhopal: A closer look at the world's deadliest industrial disaster*, Bloomington, IN: Trafford Publishing

Durose, M.R. Smith, E.L. and P.A. Langan. (2007) *Contacts between police and the public, 2005*, Washington, DC: Bureau of Justice Statistics, April, NCJ 215243.

Earley, P. (1988) *Family of spies: Inside the John Walker spy ring*, New York: Bantam.

Earley, P. (1998) *Confessions of a spy: The real story of Aldrich Ames*, New York: Berkeley Publishing Group.

Ellis, M. (1994) 'J. Edgar Hoover and the "red summer" of 1919', *Journal of American Studies*, vol 28, pp. 39-59.

Engels, F. (1942) *The origin of the family, private property and the state*, New York: International Publishers.

Evan, W. M. (1962) 'Due process of law in military and industrial organization', *Administrative Science Quarterly*, Vol 7, pp. 187-207.

Evans, P.B., Rueschemeyer, D. and Skocpol, T. (eds) *Bringing the state back in*, Cambridge: Cambridge University Press.

Faucher, P. and Fitzgibbins, K. (1989) 'Dissent and the state in Latin America', in C.E.S. Franks (ed) *Dissent and the state*, Don Mills, ON: Oxford University Press, pp. 138-68.

Fein, H. (1993) 'Accounting for genocide after 1945: theories and some findings', *International Journal of Group Rights*, vol 1, pp. 79-106.

Feld, B.C. (1971) 'Police violence and protest', *Minnesota Law Review*, vol 55, pp. 731-78.

Ferracuti, F. (1982) 'A sociopsychiatric interpretation of terrorism', *Annals of the American Academy of Political and Social Science*, vol 463, pp. 129-40.

Ferracuti, F. and Bruno, F. (1981) 'Psychiatric aspects of terrorism in Italy', in I.L. Barak-Glanmtz and C.R. Huff (eds) *The mad, the bad and the different: Essays in honor of Simon Dinitz*, Lexington, MA: Lexington Books, pp. 199-213.

Ferrell, J. (2001). *Tearing down the street: Adventures in urban anarchy*, New York, NY: Palgrave.

Ferrell J. and Sanders, C. (eds) (1995) *Cultural criminology*, Boston, MA: Northeastern University Press.

Fidel, K. (1975) *Militarism in developing countries*, New Brunswick, NJ: Transaction Books.

Fine, R. and Millar, R. (eds) (1985) *Policing the miner's strike*, London: Cobden Trust.

Flexner, S. and Flexner, D. (2000) *The pessimist's guide to history: An irresistible compendium of catastrophes, barbarities, massacres*, New York: Harper Perennial.

Foerstel, H.N. (1997) *Free expression and censorship in America*, Westport, CT: Greenwood.

Foerstel, H.N. (1998) *Banned in the media*, Westport, CT: Greenwood.

Fogelson, R. (1977) *Big city police*, Cambridge, MA: Harvard University Press.

Fowler, N. (1979) *After the riots*, London: Davis-Paynter.

Franks, C.E.S. (1989) *Dissent and the state*, Toronto: Oxford University Press.

Frenkel-Brunswik, E. (1952) 'Interaction of psychological and sociological factors in political behavior', *American Political Science Review*, vol 46, no 1, pp. 44-65.

Fricker, M. and Pizzo, S. (1992) 'Outlaws at justice', *Mother Jones*, May/June, pp. 30-8.

Fridell, L. (1985) 'Justifiable use of measures in research on deadly force', *Journal of Criminal Justice*, vol 17, no 3, pp. 157-66.

Friedrichs, D.O. (1995) 'State crime or governmental crime: making sense of the conceptual confusion', in J.I. Ross (ed) *Controlling state crime*, New York: Garland, pp. 53-79.

Friedrichs, D.O. (1996) *Trusted criminals: White collar crime in contemporary society*, New York: Wadsworth.

Friedrichs, D.O. (1998a) *State crime* (vol 1), Aldershot: Ashgate.

Friedrichs, D.O. (1998b) *State crime* (vol 2), Aldershot: Ashgate.

Fyfe, J. (1978) 'Shots fired: an analysis of New York City firearms discharge', Doctoral dissertation, Albany, NY: State University of New York.

Fyfe, J. (1979) 'Administrative interventions on police shooting discretion', *Journal of Criminal Justice*, vol 1, pp. 309-23.

Fyfe, J. (1988) 'Police use of deadly force: research and reform', *Justice Quarterly*, vol 5, no 2, pp. 165-205.

Galbraith, J.K. (1969) *How to control the military*, Garden City: Doubleday.

Gamson, W. (1968) *Power and discontent*, Homewood, IL: Dorsey.

Garber, M. and Walkowitz, R. (eds) (1995) *Secret agents: The Rosenberg case, McCarthyism and fifties America*, New York: Routledge.

Gardiner, J.A. and Lyman, T.R. (1978) *Decisions for sales, corruption and reform in land use and building regulations*, New York: Praeger.

Gaventa, J. (1980) *Power and powerlessness*, Urbana, IL: University of Illinois Press.

Geary, R. (1985) *Policing industrial disputes: 1893 to 1985*, Cambridge: Cambridge University Press.

Geller, W.A. (1982) 'Deadly force: what we know', *Journal of Police Science and Administration*, vol 10, pp. 151-77.

Gibbons, D.C. (1987) *Society, crime, and criminal behavior*, Englewood Cliffs, NJ: Prentice Hall.

Gill, P. (1995) 'Controlling state crimes by national security agencies', in J.I. Ross (ed) *Controlling state crime: An introduction*, New York: Garland, pp. 81-114.

Goldstein, J.S. (1996) *International relations* (2nd edn), New York: Addison-Wesley Longman.

Goldstein, R.J. (1978) *Political repression in modern America*, Cambridge, MA: Schenkman.

Grabosky, P.N. (1989) *Wayward governance: Illegality and its control in the public sector*, Canberra: Australian Institute of Criminology.

Grace, E. and Leys, C. (1989) 'The concept of subversion and its implications', in C.E.S. Franks (ed) *Dissent and the state*, Toronto: Oxford University Press, pp. 62-85.

Green, G.S. (1990) *Occupational crime*, Chicago, IL: Nelson-Hall.

Greider, W. (1992) *Who will tell the people: The betrayal of American democracy*, New York: Simon & Schuster.

Grey, S. (2006) *Ghost plane: The true story of the CIA rendition and torture program*, New York: St Martin's Press.

Grosman, B.A. (1972) 'Political crime and emergency measures in Canada', in F. Adler and G.O.W. Mueller (eds) *Politics, crime and the American scene*, San Juan, Puerto Rico: North-South Center Press, pp. 141-6.

Gross, F. (1972) *Violence in politics: Terror and political assassination in Eastern Europe and Russia*, The Hague: Mouton.

Gurr, T.R. (1966) *Cross-national studies of civil violence*, Washington, DC: American University, Center for Research in Social Systems.

Gurr, T.R. (1970) *Why men rebel*, Princeton, NJ: Princeton University Press.

Gurr, T.R. (1988) 'War, revolution and the growth of the coercive state', *Comparative Political Studies*, vol 21, no 1, pp. 45-65.

Gutmann, D. (1979) 'Killers and consumers: the terrorist and his audience', *Social Research*, vol 46, pp. 516-26.

Habermas, J. (1975) *Legitimation crisis*, Boston, MA: Beacon.

Hacker, F.J. (1976) *Crusaders, criminals, and crazies: Terror and terrorism in our time*, New York: Norton.

Hagan, F. (1990) *Introduction to criminology: Theories, methods, and criminal behavior*, Chicago, IL: Nelson-Hall.

Hagan, F. (1994) *Introduction to criminology: Theories, methods, and criminal behavior* (3rd edn), Chicago, IL: Nelson-Hall.

Hagan, F. (1997) *Political crime: Ideology and criminality*, Boston, MA: Allyn & Bacon.

Hahn, H. and Feagin, J.R. (1970) 'Riot-precipitating police practices: attitudes in urban ghettos', *Phylon*, vol 31, pp. 183-93.

Haldeman, H.R. (1994) *The Haldeman diaries: Inside the Nixon White House*, New York: Simon & Schuster.

Halperin, M., Burosage, R.I. and Marwick, C.M. (1977) *The lawless state: The crimes of the US intelligence agencies*, New York: Penguin.

Hamilton, L.C. (1978) 'Ecology of terrorism: a historical and statistical study', Doctoral dissertation, University of Colorado.

Hamm, M.S. (1995) *The abandoned ones: The imprisonment and uprising of the Mariel boat people*, Boston, MA: Northeastern University Press.

Hamm, M.S. (1997) *Apocalypse in Oklahoma: Waco and Ruby Ridge revenged*, Boston: Northeastern University Press.

Haritos-Fatouros, M. (1988) 'The official torturer: a learning model for obedience to the authority of violence', *Journal of Applied Social Psychology*, vol 18, pp. 1107-20.

Harring, S. (1983) *Policing a class society*, New Brunswick, NJ: Rutgers University Press.

Havill, A. (2001) *The spy who stayed out in the cold: The secret life of FBI double agent Robert Hanssen*, New York: St Martin's Press.

Hazelhurst, K.M. (1991) 'Passion and policy: Aboriginal deaths in custody in Australia, 1980-1989', in G. Barak (ed) *Crimes by the capitalist state*, Albany, NY: State University of New York Press, pp. 21-48.

Head, M. (2011) *Crimes against the state*, Farnham: Ashgate.

Henry, S. (1991) 'The informal economy: a crime of omission by the state', in G. Barak (ed) *Crimes by the capitalist state*, Albany, NY: State University of New York Press, pp. 253-72.

Hepburn, J. (1985) 'The exercise of power in coercive organizations: a study of prison guards', *Criminology*, vol 23, no. 1, pp. 145-64.

Herman, E. (1982) *The real terror network*, Boston, MA: South End.

Herman, E. and Chomsky, N. (1988) *Manufacturing consent: The political economy of the mass media*, New York: Pantheon.

Herring, G.C. (ed) (1993) *The pentagon papers* [abridged edn], New York: McGraw Hill.

Higham, S., J. Stephens, and Williams, M. (2004) 'Guantanamo – a holding cell in the war on terror', *Washington Post*, May 2, p. A1.

Hitchens, C. (2001) *The trial of Henry Kissinger*, London: Verso.

Holsti, O. R., Brody, R.A. and North, R.C. (1964) 'Measuring affect and action in international reaction models: Empirical materials from the 1962 Cuban Crisis', *Journal of Peace Research*, vol 1, no. 1, pp. 170-89.

Home Affairs Committee (1980) *Deaths in custody*, London: HMSO.

Hornblum, A. (2010) *The invisible Harry Gold: the man who gave the Soviets the atom bomb*, Stanford, CT: Yale University Press.

Horvath, F. (1987) 'The police use of deadly force: a description of selected characteristics of intrastate incidents', *Journal of Police Science and Administration*, vol 15, pp. 26-238.

Hubbard, D.G. (1971) *The skyjacker: His flights of fantasy*, New York: Macmillan.

Hubbard, D.G. (1983) 'The psychodynamics of terrorism', in Y. Alexander and T. Adeniran (eds) *International violence*, New York: Praeger, pp. 43-53.

Huntington, S.P. (1957) *The soldier and the state*, New York: Random House.

Hurst, J.W. (1983) 'Treason' in *Encyclopedia of crime and justice*, New York: Free Press, pp. 1559-62.

Hurwitz, L. (1995) 'International state-sponsored organizations to control state crime: the European Convention on Human Rights', in J.I. Ross (ed) *Controlling state crime*, New York: Garland, pp. 283-316.

IJOGT (*International Journal of Group Tensions*) (1982a) 'Psychology of leaders of terrorist groups', International Scientific Conference on Terror and Terrorism: International Terrorism, *International Journal of Group Tensions*, vol 12, pp. 84-104.

IJOGT (1982b) 'Psychology of the followers', International Scientific Conference on Terror and Terrorism: International Terrorism, *International Journal of Group Tensions*, vol 12, pp. 105-21.

Ingelhart, R. (1977) *Silent revolution*, Princeton, NJ: Princeton University Press.

Ingraham, B.L. (1979) *Political crime in Europe: A comparative study of France, Germany, and England*, Berkeley, CA: University of California Press.

Ingraham, B.L. and Tokoro, K. (1969) 'Political crime in the United States and Japan', *Issues in Criminology*, vol 4, no 2, pp. 145-69.

Jakubs, D. (1977) 'Political violence in times of political tension: the case of Brazil', in D. H. Bayley (ed.) *Police and society*, Beverly Hills, CA: Sage Publications, pp. 85-106.

Janowitz, M. (1960) *The professional soldier*, New York: Free Press.

Janowitz, M. (1977) *Military institutions and coercion in the developing nations*, Chicago: University of Chicago Press.

Jenkins, B. (1979) 'The potential for nuclear terrorism', in M. H. Greenberg and A. R. Norton, (eds.) *Studies in nuclear terrorism*, Boston: G. K. Hall.

Jenkins, B. (1982) *Terrorism and beyond: An international conference on terrorism and low level conflict*, Santa Monica, CA: RAND.

Jenkins, P. (1988) 'Whose terrorists? Libya and state criminality', *Contemporary Crises*, vol 12, pp. 1-11.

Jenkins, P. (2003) *Images of terror: What we can and can't know about terrorism*, Hawthorne, NY: Aldine de Gruyter.

Johnson, C. (1982) *Revolutionary change*, Stanford, CA: Stanford University Press.

Johnson, R. and Leighton, P. (1999) 'American genocide: the destruction of the black underclass', in C. Summers and E. Markusen (eds) *Collective violence: Harmful behavior in groups and governments*, Lanham, MD: Rowman & Littlefield, pp. 95-140.

Jongman, A.J. (1983) 'A world directory of "terrorist" organizations and other groups, movements and parties involved in political violence as initiators or targets of armed violence', in A.P. Schmid, *Political terrorism: A research guide to concepts, theories, data bases and literature*, New Brunswick, NJ: Transaction, pp. 284-417.

Joseph, J. (1994) *Signs of life: Channel surfing through 90s culture*, San Francisco, CA: Manic D Press.

Kania, R.E. and Mackay, W.C. (1977) 'Police violence as a function of community characteristics', *Criminology*, vol 15, pp. 27-48.

Kaplan, A. (1978) 'The psychodynamics of terrorism', *Terrorism: An International Journal*, vol 1, pp. 237-54.

Kappeler, V.E., Sluder, R.D. and Alpert, G.P. (1994) *Forces of deviance*, Prospect Heights, IL: Waveland.

Kasinitz, P. (1983) 'Neo-Marxist views of the state', *Dissent*, vol 30, pp. 337-46.

Kaufman, M.T. (2003) 'In memoriam Robert King Merton', *Criminologist*, vol 28, no 3, May/June, pp. 30-1.

Kauzlarich, D. and Kramer, R.C. (1993) 'State-corporate crime in the US nuclear weapons production complex', *Journal of Human Justice*, vol 5, pp. 4-28.

Kauzlarich, D. and Kramer, R.C. (1998) *Crimes of the American nuclear state*, Boston, MA: Northeastern University Press.

Kauzlarich, D. and Matthews, R. (2006) 'Taking stock of theory and research', in R.J. Michalowski and R.C. Kramer (eds) *State-corporate crime: Wrongdoing at the intersection of business and government*, New Brunswick, NJ: Rutgers University Press, pp. 239-49.

Keenan, J.P. (1987) 'A new perspective on terrorism: theories and hypotheses', Paper presented at the annual meeting of the American Society of Criminology, Montreal.

Kelly, R.J. (1972) 'New political crimes and the emergence of revolutionary nationalist ideologies', in F. Adler and G.O.W. Mueller (eds) *Politics, crime and the international scene: An inter-American focus*, San Juan, Puerto Rico: North-South Center Press, pp. 23-35.

Kelman, H. (1983) 'Conversations with Arafat', *American Psychologist*, vol 70, pp. 203-16.

Kelman, H. C. and V. L. Hamilton. (1989) *Crimes of obedience*, New Haven: Yale University Press.

Kerness, B. and M. Ehehosi. 2001. *Torture in U.S. Prisons: Evidence of U.S. Human Rights Violations*, Philadelphia: American Friends Service Committee.

Kettle, M. and Hodges, L. (1982) *Uprising! The police, the people and the riots in Britain's cities*, London: Pan Books.

Khan, R.A. and McNiven, J.D. (1991) *An introduction to political science* (4th edn), Scarborough, ON: Nelson Canada.

Kirchheimer, O. (1961) *Political justice: The use of legal procedure for political ends*, Princeton, NJ: Princeton University Press.

Kittrie, N.N. (1972) 'International law and political crime', in F. Adler and G.O.W. Mueller (eds) *Politics, crime and the international scene: An inter-American focus*, San Juan, Puerto Rico: North-South Centre Press, pp. 91-5.

Kittrie, N.N. (2000) *Rebels with a cause*, Boulder, CO: Westview.

Kittrie, N.N. and Wedlock, Jr., E.D. (1986) *The tree of liberty: A documentary history of rebellion and political crime in America*, Baltimore MD: Johns Hopkins University Press.

Klein, N. (2000) *No logo*, New York: Picador.

Kneece, J. (1986) *Family treason: The Walker spy ring case*, New York: Stein and Day.

Knutson, J. (1981) 'Social and psychodynamic pressures toward a negative identity: the case of an American revolutionary terrorist', in Y. Alexander and J.M. Gleason (eds) *Behavioral and quantitative perspectives on terrorism*, Toronto: Pergamon, pp. 105-52.

Kohn, S.M. (1994) *American political prisoners: Prosecutions under the Espionage and Sedition Acts*, Westport, CT: Praeger Publishers.

Koistra, P.G. (1985) 'What is a political crime?', *Criminal Justice Abstracts*, vol 17, pp. 100-15, March.

Kramer, R.C. (1982) 'Corporate crime: an organizational perspective', in P. Wickman and T. Dailey (eds) *White-collar and economic crime*, Lexington, MA: Lexington Books, pp. 75-94.

Kramer, R.C. (1992) 'The space shuttle Challenger explosion: a case study of state-corporate crime', in K. Schlegel and D. Weisburd (eds) *White-collar crime reconsidered*, Boston, MA: Northeastern University Press, pp. 214-43.

Kramer, R.C. and Michalowski, R.J. (1990) 'State-corporate crime', Paper presented at the annual meeting of the American Society of Criminology, Baltimore, MD.

Kramer, R.C., Michalowski, R.J. and Kauzlarich, D. (2000) 'The origins and development of the concept and theory of state-corporate crime', *Crime and Delinquency*, vol 48, no 2, pp. 263-82.

Krammer, A. (1997) *Undue process: The untold story of America's German alien internees*, Boulder, CO: Rowman & Littlefield.

Kuper, L. (1985) *The prevention of genocide*, New Haven, CT: Yale University Press.

Lancaster, J. (2001) 'Hill is due to take up anti-terror legislation; Bill prompts worries of threat to rights', *The Washington Post*, October 9.

Lang, K. (1972) *Military institutions and the sociology of war*, Beverly Hills, CA: Sage Publications.

Langford, J.W. and Tupper, A. (eds) (1994) *Corruption, character, and conduct: Essays on Canadian government ethics*, Toronto: Oxford University Press.

Laqueur, W. (1977) *Terrorism*, Boston, MA: Little, Brown.

Laqueur, W. (1985) *A world of secrets*, New York: Twentieth Century Fund.

Lewis, A. (2004) 'A President beyond the law', in M. Ratner and E. Ray (eds.) *Guantanamo: What the world should know*, White River Junction, VT: Chelsea Green, pp. ix-xi.

Lichbach, M.I. (1987) '"Deterrence or Escalation": The puzzle of aggregate studies of repression and dissent', *Journal of Conflict Resolution*, vol 31, no 2, pp. 266-97.

Lukes, S. (1974) *Power: A radical view*, London: Macmillan.

Malvern, P. (1985) *Persuaders: Influence peddling, lobbying, and political corruption in Canada*, Toronto: Methuen.

Manheim, J.B. and Rich, R.C. (1986) *Empirical political analysis*, New York: Longman.

Manning, P.K. (1980) 'Violence and the police role', *Annals of the American Academy of Political and Social Science*, vol 452, pp. 135-44.

Mannle, H.W. and Hirschel, J.D. (1988) *Fundamentals of criminology* (2nd edn), Englewood Cliffs, NJ: Prentice Hall.

Marchetti, V. and Marks, J.D. (1975) *The CIA and the cult of intelligence*, New York: Dell.

Margolin, J. (1977) 'Psychological perspectives in terrorism', in Y. Alexander and S.M. Finger (eds) *Terrorism: Interdisciplinary perspectives*, New York: John Jay Press, pp. 270-82.

Markovitz, A.S. and Silverstein, M. (eds) (1988) *The politics of scandal*, New York: Holmes and Meire.

Marshall, J., Scott, P.D. and Hunter, J. (1987) *The Iran-Contra connection: Secret teams and covert operations in the Reagan era*, Boston, MA: South End.

Martin, B. (1984) *Uprooting war*, London: Freedom Press.

Martin, B. (1995) 'Eliminating state crime by abolishing the state', in J.I. Ross (ed) *Controlling state crime*, New York: Garland, pp. 389-417.

Marx, G.T. (1970a) 'Issueless riots', *Annals of the American Academy of Political and Social Science*, vol 39, pp. 21-33.

Marx, G.T. (1970b) 'Civil disorder and agents of social control', *Journal of Social Issues*, vol 26, pp. 19-57.

Marx, G.T. (1988) *Undercover: Police surveillance in America*, Berkeley, CA: University of California Press.

Marx, K. and Engels, F. (1848/1948) *The Communist manifesto*, New York: International Publishers.

Mason, T. D. and Krane, D.A. (1989) 'The political economy of death squads: toward a theory of impact of state sanctioned terror', *International Studies Quarterly*, vol 33, no 1, pp. 175-98.

Mass, P. (1973) *Serpico*, New York: Viking.

Matthews, R. and Kauzlarich, D. (2000) 'The crash of ValuJet flight 592: a case study in state-corporate crime', *Sociological Focus*, vol 3, pp. 281-98.

Matthiesen, P. (1991) *In the spirit of Crazy Horse*, New York: Penguin.

McAlary, M. (1987) *Buddy boys*, New York: Charter Books.

McCarthy, B. J. (1996) 'Keeping an eye on the keeper: prison corruption and its control', in M. C. Braswell, B. R McCarthy, and B. J. McCarthy (eds.) *Justice, Crime, and Ethics* (2nd edn), Cincinnati, OH: Anderson, pp. 229-41.

McCauley, C.R. and Segal, M.E. (1987) 'Social psychology of terrorist groups', in C. Hendrick (ed) *Annual review of social and personality psychology: Group processes and intergroup relations*, Newbury Park, CA: Sage Publications, pp. 231-56.

Meacham, J. (2008) *American lion: Andrew Jackson in the White House*, New York: Random House.

Merton, R.K. (1938) 'Social structure and anomie', *American Sociological Review*, vol 3, pp. 672-82.

Merton, R.K. (1964) 'Anomie, anomia, and social interaction: contexts of deviant behavior', in M.B. Clinard (ed) *Anomie and deviant behavior*, New York: Free Press, pp. 397-408.

Merton, R.K. (1966) 'Social problems and sociological theory', in R.K. Merton and R.A. Nisbet (eds) *Contemporary social problems*, New York: Harcourt Brace, pp. 775-823.

Michalowski, R.J. (1985) *Order, law, and crime*, New York: Random House.

Michalowski, R.J. and Kramer R.C. (eds) (2006a) *State-corporate crime: Wrongdoing at the intersection of business and government*, Piscataway, NJ: Rutgers University Press.

Michalowski, R.J. and Kramer, R.C. (2006b) 'The critique of power', in R.J. Michalowski and R.C. Kramer (eds) *State-corporate crime: Wrongdoing at the intersection of business and government*, Piscataway, NJ: Rutgers University Press, pp. 1-17.

Mickolus, E. (1981) Combating international terrorism: A quantitative analysis. PhD dissertation, Yale University.

Miligram, S. (1974) *Obedience to authority*, London: Harper & Row.

Miligram, S. (1977) *The individual and the social world*, Boston, MA: Addison-Wesley.

Miller, R.R. (2000) 'Controlling state crime in Israel: the dichotomy between national security versus coercive powers', in J.I. Ross (ed) *Varieties of state crime and its control*, Monsey, NY: Criminal Justice Press, pp. 89-118.

Miller, W.B. (1973) 'Ideology and criminal justice policy: some current issues', *The Journal of Criminal Law and Criminology*, vol 64, pp. 142-54.

Mills, C.W. (1956) *The power elite*, New York: Oxford University Press.

Miron, M.S. (1976) 'Psycholinguistic analysis of the SLA', *Assets Protection*, vol 1, pp. 14-19.

Mitchell, C., Stohl, M., Carleton, D. and Lopez, G.A. (1986) 'State terrorism: issues of concept and measurement', in M. Stohl and G.A. Lopez (eds) *Government violence and repression*, Westport, CT: Greenwood, pp. 1-26.

Mitchell, T.H. (1985) 'Politically-motivated terrorism in North America: the threat and the response', Doctoral dissertation, Carleton University.

Moran, R. (1974) 'Political crime', Doctoral dissertation, University of Pennsylvania.

Morf, G. (1970) *Terror in Québec*, Toronto: Clarke, Irwin and Company Ltd.

Mullins, C.W. (2006) 'Bridgestone-Firestone, Ford and the NHTSA', in: R.J. Michalowski and R.C. Kramer (eds) *State-corporate crime: Wrongdoing at the intersection of business and government*, Piscataway, NY: Rutgers University Press, pp. 134-48.

Navanksy, V. (1991) *Naming names*, New York: Viking Penguin.

Neville, J.F. (1995) *Press, the Rosenbergs and the Cold War*, Santa Barbara, CA: Greenwood Press.

Newfield, J. and W. Barret (1988) *City for sale*, New York: Harper and Row.

Noonan, J. (1984) *Bribes*, New York: Macmillan.

Nordlinger, E. (1977) *Soldiers in politics: Military coups and government*, Englewood Cliffs, NJ: Prentice Hall, Inc.

Nye, J., Jr, Zelikow, P. and King, D.C. (1997) *Why people don't trust the government*, Cambridge, MA: Harvard University Press.

Packer, H.L. (1962) 'Offenses against the state', *The Annals of the American Academy*, vol 339, pp. 77-89.

Parenti, M. (1995) *Democracy for the few* (2nd edn), New York: St Martin's Press.

Pearce, F. (1976) *Crimes of the powerful*, London: Pluto.

Pearce, F. and Tombs, S. (1998) *Toxic capitalism: Corporate crime and the chemical industry*, Brookfield, VT: Ashgate Books.

Pearlstein, R.M. (1991) *The mind of a political terrorist*, Wilmington, DE: Scholarly Resources.

Pitcher, B. and Hamblin, R. (1982) 'Collective learning in ongoing political conflicts', *International Political Science Review*, vol 3, pp. 71-90.

Pollis, A. and Schwab, P. (1979) 'Human rights: a western construct with limited applicability', in A. Pollis and P. Schwab (eds) *Human rights: Cultural and ideological perspectives*, New York: Praeger, pp. 1-18.

Polsby, N. (1980) *Community power and political theory* (revised edn), New Haven, CT: Yale University Press.

Post, J.M. (1986) 'Hostilité, conformité,, fraternité: the group dynamics of terrorist behavior', *International Journal of Group Psychotherapy*, vol 36, pp. 211-24.

Post, J.M. (1990) 'Terrorist psycho-logic: terrorist behavior as a product of psychological forces', in W. Reich (ed) *Origins of terrorism*, Cambridge: Cambridge University Press, pp. 25-40.

Power, J. (1981) *Amnesty International: The human rights story*, New York: McGraw-Hill.

Pratt, T. C., Maahs, J. and Hemmens, C. (1999) 'The history of the use of force in corrections', in C. Hemmens and E. Atherton (eds.) *Use of force: Current practice and policy*, Lanham, MD: American Correctional Association, pp. 13-22.

Proal, L. (1898/1973) *Political crime*, Montclair, NJ: Paterson Smith.

Quinney, R. (1970) *The social reality of crime*, Boston, MA: Little, Brown.

Quinney, R. (1974) *Critique of legal order: Crime control in capitalist society*, Boston, MA: Little, Brown.

Quinney, R. (1977) *Class, state, and crime*, New York: David McKay.

Ranelagh, J. (1987) *The Agency: The rise and decline of the CIA* (revised and updated), New York: Simon & Schuster.

Ratner, M. and E. Ray. (2004) *Guantanamo: What the world should know*, White River Junction, VT: Chelsea Green.

Ratner, R.S. and McMullen, J. (1983) 'Social control and the rise of the "exceptional state" in Britain, the United States and Canada', *Crime and Social Justice*, vol 19, pp. 31-43.

Redden, J. (2000) *Snitch culture: How citizens are turned into the eyes and ears of the state*, Venice, CA: Feral House.

Reeve, S. (1999) *The new jackels*, Boston, MA: Northeastern University Press.

Reich, W. (1990) 'Understanding terrorist behavior: the limits and opportunities of psychological inquiry', in W. Reich (ed) *Origins of terrorism*, Cambridge: Cambridge University Press, pp. 261-81.

Reilly, W.G. (1973) 'Canada, Québec and theories of internal war', *American Review of Canadian Studies*, vol 3, pp. 67-75.

Reiman, J. (1998) *The rich get richer and the poor get prison* (5th edn), Boston, MA: Allyn & Bacon.

Reiner, R. (1980) 'Forces of disorder: how the police control "riots"', *New Society*, vol 10, pp. 51-4.

Reiss, A.J., Jr (1968) 'Police brutality: answers to key questions', *Trans-Action*, vol 10, p. 19.

Richards, S.C. and Avey, M. (2000) 'Controlling state crime in the United States of America: what can we do about the thug state?', in J.I. Ross (ed) *Varieties of state crime and its control*, Monsey, NY: Criminal Justice Press, pp. 31-57.

Roberg, R.R. and Kuykendall, J.L. (1993) *Police and society*, Belmont, CA: Wadsworth.

Robertson, G. (2000) *Crimes against humanity: The struggle for global justice*, New York: New Press.

Roebuck, J. and Weeber, S.C. (1978) *Political crime in the United States*, New York: Praeger.

Romano, A.T. (1984) 'Terrorism: an analysis of the literature', Doctoral dissertation, Fordham University.

Ross, J.I. (1988a) 'An events data base on political terrorism in Canada: some conceptual and methodological problems', *Conflict Quarterly*, vol 8, no 2, pp. 47-65.

Ross, J.I. (1988b) 'Attributes of political terrorism in Canada, 1960-1985', *Terrorism: An International Journal*, vol 11, no 3, pp. 213-33.

Ross, J.I. (1991) 'The nature of contemporary international terrorism', in D. Charters (ed) *Democratic responses to terrorism*, Ardsley-on-Hudson, NY: Transnational Publishers, pp. 17-42.

Ross, J.I. (1992) 'Review of Gregg Barak's, *Crimes by the capitalist state*', *Justice Quarterly*, vol 9, pp. 347-54.

Ross, J.I. (1993a) 'Structural causes of oppositional political terrorism: towards a causal model', *Journal of Peace Research*, vol 30, no 3, pp. 317-29.

Ross, J.I. (1993b) 'Research on contemporary oppositional political terrorism in the United States: merits, drawbacks, and suggestions for improvement', in K.D. Tunnell (ed) *Political crime in contemporary America: A critical approach*, New York: Garland, pp. 101-20.

Ross, J.I. (1994) 'The psychological causes of oppositional political terrorism: toward an integration of findings', *International Journal of Group Tensions*, vol 24, no 2, pp. 157-85.

Ross, J.I. (ed) (1995/2000) *Controlling state crime* (2nd edn), New Brunswick, NJ: Transaction Books.

Ross, J.I. (ed) (1995/2004) *Violence in Canada: Sociopolitical perspectives* (2nd edn), New Brunswick, NJ: Transaction Books.

Ross, J.I. (1995a) 'Controlling state crime: toward an integrated structural model', in J.I. Ross (ed) *Controlling state crime: An introduction*, New York: Garland, pp. 3-33.

Ross, J.I. (1995b) 'Police violence in Canada', in J.I. Ross (ed) *Violence in Canada: Sociopolitical perspectives*, Don Mills, ON: Oxford University Press, pp. 223-51.

Ross, J.I. (1995c) 'The rise and fall of Québécois Separatist terrorism: a qualitative application of factors from two models', *Studies in Conflict and Terrorism*, vol 18, no 4, pp. 285-97.

Ross, J.I. (1996) 'A model of the psychological causes of oppositional political terrorism', *Peace and Conflict: Journal of Peace Psychology*, vol 2, no 2, pp. 129-41.

Ross, J.I. (ed) (1998/2009) *Cutting the edge: Current perspectives on radical/critical criminology and criminal justice* (2nd edn), New Brunswick, NJ: Transaction Publishers.

Ross, J.I. (1998) 'Radical and critical criminology's treatment of municipal policing', in J.I. Ross (ed) *Cutting the edge: Current perspectives on radical/critical criminology and criminal justice*, Greenwood, CT: Praeger, pp. 95-106.

Ross, J.I. (1999) 'Beyond the conceptualization of terrorism', in C. Summers and E. Markusen (eds) *Collective violence: Harmful behavior in groups and governments*, Lanham, MD: Rowman & Littlefield, pp. 169-92.

Ross, J.I. (ed) (2000a) *Making news of police violence: Comparing Toronto and New York City*, Greenwood, CT: Praeger.

Ross, J.I. (ed) (2000b) *Varieties of state crime and its control*, Monsey, NY: Criminal Justice Press.

Ross, J.I. (2000c) 'Controlling state crime in the United Kingdom', in J.I. Ross (ed) *Varieties of state crime and its control*, Monsey, NY: Criminal Justice Press, pp. 11-30.

Ross, J.I. (2001) 'Police crime and democracy: demystifying the concept, research and presenting a taxonomy', in S. Einstein and M. Amir (eds) *Policing, security and democracy: Special aspects of 'democratic policing'*, Huntsville, TX: Office of International Criminal Justice, pp. 177-200.

Ross, J.I. (2003) *The dynamics of political crime*, Thousand Oaks, CA: Sage Publications.

Ross, J. I. (2005) 'What works when? Some preliminary thoughts on controlling the major state criminogenic agencies in Democratic States', in E. Vetere and D. Pedro (eds.) *Victims of crime and abuse of power. Festschrift in honour of Irene Melup*, Congress on Crime Prevention and Criminal Justice, pp. 610-23.

Ross, J.I. (2006) *Political terrorism: An interdisciplinary approach*, New York: Peter Lang Publishers.

Ross, J. I. (2007) 'Guantánamo detainees', in G. Barak (ed.) *Battleground criminal justice*, Westport, CT: Greenwood Press, pp. 320-29.

Ross, J.I. (2008) *Special problems in corrections*, Upper Saddle, NJ: Prentice Hall.

Ross, J. I. (2009) *Cybercrime*, New York, NY: Chelsea House/Facts on File.

Ross, J. I. (2012) *Policing issues: Challenges and controversies*, Sudbury, MA: Jones and Bartlett.

Ross, J.I. and Gurr, T.R. (1989) 'Why terrorism subsides: a comparative study of Canada and the United States', *Comparative Politics*, vol 21, pp. 406-26.

Ross, J.I. and Richards, S.C. (2002) *Behind bars: Surviving prison*, Indianapolis, IN: Alpha Books.

Ross, J.I. and Rothe, D.L. (2007) 'Swimming upstream: teaching state crime to students at American universities', *Journal of Criminal Justice Education*, vol 18, no 3, pp. 460-475.

Ross, J.I. and Rothe, D.L. (2008) 'Ironies of controlling state crime', *International Journal of Law, Crime and Justice*, vol 36, no 3, pp. 196-210.

Ross, J.I., Barak, G., Kauzlarich, D., Hamm, S., Friedrichs, D., Matthews, R., Pickering, S., Presdee, M., Kraska, P. and Kappeler, V. (1999) 'The state of state crime research', *Humanity and Society*, vol 23, no 3, pp. 273-81.

Rothe, D.L. (2009) *State criminality: The crime of all crimes*, Lanham, MD: Lexington Books.

Rothe, D.L. and Ross, J.I. (2008) 'The marginalization of state crime in contemporary introductory textbooks on criminology', *Critical Sociology*, vol 34, no 5, pp. 741-52.

Rothe, D. L. and Ross, J.I. (2010) 'Private military contractors, crime, and the terrain of unaccountability', *Justice Quarterly*, vol 27, no 4, pp. 593-617.

Rothmiller, M. and Goldman, I.G. (1992) *LA secret police: Inside the LAPD elite spy network*, New York: Pocket Books.

Russell, C.A. and Miller, B.H. (1983) 'Profile of a terrorist', in L.Z. Freedman and Y. Alexander (eds) *Perspectives on terrorism*, Wilmington, DE: Scholarly Resources, pp. 45-60.

Sagarin, E. (1973) 'Introduction', in L. Proal, *Political crime* (reprint edn), Montclair, NJ: Paterson Smith, pp v-xvi.

Saltstone, S.P. (1991) 'Some consequences of the failure to define the phrase "national security"', *Conflict Quarterly*, vol 11, no 3, pp. 36-54.

Sawatsky, J. (1980) *Men in the shadows: The RCMP Security Service*, Toronto: Doubleday.

Sawatsky, J. (1984) *Gouzenko: The untold story*, Toronto: Macmillan.

Sayari, S. (1985) *Generational change in terrorist movements: The Turkish case*, Santa Monica, CA: RAND.

Schafer, S. (1971) 'The concept of the political criminal', *The Journal of Criminal Law, Criminology, and Police Science*, vol 62, no 3, pp. 380-7.

Schafer, S. (1974) *The political criminal*, New York: Free Press.

Scharf, P. and Binder, A. (1983) *The badge and the bullet: Police use of deadly force*, New York: Praeger.

Scheingold, S. (1998) 'Constructing the new political criminology: power, authority, and the post-liberal state', *Law and Social Inquiry*, vol 23, no 4, pp. 857-95.

Scheppele, K.L. (2006) 'North American emergencies: the use of emergency powers in Canada and the United States', *International Journal of Constitution Law*, vol 4, no 2, pp. 213-43.

Schmalleger, F. (2002) *Criminal law today*, Upper Saddle River, NJ: Prentice Hall.

Schmid, A. (1983) *Political terrorism: A guide to concepts, theories, data bases and literature*, New Brunswick, NJ: Transaction Books.

Schmid, A. (1988) *Political terrorism: A new guide to actors, authors, concepts, data bases, theories and literature*, Amsterdam: SWIDOC/Transaction.

Schwendinger, H. and Schwendinger, J. (1975) 'Defenders of order or guardians of human rights?', in I. Taylor, P. Walton and J. Young (eds) *Critical criminology*, London: Routledge & Kegan Paul, pp. 113-46.

Scott, J.C. (1985) *Weapons of the weak: Everyday forms of peasant resistance*, New Haven, CT: Yale University Press.

Scraton, P. (1985) *The state of the police*, London: Pluto.

Scraton, P. and Chadwick, K. (1985) *In the arms of the law: Deaths in custody*, London: Cobden Trust.

Senate Select Committee on Intelligence (1989) *The FBI and CISPES*, 101st Congress, 1st session, July, Committee Print: 1.

Shane, S. (2006) 'Seeking an exit strategy for Guantanamo', *The New York Times*, June 18, section 4, 1, 4.

Shank, G. (1980) 'State and corporate crime: an introduction', *Social Justice*, vol 16, no 2, pp i-vi.

Shanker, A. (1992) 'Where we stand: The Hamlet, North Carolina fire', *New York Times*, January 5, p. 7.

Sharkansky, I. (1995) 'A state action may be nasty but it is not likely to be a crime', in J.I. Ross (ed) *Controlling state crime*, New York: Garland, pp. 35-52.

Sherman, L.W. (1978) *Scandal and reform: Controlling police corruption*, Berkeley, CA: University of California Press.

Sherman, L.W. (1980a) 'Executions without trial', *Vanderbilt Law Review*, vol 33, pp. 71-100.

Sherman, L.W. (1980b) 'Perspectives on police and violence', *Annals of the American Academy of Political and Social Science*, vol 452, pp. 1-12.

Simon, D. and Eitzen, D.S. (1999) *Elite deviance* (6th edn), Boston, MA: Allyn & Bacon.

Simon, H. (1982) *Models of bounded rationality*, Cambridge, MA: MIT Press.

Skocpol, T. (1979) *States and social revolution*, Cambridge, MA: Harvard University Press.

Snepp, F. (1977) *Decent interval: An insider's account of Saigon's indecent end*, New York: Random House.

Snepp, F. (1999) *Irreparable harm: A firsthand account of how one agent took on the CIA in an epic battle*, New York: Random House.

Spencer, J. (2000) 'The case for a code of criminal procedure', *Criminal Law Review*, July, 519–31.

Spjut, R.J. (1974) 'Defining subversion', *British Journal of Law and Society*, vol 6, no 2, pp. 254-61.

Stark, R. (1972) *Police riots*, Belmont, CA: Wadsworth.

Stepan, A. (1973) 'The new professionalism of internal warfare and military role expansion', in A. Stepan (ed.) *Authoritarian Brazil: Origins, policies, and future*, New Haven, CT: Yale University Press, pp. 45-65.

Sterling, C. (1981) *The terror network*, New York: Holt, Rinehart and Winston.

Stevens, D.J. (2009) *An introduction to American policing*, Sudbury, MA: Jones and Bartlett.

Stone, G.R. (1983) 'Sedition', in *Encyclopedia of crime and justice*, New York: Free Press, pp. 1425-31.

Stone, G.R. (2004) *Perilous times: Free speech in wartime*, New York: Norton.

Sutherland, D. (1980) *The fourth man: The definitive story of Blunt, Philby, Burgess, and Maclean*, London: Secker & Warburg.

Sutherland, E.H. (1947) *Principles of criminology* (4th edn), Philadelphia, PA: J.B. Lippincott.

Sutherland, E.H. (1949a) *White collar crime*, New York: Holt, Rinehart and Winston.

Sutherland, E.H. (1949b) 'The white collar criminal', in V.C. Branham and S.B. Kutash (eds) *Encyclopedia of criminology*, New York: Philosophical Library, pp. 511-15.

Sykes, G.M. (1980) *The future of crime*, Rockville, MD: National Institute of Mental Health.

Sykes, G.M. and Cullen, F. (1992) *Criminology* (2nd edn), Toronto: Harcourt, Brace Jovanovich.

Sykes, G.M. and Matza, D. (1957) 'Techniques of neutralization: a theory of delinquency', *American Sociological Review*, vol 22, pp. 667-70.

Taft, P. and Ross, P. (1979) 'American labor violence: its causes, character, and outcome', in H.D. Graham and T.R. Gurr (eds) *Violence in America: Historical and comparative perspectives*, Beverly Hills, CA: Sage Publications, pp. 187-242.

Targ, H.R. (1979) 'Societal structure and revolutionary terrorism: a preliminary investigation', in M. Stohl (ed) *The politics of terrorism*, New York: Marcel Dekker, pp. 119-43.

Taylor, M. (1988) *The terrorist*, London: Brassey's Defence Publishers.

Theoharis, A. (1978) *Spying on Americans: Political surveillance from Hoover to the Huston Plan*, Philadelphia, PA: Temple University Press.

Thomas, C.W. and Hepburn, J.R. (1983) *Crime, criminal law, and criminology*, Dubuque, IA: William C. Brown.

Thomas, D.S. (ed) (1972) *Treason and libel*, Boston, MA: Routledge & Kegan Paul.

Thornton, T.P. (1964) 'Terror as a weapon of political agitation', in H. Eckstein (ed) *Internal war: Problems and approaches*, New York: Free Press of Glencoe, pp. 82-8.

Thurlow, R. (1994) *The secret state: British internal security in the twentieth century*, Cambridge, MA: Blackwell.

Tilly, C. (1978) *From mobilization to revolution*, Reading, MA: Addison-Wesley.

Tilly, C. (1985) 'War making and state making as organized crime', in P.B. Evans, D. Rueschemeyer and T. Skocpol (eds) *Bringing the state back in*, Cambridge: Cambridge University Press.

Tilly, C. (1993) *Coercion, capital, and European states*, Cambridge, MA: Blackwell.

Tombs, S. and Whyte, D. (eds.) (2003) *Unmasking the crimes of the powerful: Scrutinizing states and corporations*, New York: Peter Lang.

Torrance, J. (1977) 'The response of Canadian governments to violence', *Canadian Journal of Political Science*, vol 10, pp. 473-96.

Torrance, J. (1995) 'The responses of democratic governments to violence', in J.I. Ross (ed) *Violence in Canada: Sociopolitical perspectives*, Toronto: Oxford University Press, pp. 313-43.

Tunnell, K.D. (1992) *Choosing crime: The criminal calculus of property offenders*, Chicago, IL: Nelson-Hall.

Tunnell, K.D. (1993a) 'Political crime and pedagogy: a content analysis of criminology and criminal justice texts', *Journal of Criminal Justice Education*, vol 4, no 1, pp. 101-14.

Tunnell, K.D. (ed) (1993b) *Political crime in contemporary America: A critical approach*, New York: Garland.

Tunnell, K.D. (1995a) 'Crimes of the capitalist state against labor', in J.I. Ross (ed) *Controlling state crime*, New York: Garland, pp. 207-33.

Tunnell, K.D. (1995b) 'Worker insurgency and social control: violence by and against labor in Canada', in J.I. Ross (ed) *Violence in Canada*, Toronto: Oxford University Press, pp. 78-96.

Turk, A.T. (1982a) *Political criminality*, Beverly Hills, CA: Sage Publications.

Turk, A.T. (1982b) 'Social dynamics of terrorism', *Annals of the American Association of Political and Social Sciences*, vol 463, pp. 119-28.

Turk, A.T. (1984) 'Political crime', in R.F. Meir (ed) *Major forms of crime*, Beverly Hills, CA: Sage Publications, pp. 119-35.

Tzu, S. (1963) *The art of war* (translated by Samuel T. Griffith), New York: Oxford University Press.

Ujevich, R. M. (1969) *Military justice: A summary of its legislative and judicial development*, Washington, DC: Library of Congress.

Vaughn, D. (1996) *The Challenger launch decision*, Chicago, IL: University of Chicago Press.

Warr, M. (1995) 'Public perceptions of crime and punishment', in J.F. Sheley (ed) *Criminology* (2nd edn), Belmont, CA: Wadsworth, pp. 15-31.

Webster's new collegiate dictionary (1980) Toronto: Thomas Allen & Son.

Weinberg, L. and Davis, P.B. (1989) *Introduction to political terrorism*, New York: McGraw-Hill.

Weinberg, L. and Eubank, W.L. (1987) 'Italian women terrorists', *Terrorism: An International Journal*, vol 9, pp. 241-62.

Westley, W.A. (1953) 'Violence and the police', *American Journal of Sociology*, vol 59, pp. 34-41.

Westley, W.A. (1970) *Violence and the police: A sociological study of law, custom and morality*, Cambridge, MA: MIT Press.

Wexley, J. (1977) *The judgement of Julius and Ethel Rosenberg*, New York: Ballantine.

White, M. (2007) *Current issues and controversies in policing*, New York: Pearson-Allyn & Bacon.

Whyte, J.D. and MacDonald, A. (1989) 'Dissent and national security and dissent some more', in C.E.S. Franks (ed) *Dissent and the state*, Toronto: Oxford University Press, pp. 21-39.

Willimett, Terry C. (1980) 'Social control in the military in Canada', in Richard Ossenberg (ed.) *Power and Change in Canada*, Toronto: McClelland and Stewart, pp. 246-84.

Wolfe, A. (1973) *The seamy side of democracy: Repression in America*, New York: David McKay.

Woodward, B. (1987) *Veil: The secret wars of the CIA 1981-1987*, New York: Pocket Books.

Woodward, B. and Bernstein, C. (1974) *All the president's men*, New York: Simon & Schuster.

Worden, R.E. (1995) 'The "causes" of police brutality: theory and evidence on police use of force', in W.A. Geller and H. Toch (eds) *And justice for all*, Washington, DC: Police Executive Research Forum, pp. 31-60.

Wright, J.P., Cullen, F.T. and Blankenship, M.B. (1995) 'The social construction of corporate violence: media coverage of the Imperial Food Products fire', *Crime and Delinquency*, vol 41, pp. 20-36.

Wright, S. (1998) *An appraisal of technologies of political control*, Report to the European Parliament, 6 January, Luxembourg.

Yar, M. (2006) *Cybercrime and society*, London: Sage Publications.

Zilinskas, R. A. (1995/2000) *Preventing state crimes against the environment during military operations, controlling state crime: An introduction*, New York: Garland, pp. 235-82.

Zinn, H. (1980/2010) *A people's history of the United States*, New York: Harper Perennial.

Zwerman, G. (1988) 'Domestic counter terrorism', *Social Justice*, vol 16, pp. 31-63.

Index

The letter 'f' indicates a figure, 't' a table, and 'n' an endnote

Lightning Source UK Ltd.
Milton Keynes UK
UKHW031155090519

342389UK00008B/255/P